The Clinician's Guide to Collaborative Caring in Eating Disorders

Caring for a loved one with an eating disorder is a difficult task; carers often find it hard to cope, and this can contribute to the maintenance of the disorder. *The Clinician's Guide to Collaborative Caring in Eating Disorders* shows how active collaboration between professional and non-professional carers can maximise the quality of life for both the sufferer and all other family members.

The book provides straightforward guidance for clinicians who work with families and carers. It suggests ways of ensuring that interpersonal elements that can maintain eating disorders are minimised and indicates skills and knowledge that can be taught to the carer both for managing their personal reaction to the illness, and for providing a practically and emotionally supportive environment that is conducive to change. The appendices of the book contain a *Toolkit for Carers*, a series of worksheets designed to help carers recognise their own unique caring styles.

This book is worthwhile reading for all health professionals working with people with eating disorders. It is relevant across a variety of settings and client groups including inpatients, outpatients, community and day patients.

Janet Treasure is a Psychiatrist at the Maudsley Hospital and a Professor at King's College London.

Ulrike Schmidt is a Consultant Psychiatrist at the Maudsley Hospital and Professor at the Institute of Psychiatry, King's College London.

Pam Macdonald is working on a PhD at the Institute of Psychiatry, King's College London.

The Clinician's Guide to Collaborative Caring in Eating Disorders

The new Maudsley method

Edited by Janet Treasure,
Ulrike Schmidt and
Pam Macdonald

Routledge
Taylor & Francis Group

LONDON AND NEW YORK

First published 2010
by Routledge
27 Church Road, Hove, East Sussex BN3 2FA

Simultaneously published in the USA and Canada
by Routledge Inc
711 Third Avenue, New York NY 10017 (8th Avenue)

*Routledge is an imprint of the Taylor & Francis Group,
an informa business*

Copyright © 2010 Selection and editorial matter, Janet Treasure,
Ulrike Schmidt and Pam Macdonald; individual chapters, the
contributors

Typeset in Times by
RefineCatch Limited, Bungay, Suffolk
Animal cartoons by Gary Holmes

Paperback cover design by Anú Design

All rights reserved. No part of this book may be reprinted or
reproduced or utilised in any form or by any electronic,
mechanical, or other means, now known or hereafter
invented, including photocopying and recording, or in any
information storage or retrieval system, without permission in
writing from the publishers.

British Library Cataloguing in Publication Data
A catalogue record for this book is available from the British Library

Library of Congress Cataloging-in-Publication Data
The clinician's guide to collaborative caring in eating disorders : the
   new Maudsley method / edited by Janet Treasure, Ulrike Schmidt,
   and Pam Macdonald.
       p. ; cm.
   Includes bibliographical references and index.
   1. Eating disorders. 2. Caregivers. I. Treasure, Janet. II. Schmidt,
   Ulrike, 1955– III. Macdonald, Pam, 1959–.
   [DNLM: 1. Eating Disorders–therapy. 2. Family Therapy–methods.
   WM 175 C6415 2009]
   RC552.E18C565 2009
   616.85'26—dc22

                                                    2009011375

ISBN: 978–0–415–48424–4 (hbk)
ISBN: 978–0–415–48425–1 (pbk)

Contents

PART V
Conclusion and appendices

Contributors

Emma Baldock has a PhD in medical ethics, funded by the Wellcome Trust, and for which she was based at the Eating Disorders Research Unit and Centre for Medical Law and Ethics, King's College London. She is now training in clinical psychology at the Institute of Psychiatry, London.

Liz Goddard is a PhD student and research worker employed in the Eating Disorders Research Unit, King's College London. She is a project coordinator on a multi-site national carers project involving specialist eating disorder inpatient units around the UK.

Miriam Grover is a senior practitioner in cognitive behaviour therapy. Originally from a nursing background, she is a PhD student at the Institute of Psychiatry, London. The focus of her thesis is investigating the efficacy and acceptability of new technologies in treating people with eating disorders and their carers.

Veronica Kamerling is the mother of two daughters with an eating disorder, one of whom suffered with anorexia, the other with bulimia and binge eating disorder. She now runs the London Carers' Group for those looking after someone with an eating disorder. Her work is centred around helping carers.

Olivia Kyriacou has worked as a research psychologist in eating disorders in the United States and the UK since 1999. She completed her PhD at the Eating Disorders Research Unit, King's College London, in 2008, exploring the role of fathers and carers' experiences in eating disorders.

Carolina Lopez is a clinical psychologist who has worked with adolescents and patients with eating disorders since 1999. She is an academic member of the Faculty of Medicine of the University of Chile and completed her PhD in the Eating Disorders Research Unit, King's College London, in 2008.

Pam Macdonald is a PhD student working on a DVD skills-based training project at the Institute of Psychiatry, London. She also supports carers by coaching them using the principles of motivational interviewing. She has been a carer herself and is now involved in training carers to become coaches.

Nadia Micali is a child and adolescent psychiatrist specialising in eating disorders and National Institute for Health Research (NIHR) clinician scientist, Department of Child and Adolescent Psychiatry and Eating Disorders Research Unit, King's College London. Her research interests are the effects of maternal eating disorders on childhood development and risk factors for eating disorders.

Fabrice Monneyron is a child and adolescent psychiatrist working in Maurice Corcos' Eating Disorder Department, at the Institut Mutualiste Montsouris, Paris. He is currently conducting a PhD at the Eating Disorders Research Unit, King's College London, assessing mother–daughter dyads with a history of an eating disorder.

Simone Raenker has a research post at the Eating Disorders Research Unit, King's College London. She is a project coordinator on a multi-site national carers project involving specialist eating disorder inpatient units around the UK. In her PhD, she is investigating the role of fathers in eating disorders.

Ulrike Schmidt is Professor of Eating Disorders at the Institute of Psychiatry and Honorary Consultant Psychiatrist at the South London and Maudsley National Health Service (NHS) Foundation Trust. Her research interests include all aspects of eating disorders, and in particular the evaluation of psychological treatments.

Ana Rosa Sepúlveda, a postdoctoral fellow at the Institute of Psychiatry, London, coordinated a collaborative skills-based family training project. She has been teaching MSc and PhD courses at the School of Psychology, Autonoma University, Madrid since 2003. She now works as clinical psychologist on an Eating Disorders Day Unit, H. Santa Cristina, in Madrid.

Gráinne Smith, former primary head teacher, is co-author of *Skills-based Caring. . . .* as well as author of *Anorexia and Bulimia in the Family* and *Families, Carers and Professionals: Building Constructive Conversations*. A former carer, she now supports others through helplines, workingtogether-care.com, and helping facilitate at NEEDS (North East Eating Disorders Support) Scotland meetings.

Gill Todd worked in the field of eating disorders at the Maudsley Hospital for 22 years initially with Professor Gerald Russell, as staff nurse, and later with Professor Janet Treasure as clinical nurse leader. She also established the National Carers' Conference and the Royal College of Nursing Special Interest Group in Eating Disorders.

Janet Treasure is a psychiatrist who has specialised in the treatment of eating disorders for over 25 years. A key figure at the Maudsley Hospital, London, a leading centre in clinical management and training of eating disorders, she is also active in research, having written over 150 peer-reviewed papers.

Wendy Whitaker is a senior social worker with Professor Janet Treasure's Eating Disorders team at South London and Maudsley NHS Foundation Trust. Areas of expertise include family work, carers' skills-based training and running carers' groups. She provides training in these areas and has contributed to several articles and chapters on eating disorders and carer work.

Jenna Whitney is currently training to be a clinical psychologist. She will complete her course at the Institute of Psychiatry, London, in October 2009. In 2006, she obtained her PhD in psychological medicine at the Institute of Psychiatry examining the experience of caring for people with eating disorders.

Christopher Williams, MBChB, BSc, MMedSc, MD, FRCPsych, BABCP, is an accredited practitioner and Senior Lecturer in Psychiatry, University of Glasgow and Honorary Consultant Psychiatrist, NHS Greater Glasgow and Clyde, Psychological Medicine, Gartnavel Royal Hospital, Glasgow.

Preface and acknowledgements

This book describes a collaborative approach between health-care professionals and non-professionals (family members, partners, friends) who care for people with different eating disorders, including anorexia nervosa, bulimia nervosa and mixed forms of eating disorders. (In some sections of this book we talk broadly of carers, in other parts where it seems more appropriate we talk of families or parents. We use these terms interchangeably.) It developed through a gradual iterative process between people with eating disorders, their families, the clinical and academic teams at the Maudsley Hospital and King's College London and the various authorities that the team consulted. The idea for this book germinated out of clinical need. We knew that it was important to actively involve the families of our patients in treatment, since they usually took on the main burden of caring. Our research indicated that the families were stressed by their caring role and had many needs that were not met by the health professionals and services they and their family member with an eating disorder came in contact with. We then began to undertake research to understand how caring for someone with an eating disorder produced stress and what carers needed to ameliorate this.

A major dilemma of anorexia nervosa is the tension caused by the obvious signs of illness to the outside world and the patients' denial that there are any problems. We read that motivational interviewing can help people move towards change and so we invited Dr Steve Rollnick to come to our ward and teach the team the skills of Motivational Interviewing (Miller & Rollnick, 1991; Rollnick et al., 1999; Miller & Rollnick, 2002). We found that models of health behaviour change such as the trans-theoretical stage of change model, along with the techniques of motivational interviewing, were invaluable resources in our work with individuals with eating disorders. Members of our team later travelled to the home of motivational interviewing in Albuquerque, New Mexico, and met with Dr Bill Miller. Dr Robert Meyers demonstrated the principles of community reinforcement training for families (Meyers et al., 1998). This approach involves working with those motivated families who have an unmotivated family member with an illness.

This caused considerable excitement due to its obvious applications to people with eating disorders, and consequently, we introduced some of these techniques into our work with families. Professor John Weinman at Guy's Hospital introduced us to models of health behaviour change and illness representations. Dr Chris Williams has worked with us to help structure our materials into his user-friendly model of cognitive behavioural therapy, which identifies the vicious cycles that keep problems going. Finally, we found that one of the core components of the core skills of the carers workshops was compassion. Thereafter, we found the work of Paul Gilbert describing the social aspects of psychopathology and how this could be incorporated into treatment added an interesting new dimension to our work (Gilbert & Irons, 2005).

Once we had developed an empirically based model and outline of the strategies and technical interventions, we then had to implement it. Gill Todd, the nurse leader on our service, is a 'can do' sort of person and has a particular interest in working with carers. We soon had time and space and the backing of the service behind this enterprise. We were blessed to have Kay Gavan working with our service as a social worker. Kay is an archetypal wise woman. She came with a great deal of expertise on interventions to decrease expressed emotion in families, having worked with Professor Julian Leff. She has the perfect temperament to be a motivational therapist . . . slow to chide and swift to bless, and with lashings of 'agape', the type of spiritual love that Bill Miller says is critical in moving people towards change. This meant that families readily offered up their problems and difficulties, which were met with a soft smile. Kay has now begun her third stage of life back in Ireland and we have been working hard to encapsulate her lifetime's wisdom and experience.

Jenna Whitney helped to build some of the theoretical background to the intervention described in this book. Through her research endeavour, we were able to construct models to understand the process of caring for someone with an eating disorder, which in turn, informed our intervention. Jenna also evaluated the day patient work with families of people with anorexia nervosa as part of her PhD, which was funded by a Nina Jackson fellowship. Detailed interviews were undertaken with family members being asked what they found helpful and not so helpful about the family intervention. Some examples from this research are used to illustrate aspects of the intervention in this book. This feedback from families has helped shape what we do and how we do it. We are very grateful to all the families who agreed to have their feedback and reflections appear in this manual for teaching purposes and for the benefit of others.

We had support from the Health Foundation to research different models of working with adolescents with bulimia nervosa. Sarah Perkins and Suzanne Winn examined how the families coped with this problem and identified their needs and difficulties. More recently Ana Rosa Sepúlveda, a postdoctoral student from Spain, and Carolina Lopez, a PhD student from Chile, have set up the evaluation process for the carers' workshops. Wendy Whitaker and Gill Todd have helped with their delivery. We now have graduates from the first workshops who have taken a particular interest in more training to become 'expert carers'. Pat Sacks and Veronica Kamerling are now helping to run the new series of workshops. Natalie Loader has also joined the workshop-teaching faculty. She brings insights to the enterprise of someone who has recovered from anorexia nervosa herself and also acted as a carer for her sister. Pam Macdonald is another person who juggles with various hats. She has been a carer herself and is now embarking on a PhD to understand the processes involved in more detail. She has been delivering telephone coaching to families who have been enrolled in a distance learning form of support in which DVDs take the place of some of the aspects of the training workshops.

Support from the South London NHS Foundation Trust's Research and Development Fund allowed us to develop a web-based programme for carers with eating disorders build on the philosophy, model and techniques described above. We were lucky to have the expertise of the following experts on our development team: Gráinne Smith, a carer, writer and wonderful poet, Catherine McCloskey, a recovered sufferer, Dr Ivan Eisler, who has pioneered the Maudsley Model of family therapy for adolescents with anorexia nervosa, and Dr Chris Williams. This programme, which won a London Innovation Award for Service Development, is being evaluated by our PhD student and outpatient team leader Miriam Grover.

Emma Baldock is an expert in medical ethics who did her PhD supported by a Wellcome Trust Bioethics PhD fellowship; in her chapter, she discusses issues of confidentiality and information sharing which carers often find to be a problematic area.

We have presented aspects of all this work to families attending the National Carers' Conference, jointly run by beat and the South London and Maudsley NHS Foundation Trust. We want to thank all families who have helped by giving us questions, ideas and feedback. This partnership has been very productive and we hope that it will benefit families in the future.

Finally, this work was part of the ARIADNE (Applied Research into Anorexia Nervosa and Not Otherwise Specified Eating Disorders) programme, funded by a Department of Health (DH) NIHR Programme Grant for Applied Research (Reference number RP-PG-0606-1043) to U. Schmidt, J. Treasure, K. Tchanturia, H. Startup, S. Ringwood, S. Landau, M. Grover, I. Eisler, I. Campbell, J. Beecham, M. Allen and G. Wolff. The views expressed herein are not necessarily those of the DH or NIHR.

This work was also supported by a grant from the NIHR Biomedical Research Centre for Mental Health, South London and Maudsley NHS Foundation Trust and Institute of Psychiatry, King's College London.

References

Gilbert, P. & Irons, C. (2005). Focused therapies and compassionate mind training for shame and self-attacking. In P. Gilbert (ed.) *Compassion: Conceptualisations, Research and Use in Psychotherapy*. London: Routledge.

Meyers, R. J., Miller, W. R., Hill, D. E. & Tonigan, J. S. (1998). Community reinforcement and family training (CRAFT): Engaging unmotivated drug users in treatment. *Journal of Substance Abuse* 10: 291–308.

Miller, W. & Rollnick, S. (1991). *Motivational Interviewing: Preparing People to Change Addictive Behaviour*. New York: Guilford.

Miller, W. & Rollnick, S. (2002). *Motivational Interviewing*, 2nd edn. New York: Guilford.

Rollnick, S., Mason, P. & Butler, C. (1999). *Health Behaviour Change*. Edinburgh: Churchill Livingstone.

Part I

Introduction to collaborative care between carers of people with eating disorders and professional services

We begin by providing a general overview in Chapter 1 of what to expect in the book – its goals, aims and target audience. The reader is introduced to the concept of how, when and in what way carers can participate in treatment along with a discussion on the essential links between professionals, carers and people with eating disorders. The chapter closes with an overview of the book's overall aims, which are first and foremost to provide a clear manual that describes the content and various forms of working collaboratively with families.

Although it is beyond the scope of this book to provide detailed analyses of the underlying causal processes of eating disorders, Chapter 2 nevertheless offers basic general details on the clinical presentations of eating disorders and their causal processes. We look at family factors as moderators of treatment outcomes and cite numerous examples of evidence-based guidelines for the interested reader to investigate further.

In Chapter 3 we listen to the voices of two carers, whose daughters have since recovered and who themselves continue to work tirelessly in promoting the collaborative caring cause. In this chapter, they describe the experiences and needs of carers by drawing not only upon their own infinite experience, but also on that of the countless other carers they have worked with throughout the past several years.

Part I closes with a chapter giving an ethico-legal account of working with carers in eating disorders.

Chapter 1

Introduction

Janet Treasure

It is generally acknowledged that involving the families of adolescents with eating disorders is essential good practice. There is less certainty about the involvement of families of adults. The degree of involvement of parents and partners in outpatient treatment for adults depends on several factors:

- the interest of the patient and/or family member or close other
- practical considerations such as whether the person with the eating disorder lives with their family or close other or at least has close contact with them
- the progress of treatment
- the level of risk.

Thus, it is possible for many patients to recover from their eating disorder with individual therapy alone. However, the more ill the patient, the higher the risk and the less willing or able the person is to care for their own nutritional need, the more the help of the family is needed to participate in treatment.

What this book is about

In this book we discuss an approach to working with family members that can be used across both the age and diagnostic spectrum. This form of intervention can be used for the full range of severity and in a variety of settings and services that may be employed: self-guidance, distance support, carer group workshops and day patient, outpatient and inpatient settings. It should, therefore, be of value to a range of professionals who work in each of these settings.

This approach has been developed with key stakeholders including carers and people with eating disorders themselves. In the book we discuss the ethics and the theories that underpin the approach. Finally, we describe how to implement the various interventions.

It is usually helpful to involve families and other carers in the initial assessment, if possible. Part of the assessment process involves a consideration of the needs of carers themselves. Further help is offered as needed. At minimum, information about the illness and how best to manage it, is offered with guidance offered in person, or via telephone or email.

A more intensive intervention can be given in the form of workshops held for groups of up to twelve carers. These can be used by family members and partners of people with anorexia nervosa, bulimia nervosa or eating disorder not otherwise specified. These involve twelve hours of training delivered in two-hour sessions. The advantage of this form of delivery is that there can be more time and focus on the acquisition of skills and there is the opportunity for peer support and learning.

A more intensive intervention is a three-day workshop held with two or three families. This was developed to facilitate the transition from inpatient care to community care and to moderate the risk of relapse, which occurs in over 50 per cent of patients. In the case of the more severe patients, it is important to adopt a holistic approach by undertaking 'bridging' work with both family members as well as any local services that the individual may encounter in the community. In severe cases the problem is multidetermined and so management and treatment needs to address the multiple risk factors that contribute to the problem, some of which are in the social network. A multisystemic approach with a careful and ecologically based functional analysis of identified problems can be helpful which may need some form of outreach work. Such an approach has been found to be effective for adolescents with serious emotional disturbance (Henggeler et al., 2002).

Who should read this book?

This book has been written primarily for all health professionals who work with people with eating disorders in any setting such as inpatient, outpatient, community or day patient. The model of working that we advocate involves active collaboration between professional and non-professional carers, working together to maximise the quality of life for all family members. The basic aim is to provide families with the knowledge and skills that can help them not only manage their own reaction to the illness but also provide an environment (emotionally and practically) that is conducive to change.

As discussed earlier the needs of family members or other carers do not differ from the needs of health professionals working with this patient group, in terms of information about the illness and skills used to manage it. The unhelpful patterns of interactions that are set up within families resemble those that occur within our specialist eating disorder teams. These reactions form as a consequence of the powerful mixed emotions that the symptoms evoke in anyone and in any place where there is prolonged contact with people with eating disorders, such as inpatient, day patient and even outpatient settings. Consequently, we anticipate that this book will be useful for all professionals working with people with eating disorders, even if the main focus of their work is not with families.

Family members may also find that reading the book is helpful in order to deepen their understanding of the illness. Family members tell us that they are desperate for reliable information about how to help their loved one. The commitment, energy and resourcefulness of family members are astounding. Yet all of us, health professional or not, can soon become discouraged if our attempts to help seem to get nowhere.

How, when and in what way can carers participate in treatment?

Carers often provide the initial impetus in guiding their loved one towards treatment. Moreover, they remain a consistent presence throughout the illness and into recovery. During a process that can extend over many years, they shoulder the burden of continuing care while coping with the transitions between different forms of services and treatment.

The form and content varies of how, when and what information and skills are required. We have distilled this information into a book specifically written for carers (Treasure et al., 2007). It provides a detailed practical guide for carers (parents and professionals) involved in the day-to-day management of such cases. This book can be used as a basic outline of the curriculum for carers.

Links between professionals, parents and people with eating disorders

Family members often find themselves stigmatised and treated as if they had contributed to the problem. Parents can be excluded by some services from participating in caring for their daughter while she is in more 'expert' hands. Family members are often puzzled and confused because there can be profound differences in the ethos of specialised treatment teams. The parents' role and the expectations made of them in such settings may vary greatly. In some child and adolescent teams, for example, there may be a minimal interest in working with the individual but this position can abruptly reverse once their child turns 18 and is linked into adult services.

Aside from practical and management issues within this period of transition, there is wide variability in the treatment method and ethos within the different services. Often the family is the central focus of attention in Child and Adolescent Services. Adult services have more of a focus on individual responsibility and the family may be excluded from treatment. This abrupt change in emphasis can be confusing and disconcerting, both for the individual and her parents. The model of treatment that we describe in this book provides a bridge that can link these two approaches where necessary. We describe how to give the parents an opportunity to contribute to their offspring's welfare in a developmentally appropriate manner.

Aims of this book

- The overall aim of this book is to help professionals work with the families and loved ones of people with an eating disorder with a spirit in which families are seen as part of the solution rather than as part of the problem.
- To provide a theoretical explanation of how carers may be coping with this role.
- To describe and analyse how reactive family processes can act as one of the factors that can maintain an eating disorder.
- To describe how we work in a collaborative way with the broad spectrum of families to share information and skills to facilitate their role.
- To disseminate information and skills to carers which enables them to step back from the interpersonal processes that maintain anorexia nervosa.
- The overarching final aim is to have a clear manual, which describes the content and various forms of working with families so that the interpersonal elements that maintain eating disorder symptoms are minimised. We hope that this will provide one of the stepping-stones required to produce high quality evidence about treatment by clearly defining our treatment model in the form of a manual. The wide case mix in eating disorders means that how, when and by how much, the techniques described in this book are appropriate for use in an individual case will need to be judged flexibly. Thus, there needs to be some form of clinical assessment as to whether and by how much the interpersonal aspects of maintenance are relevant to an individual case and the optimal way this can be addressed.

References

Henggeler, S. W., Schoenwald, S. K., Rowland, M. D. & Cunningham, P. B. (2002). *Serious Emotional Disturbance in Children and Adolescents: Multisystemic Therapy*. New York: Guilford.

Treasure, J., Smith, G. & Crane, A. (2007). *Skills-based Learning for Caring for a Loved One with an Eating Disorder: The New Maudsley Method*. London: Routledge.

Chapter 2

Eating disorders and the concept of working with families and other carers

Janet Treasure and Ulrike Schmidt

Introduction

Living with a loved one with an eating disorder can have a significant impact on the mental and physical health of individual family members. Carers frequently report that they lack the skills and resources required to care for their loved one with an eating disorder. Consequently, in this chapter we summarise the background that relates to the reasons for working with family members and other carers of people with eating disorders. We include some basic details about the clinical presentation and the underlying causal processes in eating disorders, but a full discussion of these is beyond the scope of this chapter. We review what information there is from evidence-based guidelines and randomised trials with regards to working with families. We also discuss the wider body of evidence such as that from naturalistic outcome studies, pertaining to family factors in the maintenance of eating disorder. Finally, we describe the history and evolution of family-based interventions.

Clinical presentation of eating disorders

Anorexia nervosa is a disorder which typically arises during a fairly narrow developmental window from adolescence to young adulthood. The most common age for it to develop is at about 15. The timing of onset is often linked to the later phases of puberty. It is unusual for the illness to begin after the age of 25. In most cases that appear to start in adult life, there has been an earlier mild phase of the illness during adolescence. There are two subtypes of anorexia nervosa – a restricting type, where there is continuous avoidance of calories, and a binge purge type where there is periodic disinhibition, with over-eating and under-eating alternating. The binge purge type of anorexia nervosa has many similarities with bulimia nervosa.

The onset of bulimia nervosa is usually slightly later than that of anorexia nervosa. In about one-third of cases, however, there is a preliminary phase of anorexia nervosa preceding the development of bulimic symptoms. Bulimia nervosa often goes untreated for years, as unlike anorexia nervosa, it is invisible to the outside world. Other forms of bulimic disorders, such as binge eating disorder, have a much wider window of onset.

Thus, the clinical presentation of eating disorders can be very mixed. Cases often do not respect diagnostic boundaries and transition from one form of eating disorder to the other over the life course occurs in many cases (Fairburn & Harrison, 2003; Anderluh et al., 2008).

In clinical practice, the following broad categories of anorexia nervosa cases are seen:[1]

- *Recent onset cases of anorexia nervosa:* these are young people within a year or two of onset who usually present to Child and Adolescent Services. The majority of these will have an excellent outcome and make a full recovery. A proportion of these will develop a form of bulimic disorder.
- *Standard cases of anorexia nervosa:* a large proportion of the cases presenting to Adult Eating Disorders Services (and a proportion of those presenting to Child and Adolescent Services) have more protracted symptoms of clinical significance. The response to treatment is usually less good than for the recent onset cases.
- *Treatment resistant anorexia nervosa:* a small proportion of cases have a severe and chronic form of the illness that does not respond to standard interventions and produces life endangering complications.

A similar pattern occurs in the bulimic disorders with the exception that recent onset cases less commonly transform into anorexia nervosa and the complications of the treatment resistant form of bulimia nervosa are less life threatening and so inpatient care is rarely used.

Anorexia nervosa may be a passing phase that can be as short as a few months, but at the other end of the spectrum, it can persist throughout adult life. In clinical populations 40 per cent continue as cases at four years (Deter & Herzog, 1994), whereas in community samples of treated and untreated cases, about two-thirds are fully recovered after five years (Keski-Rahkonen et al., 2007). The course of anorexia nervosa can be unstable. Over half the cases can transform into a bulimic form of illness (Anderluh et al., 2008). Consequently, a person may remain underweight and periodically over-eat or may restore their weight and have symptoms of bulimia nervosa. The bulimic phase of the illness can merely be a transient phase during weight restoration or it can evolve into a persistent problem. Therefore, the management of symptoms of bulimia has to be considered in addition to that of the symptoms of anorexia nervosa. Bulimia nervosa less rarely transforms to anorexia nervosa. The course can also be protracted.

Causal processes

Multiple genetic and environmental factors contribute to the risk of developing an eating disorder, but precisely how these interact to produce the different forms of eating disorders is, as yet, unknown. Jacobi et al. (2004) conducted a systematic review of all the available risk factor studies on eating disorders available at the time and classified the risk factors based on the strength of the evidence and the specificity to eating disorders compared with other psychiatric conditions (Jacobi et al., 2004). A different risk profile emerges for anorexia and bulimia nervosa. The only two high potency risk factors for anorexia nervosa (AN) were being female and exercising before onset. Early feeding difficulties, picky eating, gastrointestinal problems, problems with sleeping, and over-involved, anxious parenting were medium potency risk factors, as were childhood perfectionism, obsessive compulsive personality disorder and negative evaluation of self. Pre-term birth, birth trauma and perinatal complications were specific risk factors for anorexia nervosa, as was obsessive compulsive disorder (OCD). Other research findings add to the picture. Negative self-evaluation, for example, often occurs in relation to others such as a sister, and jealousy is the predominant emotion aroused (Murphy et al., 2000; Karwautz et al., 2001). In another study (Pike et al., 2008), women with AN specifically reported greater severity and significantly higher rates of negative affectivity, perfectionism and family discord premorbidly and higher parental demands than women with other psychiatric disorders. Taken together, this evidence suggests that there are different developmental trajectories into anorexia nervosa. One route may be in terms of parental preoccupation with a rather small, fragile child, with early concerns round feeding and abdominal complaints and physical ill health being an early theme. Refusing to eat can then become a way of eliciting care or nurturance. A second developmental theme commonly encountered is that of negative affect, negative self-comparison to others and rigid competitive striving in conjunction with perfectionist standards for the self. Rigid control over food intake can become a way of 'winning the competition'.

In the case of bulimia nervosa (BN), being female and dieting were the only high potency risk factors, and negative self-evaluation the only medium potency risk factor (Jacobi et al., 2004). Pregnancy complications, parental obesity and weight or shape-related criticism were specific risk factors for bulimia nervosa. Thus, the causes of bulimia nervosa appear to be more embedded within cultures where there is both a free access to food and a fashion for slimness. In terms of a developmental trajectory into BN those predisposed to obesity or plumpness, who through adverse childhood experiences and/or weight or shape-related criticism by their families develop low self-esteem, may resort to extreme dieting that kicks off the bulimia.

The balance between biological and cultural risk factors may vary between conditions and across the range of eating disorders. Any explanation about the causes of eating disorders must account for why the onset of the illness is so tightly connected to the pubertal phase of development, particularly in girls, and how it is usually triggered by some form of psychological difficulty. One possibility is that the biological changes associated with maturation elicit an atypical response to stress (Connan et al., 2003) in some girls who have a particular genetic and personality make-up. Alternatively, it may be that this phase of development leads to a difference in the meaning and response to stress. The maturational milestones in the brain unique to this phase of development such as synaptic pruning in the frontal lobes may be of key importance. It is possible that all three of these mechanisms interact in a complex way. We have developed a model which explains some of the key epidemiological and neuroscience findings (Southgate et al., 2005) and we have translated this into treatment which is based on causal and maintaining factors (Schmidt & Treasure, 2006; Treasure et al., 2006).

Consequences of eating disorders

Anorexia nervosa

The acute illness has deleterious effects on several domains of life such as physical, spiritual, social, emotional and cognitive health and general well-being. Furthermore, because the normal process of development is inter-rupted, with many of the tasks and experiences of normal adolescence put on hold, there can be a profound disruption in the course of maturation. This latter complication is most marked in the group who have not responded to an earlier intervention and have had a protracted, severe course. Consequently, the management of adult cases of anorexia nervosa can be more complex because of this broader range of consequences. These consequences may in turn play a role in maintaining the illness.

Bulimia nervosa

The major domain impacted by bulimia nervosa is psychological well-being, but all other areas of life can be affected either indirectly from the mood changes or directly from the bulimia itself. It is, therefore, important that treatment not only focuses on the physical and nutritional needs but also addresses these other areas.

Importantly, all eating disorders have an interpersonal context. They have an impact on the well-being of close others. Reciprocally, the reaction of family members can have a significant effect on the outcome.

What do evidence-based guidelines tell us to do?

In medicine there is a move to develop clinical guidelines for different conditions, based upon systematic reviews of the literature and on a composite analysis of data obtained from randomised controlled trials which are regarded as the gold standard in terms of assessing which treatments work best for particular disorders, under what circumstances. The different National Institute for Health and Clinical Excellence (NICE) guidelines exemplify this approach. The NICE guidelines for eating disorders (National Collaborating Centre for Mental Health, 2003) were able to distil evidence from a reasonably large body of randomised controlled trials on bulimia nervosa and binge eating disorders and some grade A recommendations about the treatment of these disorders were made. Grade A recommendations are reliable as they are drawn from a synthesis of results from several high quality randomised controlled research trials. However, the NICE guidelines fall down badly in the case of anorexia nervosa, as the number and quality of randomised controlled trials on which to base any recommendations is limited for several reasons:

- *Some treatments are self-evident and dangerous to test:* for example, giving nourishment to someone who is on the verge of collapse from starvation, or giving fluids to someone developing renal failure because of dehydration.
- *Case mix:* the very broad range of severity and clinical needs of people with anorexia nervosa makes it difficult to design treatment trials that give the appropriate level of intervention to all participants.[2]
- *Case ambivalence:* acceptability of different interventions and dropout from research treatments are major problems.
- *Intervention:* many treatments are taken from other conditions and are not tailored to AN.

The NICE guidelines and anorexia nervosa

No grade A recommendations on the treatment of anorexia nervosa were made. Indeed the only research evidence that merited a grade B recommendation in the management of anorexia nervosa was the need to involve the family in the treatment of adolescents with anorexia nervosa.[3]

> Family interventions that directly address the eating disorder should be offered to children and adolescents with anorexia nervosa.
>
> (National Collaborating Centre for Mental Health, 2004)

The fact that the only positive evidence is for the involvement of families in the early intervention of adolescents does not imply that there is evidence that involvement of families is *not* helpful for adults with anorexia nervosa. Indeed, the situation is that there is very little evidence in the form of randomised trials that any intervention is successful for adults with anorexia nervosa. On the other hand, there is a great deal of evidence from many studies involving a large number of people that the family environment can have a marked effect on the outcome of anorexia nervosa (see below). The NICE guidelines highlighted the role of carers and the family in the management of anorexia nervosa in general.

The NICE guidelines and bulimia nervosa

There are grade A recommendations for the standard form of bulimia nervosa which state that a particular form of cognitive behavioural therapy (CBT), focused on the eating disorder, is the treatment of choice. At the time the guidelines were produced, no research evidence was available on which to base recommendations for either adolescent or treatment resistant forms of bulimia nervosa. The NICE guidelines, therefore, suggested that in the absence of evidence-based recommendations, adolescents with bulimia nervosa should be treated in a similar manner to adults with appropriate developmental adjustments. Research from our unit would agree with this approach, as a guided self-care version of CBT was quickly effective for adolescents with bulimia nervosa (Schmidt et al., 2007). However, there was a tentative suggestion that the level of expressed emotion in carers moderated this effect (see Chapter 6 for more details), so that individuals who had carers with high expressed emotion did less well with guided CBT self-care and had a better outcome with family-based treatment (Schmidt et al., unpublished data). Thus, it is probable that carers may need to be involved in treatment of bulimia nervosa under particular circumstances.

Cochrane systematic reviews

There are several Cochrane systematic reviews on prevention and treatment approaches for people with eating disorders (Bacaltchuk et al., 2000a; Bacaltchuk et al., 2000b; Hay & Bacaltchuk, 2000; Bacaltchuk & Hay, 2001; Bacaltchuk et al., 2001; Pratt & Woolfenden, 2002; Hay et al., 2003; Claudino et al., 2006; Fisher et al., 2008; Hay et al., 2008). These are updated at regular intervals and the interested reader can keep abreast of the evidence base relating to the treatment of eating disorders with these publications.

Family factors as moderators of treatment outcome

As discussed above, there is little evidence in the form of randomised controlled trials that any treatment is effective in adults with anorexia nervosa. On the other hand, there is good evidence from naturalistic, cohort studies that the outcome of anorexia nervosa is influenced by the emotional reactions of close others. Indeed, in the Australian and New Zealand guidelines, family factors were flagged up as important prognostic variables (Beumont et al., 2004). In their summary of the predictors of outcome at first referral, Beumont et al. (2004) stated that

> good outcome is associated with minimal weight loss (BMI>17kg/m^2), absence of medical complications, strong motivation to change behaviour, supportive family and friends who do not condone the abnormal behaviour. Poor outcome is indicated by vomiting in emaciated patients, onset in adulthood, co-existing psychiatric or personality disorder, disturbed family relationships and a long duration of illness.
>
> (Beumont et al., 2004)

Several studies have found that expressed emotion (EE) affects adherence to treatment and/or outcome in AN (Szmukler et al., 1985; Russell et al., 1987; van Furth et al., 1996; Eisler et al., 1997; Eisler et al., 2000; Uehara et al., 2001). Indeed, the effect size of the relationship between living with a relative with high EE and poor outcome is 0.5 (Butzlaff & Hooley, 1998), which is higher than the effect size found for schizophrenia or for mood disorders. This finding must be interpreted with caution as it is based on a single study in anorexia nervosa.

Furthermore, expressed emotion is modifiable by family-based interventions (Eisler et al., 2000; Uehara et al., 2001). Interestingly, there is an interaction between the level of expressed emotion and type of family intervention; namely, anorexia nervosa families with high expressed emotion have a better outcome with separated family therapy (where the parents are seen separately from the patient) rather than conjoint family therapy (Eisler et al., 2000). As mentioned above, in our study of interventions for adolescent bulimia nervosa, the outcome was better if carers with high expressed emotion were involved in a family-based intervention (Schmidt et al., unpublished data).

In conclusion, there is preliminary evidence from a small but consistent body of work that suggests that the type of close interpersonal interaction captured in the construct of EE may be a causal maintaining factor in anorexia nervosa.[4] This effect is probably most pronounced when there are high levels of contact between the person with anorexia nervosa, and their relatives. The interventions described in this book have a particular focus on expressed emotion and the reaction of family members to the illness.

The model of treatment that we have developed for anorexia nervosa names interpersonal factors as one of the four key maintaining processes (Schmidt & Treasure, 2006; Treasure et al., 2006). Thus, work with families complements individual work on nutrition and on cognitive and emotional processing. The treatment processes we describe here parallel those used in our individual approach used for the treatment of anorexia nervosa and bulimia nervosa such as motivational enhancement therapy and cognitive behavioural therapy (Treasure, 1997; Treasure & Schmidt, 1997).

The evolution of this approach

The interventions described in this book evolved from a platform of treatment research involving a series of clinical trials from the Maudsley Hospital, which have examined various aspects of family work with people with an eating disorder across the age range and the diagnostic spectrum.

The initial study in the Maudsley series of trials compared family therapy with individual therapy to prevent relapse after inpatient care in adolescents and adults with anorexia nervosa. No significant differences between these approaches were found in the adult onset patient group or in the group of adolescents with a longer duration of illness. This contrasted with the results in the recent onset adolescent group in which a family approach had a better effect on outcome at both one and five years (Russell et al., 1987; Eisler et al., 1997). This form of family treatment for the recent onset adolescent group has been described in a manual of the 'Maudsley model' (Lock et al., 2001).

In the next study, which again examined the efficacy of treatment to prevent relapse in adults with anorexia nervosa, a style of family therapy more closely matched to the developmental stage of adults was used. This sort of family approach was found to be more effective than psychodynamic or individual supportive therapy, particularly if the illness started during adolescence (Dare & Eisler, 1995). This adaptation of family treatment for adults was later used as one of the treatment arms in a study of outpatient care of adults with anorexia nervosa (Dare et al., 2001). Adults with anorexia nervosa were randomly allocated to three forms of specialised therapy; either family therapy, a focal form of individual psychodynamic therapy, or cognitive analytic therapy compared to treatment as usual (this was treatment by trainee psychiatrists supervised by a specialist eating disorder consultant). The outcome at one year was better in all three of the specialised treatments than in the non-specialised treatment. In the treatment as usual group, a greater number of inpatient admissions were needed. Also, the only death occurred in this group. The study had insufficient power to distinguish between the efficacy of the three specialised treatments. All three treatments had a focus on interpersonal relationships but the style and form in which this was done differed. There appears, therefore, to be evidence that a family approach for adults is as good as any other form of treatment. Most studies of psychotherapy in the treatment of anorexia have been too small to compare between treatments (Hay et al., 2003).

Working across the eating disorder spectrum

There are several key differences between the approach described for adolescents with a recent onset of anorexia nervosa (Lock et al., 2001) and the work with families of older patients and those within the bulimia spectrum. One of the primary aims of the 'Maudsley' adolescent/early intervention model is to raise parents' anxiety in order to mobilise them to take control of their daughter's eating.

This focus is less suitable for older patients and those with bulimia nervosa, where we aim to lower anxiety and distress in family members. Often these families have 'been there, done that'. They have the 'lived experience' of the life-threatening consequences of anorexia nervosa and the unrelenting persistence of the condition, despite high intensity treatments such as several inpatient admissions. In the case of people with bulimia nervosa, families are often distressed by the florid, disruptive and socially unacceptable nature of the symptoms, and are highly critical of the sufferer.

As the typical age of onset of anorexia nervosa is in the early teenage years, this means that adults with anorexia nervosa have usually had a protracted course of illness. As discussed earlier, this is a marker of a poor prognosis (Nielsen et al., 1998; Steinhausen, 2002). Often there have been many treatment episodes, all of which have failed to avert this ominous outcome. Thus, the family have had to live with and adjust to anorexia nervosa for many years. This resistant and persistent form of anorexia nervosa produces a difficult pattern of adaptation to that which is seen in the more acute adolescent presentations. The family may have become paralysed into behaving in rigid patterns that maintain the illness. It is also possible that the family's approach to the illness has led to a protracted course. Therefore, a functional analysis of patterns of interaction is important. This will be discussed in more detail in Chapter 6.

Furthermore, the style and form of intervention differs in order to match the developmental stage. It becomes less appropriate for parents to take over and control their offspring's life. Nevertheless, at times, it may be necessary for parents to take more active control, especially concerning food and eating, for practical, legal and moral reasons. Consequently, there needs to be careful judgement about when and how parents should take control, and when and where and by how much they should relinquish this control. This needs to be carefully negotiated, time limited and reviewed regularly with professionals. In the case of adult patients, the balance of the relationship between the parents and the patient is more even. Choice and decision-making is more equally shared between parents and offspring. Notwithstanding, there is some research, indicating that decision-making in people with anorexia nervosa is impaired. People with eating disorders, for example, do not make optimal choices on a standard gambling task (Tchanturia et al., 2007; Liao et al., 2009). This problem with insight is most pronounced in the severe high risk group usually with a body mass index less than 15 kg/m^2. This suggests that the next of kin need to remain more involved than in age-matched adult peers in this group. In particular it is helpful if professionals, carers and the individual work conjointly to manage the transition from an inpatient unit to the community.

We have also examined the role of the family in bulimia nervosa. People with bulimia nervosa, of whatever age, are less willing to include family members in care but relationship difficulties are commonly a focus of treatment. We have undertaken a study which compared a family-based intervention with a guided self-care intervention in which we had two sessions with a carer of adolescents (Schmidt et al., 2007, 2008). We gave carers information about the illness in the form of an information leaflet. People in the guided self-care condition appeared to improve more quickly but after one year, outcomes in both groups were similar. Families are most often involved in the bulimic form of the illness when this develops from anorexia nervosa. The approach to working with families with bulimia nervosa resembles that of working with adults with anorexia nervosa, in that parents take on less control over the eating behaviour. The interventions described in this book are suitable for people with bulimia. Bulimia nervosa is more likely to impact on adult relationships, such as with partners.

Conclusion and outlook

Eating disorders present with a wide range of clinical features and at different ages from childhood to adulthood. Importantly, all eating disorders have an interpersonal context. They have an impact not only on the well-being of the individual but also on their close others. Reciprocally, the reaction of family members can have a significant effect on the outcome.

In writing this book, we endorse a collaborative style of working. The next chapter gives the carers' perspective from two mothers who have a wide experience, having worked with beat, the national eating disorders charity, and personally cared for individuals with anorexia nervosa and bulimia nervosa.

Notes

1 This rough and ready categorisation is an oversimplification which does not take into account personality and other factors that colour the disorder and its prognosis, but we believe that nonetheless it has some clinical utility.
2 An example is the trial by Gowers et al. (2007), which compared two types of outpatient treatment with immediate inpatient treatment in adolescents with anorexia nervosa. Many of the young people allocated to inpatient treatment did not take this up, making it hard to interpret the findings of the study.
3 Grade B recommendations are based on a body of research that is altogether less strong than that required for grade A recommendations.

4 Stice (2002) in an excellent meta-analysis of risk and maintaining factors of eating disorders provided the following definition of a causal maintenance factor:

> a factor that predicts symptom persistence over time versus remission among initially symptomatic individuals is a maintenance factor. If an experimental increase or decrease in a factor among initially symptomatic individuals results in symptom expression or suppression respectively, it may be referred to as a causal maintenance factor.

References

Anderluh, M., Tchanturia, K., Rabe-Hesketh, S., Collier, D. & Treasure, J. (2008). Lifetime course of eating disorders: Design and validity testing of a new strategy to define the eating disorders phenotype. *Psychological Medicine* 39(1): 105–114.

Bacaltchuk, J. & Hay, P. (2001). Antidepressants versus placebo for people with bulimia nervosa. *Cochrane Database of Systematic Reviews*, CD003391.

Bacaltchuk, J., Hay, P. & Mari, J. J. (2000a). Antidepressants versus placebo for the treatment of bulimia nervosa: A systematic review. *Australian and New Zealand Journal of Psychiatry* 34(2): 310–317.

Bacaltchuk, J., Trefiglio, R. P., Oliveira, I. R., Hay, P., Lima, M. S. & Mari, J. J. (2000b). Combination of antidepressants and psychological treatments for bulimia nervosa: A systematic review. *Acta Psychiatrica Scandinavica* 101(4): 256–264.

Bacaltchuk, J., Hay, P. & Trefiglio, R. (2001). Antidepressants versus psychological treatments and their combination for bulimia nervosa. *Cochrane Database of Systematic Reviews* CD003385.

Beumont, P., Hay, P., Beumont, D., Birmingham, L., Derham, H., Jordan, A. et al. (2004). Australian and New Zealand clinical practice guidelines for the treatment of anorexia nervosa. *Australian and New Zealand Journal of Psychiatry* 38(9): 659–670.

Butzlaff, R. L. & Hooley, J. M. (1998). Expressed emotion and psychiatric relapse: A meta-analysis. *Archives of General Psychiatry* 55: 547–552.

Claudino, A., Hay, P., Lima, M., Bacaltchuk, J., Schmidt, U. & Treasure, J. (2006). Antidepressants for anorexia nervosa. *Cochrane Database of Systematic Reviews* CD004365.

Connan, F., Campbell, I. C., Katzman, M., Lightman, S. L. & Treasure, J. (2003). A neurodevelopmental model for anorexia nervosa. *Physiology and Behaviour* 79(1): 13–24.

Dare, C. & Eisler, I. (1995). Family therapy. In G. Szmukler, C. Dare & J. Treasure (eds) *Handbook of Eating Disorders: Theory, Treatment and Research*, 1st edn. Chichester: Wiley.

Dare, C., Eisler, I., Russell, G., Treasure, J. & Dodge, E. (2001). Psychological therapies for adults with anorexia nervosa: Randomised controlled trial of outpatient treatments. *British Journal of Psychiatry* 178: 216–221.

Deter, H. C. & Herzog, W. (1994). Anorexia nervosa in a long-term perspective: Results of the Heidelberg-Mannheim Study. *Psychosomatic Medicine* 56: 20–27.

Eisler, I., Dare, C., Russell, G., Szmukler, G., Le Grange, D. & Dodge, E. (1997). Family and individual therapy in anorexia nervosa: A 5-year follow-up. *Archives of General Psychiatry* 54: 1025–1030.

Eisler, I., Dare, C., Hodes, M., Russell, G., Dodge, E. & Le Grange, D. (2000). Family therapy for adolescent anorexia nervosa: The results of a controlled comparison of two family interventions. *Journal of Child Psychology and Psychiatry* 41: 727–736.

Fairburn, C. G. & Harrison, P. J. (2003). Eating disorders. *Lancet* 361: 407–416.

Fisher, C. A., Rushford, N. & Hetrick, S. E. (2008). Family therapy for anorexia nervosa. Cochrane Collaboration Depression, Anxiety and Neuroses Controlled Trials Register (CCDANCTR).

Gowers, S. G., Clark, A., Roberts, C., Griffiths, A., Edwards, V., Bryan, C. et al. (2007). Clinical effectiveness of treatments for anorexia nervosa in adolescents. *British Journal of Psychiatry* 191: 427–435.

Hay, P. J. & Bacaltchuk, J. (2000). Psychotherapy for bulimia nervosa and binging (review). *Cochrane Database of Systematic Reviews* CD000562.

Hay, P., Bacaltchuk, J., Claudino, A., Ben-Tovim, D. & Yong, P. Y. (2003). Individual psychotherapy in the outpatient treatment of adults with anorexia nervosa. *Cochrane Database of Systematic Reviews* CD003909.

Hay, P., Bacaltchuk, J., Byrnes, R. T., Claudino, A. M., Ekmejian, S. S. & Yong, P. Y. (2008). Individual psychotherapy in the outpatient treatment of adults with anorexia nervosa (2nd review). *Cochrane Database of Systematic Reviews* CD003909.

Jacobi, C., Hayward, C., de Zwaan, M., Kraemer, H. C. & Agras, W. S. (2004). Coming to terms with risk factors for eating disorders: Application of risk terminology and suggestions for a general taxonomy. *Psychological Bulletin* 130(1): 19–65.

Karwautz, A., Rabe-Hesketh, S., Hu, X., Zhao, J., Sham, P., Collier, D. A. et al. (2001). Individual-specific risk factors for anorexia nervosa: A pilot study using a discordant sister-pair design. *Psychological Medicine* 31: 317–329.

Keski-Rahkonen, A., Hoek, H. W., Susser, E. S., Linna, M. S., Sihvola, E., Raevuori, A. et al. (2007). Epidemiology and course of anorexia nervosa in the community. *American Journal of Psychiatry* 164: 1259–1265.

Liao, P. C., Uher, R., Lawrence, N., Treasure, J., Schmidt, U., Campbell, I. C. et al. (2009). An examination of decision making in bulimia nervosa. *Journal of Clinical and Experimental Neuropsychology* 31(4): 455–461.

Lock, J., Le Grange, D., Agras, W. S. & Dare, C. (2001). *Treatment Manual for Anorexia Nervosa: A Family Based Approach*. New York: Guilford.

Murphy, F., Troop, N. A. & Treasure, J. L. (2000). Differential environmental factors in anorexia nervosa: A sibling pair study. *British Journal of Clinical Psychology* 39(2): 193–203.

National Collaborating Centre for Mental Health (2003). *Eating disorders: Core interventions in the treatment and management of anorexia nervosa, bulimia nervosa, and related eating disorders*. National Institute for Health and Clinical Excellence (NICE). Available at www.nice.org.uk / CG009 (accessed 30 April 2009).

National Collaborating Centre for Mental Health (2004). *National Clinical Practice Guideline – Eating disorders: Core interventions in the treatment and management of anorexia nervosa, bulimia nervosa, and related eating disorders*. National Institute for Health and Clinical Excellence (NICE). Available at www.guideline.gov/summary/summary.aspx?doc_id=5066 (accessed 30 April 2009).

Nielsen, S., Møller-Madsen, S., Isager, T., Jørgensen, J., Pagsberg, K. & Theander, S. (1998). Standardized mortality in eating disorders: A quantitative summary of previously published and new evidence. *Journal of Psychosomatic Research* 44: 413–434.

Pike, K. M., Hilbert, A., Wilfley, D. E., Fairburn, C. G., Dohm, F. A., Walsh, B. T. et al. (2008). Toward an understanding of risk factors for anorexia nervosa: A case-control study. *Psychological Medicine*, 38(10): 1443–1453.

Pratt, B. M. & Woolfenden, S. R. (2002). Interventions for preventing eating disorders in children and adolescents. *Cochrane Database of Systematic Reviews* CD002891.

Russell, G. F., Szmukler, G. I., Dare, C. & Eisler, I. (1987). An evaluation of family therapy in anorexia nervosa and bulimia nervosa. *Archives of General Psychiatry*, 44: 1047–1056.

Schmidt, U. & Treasure, J. (2006). Anorexia nervosa: valued and visible. A cognitive-interpersonal maintenance model and its implications for research and practice. *British Journal of Clinical Psychology* 45(3): 343–366.

Schmidt, U., Lee, S., Beecham, J., Perkins, S., Treasure, J., Yi, I. et al. (2007). A randomized controlled trial of family therapy and cognitive behavior therapy guided self-care for adolescents with bulimia nervosa and related disorders. *American Journal of Psychiatry*, 164: 591–598.

Schmidt, U., Lee, S., Perkins, S., Eisler, I., Treasure, J., Beecham, J. et al. (2008). Do adolescents with eating disorder not otherwise specified or full-syndrome bulimia nervosa differ in clinical severity, comorbidity, risk factors, treatment outcome or cost? *International Journal of Eating Disorders* 41(6): 498–504.

Southgate, L., Tchanturia, K. & Treasure, J. (2005). Building a model of the aetiology of eating disorders by translating experimental neuroscience into clinical practice. *Journal of Mental Health* 14: 553–566.

Steinhausen, H. C. (2002). The outcome of anorexia nervosa in the 20th century. *American Journal of Psychiatry* 159: 1284–1293.

Stice, E. (2002). Risk and maintenance factors for eating pathology: A meta-analytic review. *Psychological Bulletin* 5: 825–848.

Szmukler, G. I., Eisler, I., Russell, G. F. & Dare, C. (1985). Anorexia nervosa, parental 'expressed emotion' and dropping out of treatment. *British Journal of Psychiatry* 147: 265–271.

Tchanturia, K., Liao, P. C., Uher, R., Lawrence, N., Treasure, J. & Campbell, I. C. (2007). An investigation of decision making in anorexia nervosa using the Iowa Gambling Task and skin conductance measurements. *Journal of the International Neuropsychological Society* 13: 635–641.

Treasure, J. (1997). *Anorexia Nervosa: A Survival Guide for Sufferers and Those Caring for Someone with an Eating Disorder*. Hove: Psychology Press.

Treasure, J. & Schmidt, U. (1997). *A Clinician's Guide to Management of Bulimia Nervosa (Motivational Enhancement Therapy for Bulimia Nervosa)*. Hove: Psychology Press.

Treasure, J., Tchanturia, K. & Schmidt, U. (2006). Developing a model of the treatment for eating disorder: Using neuroscience research to examine the how rather than the what of change. *Counselling and Psychotherapy Research* 5(3): 187–190.

Uehara, T., Kawashima, Y., Goto, M., Tasaki, S. I. & Someya, T. (2001). Psychoeducation for the families of patients with eating disorders and changes in expressed emotion: A preliminary study. *Comprehensive Psychiatry*, 42: 132–138.

van Furth, E. F., van, S., Martina, L. M., van Son, M. J., Hendrickx, J. J. & van, E. H. (1996). Expressed emotion and the prediction of outcome in adolescent eating disorders. *International Journal of Eating Disorders* 20: 19–31.

Chapter 3

The carers' perspective

Veronica Kamerling and Gráinne Smith

Introduction

In this chapter we discuss the carers' perspective and examine interactions, both with the person with an eating disorder and with those professionals involved in their care. In part, this is drawn from our personal experience but we also synthesise the experiences of the many other carers whom we have met through our role in the Eating Disorders Association (EDA, now beat).

The carers' experience: positive and negative

Supporting a family member through any chronic illness will affect many aspects of a carer's life over years. Caring for a loved one with an eating disorder often impacts on every part of home life – meals, shopping, sleep, finance, leisure time, social life, work, holidays and relationships. In fact at the UK National Carers' Conference in 2000, Professor Arthur Crisp went as far as to say: 'Carers often bankrupt themselves, emotionally and physically as well as financially, in their efforts to support their loved ones.' Throughout our journey we have identified some of the positive and negative aspects of caring for a loved one with an eating disorder.[1]

Negative experiences

Frustration

One step forward in the battle to beat the addictive behaviour of an eating disorder is a great achievement.[2] Unfortunately, a step or three backward frequently follows that hard-won step. This pattern is enormously frustrating for carers to watch, as is trying to cope with the fallout from a sufferer's feelings of despair and self-loathing, which can often take the form of spectacular tempers, aggression and hostility, and even threats of suicide. Consequently, it can be very difficult for carers to relax when an achievement *is* acknowledged or some progress *is* made, since it is hard to accept it as permanent.

Anxiety, fear and depression

No predictions can be made as to when a setback is encountered and so each day feels like a rollercoaster or battlefield. We read of a mortality rate of up to 20 per cent . . . the highest of any mental health problem.[3] Losing a loved one to anorexia becomes a very real possibility.

Consequently, in ensuring that their loved one eats enough to avoid life-threatening deterioration, carers are often faced with constant decisions about how best to tackle meals and other situations which might trigger yet another exhausting scene. This often takes place in circumstances where the sufferer's thinking is distorted, has lost track of reality and is in total denial of any problem whatsoever. With such a situation continuing for months and years – an average duration being several years – and feelings of endless grind, it is not surprising that carers become exhausted and frequently develop ill health themselves.

Guilt and helplessness

Most carers feel completely helpless as they try to work out how to cope with out-of-control behaviour they have probably never encountered before. Coping with intense and completely unpredictable hostility, aggression, and manipulation on a daily basis causes huge family problems. In the absence of useful information about how the illness may progress, what behaviour is common, and what coping strategies might help, carers frequently feel guilt that somehow they have failed to protect their child and/or may have possibly contributed to, or even caused the illness.

Isolation and loneliness

Carers frequently feel very isolated as the illness becomes more entrenched, and often neglect their own needs to make time for other activities. Worktime becomes more difficult as do other family members' needs. Interests, activities and friends are ignored and time for all social activities recedes. Many carers give up work and outside activities in their efforts to provide proper care for a sufferer, thereby completing a vicious circle of exhaustion and isolation.

Lack of information and confidentiality

Health professionals frequently quote 'confidentiality' as a reason for not giving information to carers. While some information is indeed confidential, between therapist and patient, total lack of information can cause huge distress to carers. A carer may have no idea of what to do, what might be the 'right' thing in any particular situation and may live in fear of doing the wrong thing.[4]

Stigma

Anorexia nervosa, with its obvious physical as well as emotional aspects, cannot be hidden on outings outside the house. Carers, especially parents, often feel that judgements may be made as to their fitness to bring up children who have developed mental health problems. Bulimia, although less obvious to an onlooker, may give rise to antisocial behaviour (such as stealing to fund out-of-control eating habits, lying to cover up activities, unpredictable tempers over trivial incidents or perceived criticism) which carers feel reflect badly on them.

Positive experiences

There are with hindsight some recognisable long-term positives in supporting someone through an eating disorder.

Achievement

When a carer has supported a loved one through all the negative aspects listed above, and possibly others not mentioned, when real progress is finally recognised, and recovery is established and becomes a real prospect, the feelings of taking part in a huge achievement are wonderful. These feelings may lead to a reassessment of life values and new confidence in coping skills for carers.

Closeness

Living through and sharing the battle against an eating disorder, supporting a loved one through all the ups and downs, trials and tribulations, of their illness while they struggle to beat it, often results in a new closeness between carers and sufferers.

New skills and strengths

Personal resources, unknown or unexplored before the experience of caring for a loved one with an eating disorder, can provide new found confidence, which may be used to help and support others on a personal and professional level. Carers who have supported a loved one over years of struggle, for example, may be able to give time, effort and energy to working on a telephone helpline, email or snail mail support, starting support groups, participating in training, talks and workshops for professionals and other carers.

Friendships

Sharing experiences with others in difficult circumstances can be a therapeutic experience. Mutual bonding that includes the highs and extreme lows
which are part of the erratic, unpredictable paths of these illnesses, can often
lead to new and enduring friendships. Where problems and progress are discussed and shared, established relationships may also develop and grow in
new ways.

Interactions between carers and professionals

It usually comes as a profound shock to parents and carers to hear that their
child or loved one has an eating disorder. They may have heard something
about the illness, may have read an article or two on the subject, but will have
no idea of the real impact on family life, as well as on the sufferer. Parents are
frequently left floundering with no information, no support and no idea of
who to turn to for help. They are often left frustrated when professionals
ignore information that they, the family, can offer about individual behaviour
associated with their loved one's illness.

Carers need to know that they can be part of the solution, rather than part
of the problem. Ignoring what carers can offer, in terms of understanding the
background and context to the illness as well as contributing to full assessment with problem behaviours that a sufferer may not disclose, means that
much useful information is lost to professionals. This may prolong the
illness if carers and families have no 'tools of the trade' to allow them to carry
out their work of support properly – and may lead to relapse and even to
tragedy.[5]

What would help?

First steps . . .

When a carer arrives in surgery to see their general practitioner (GP) about a
family member who has lost dramatic amounts of weight and who is displaying erratic behaviour, both to food and also to many other situations, they are
already feeling extremely worried. Even more unfortunate is the fact that one
core aspect of an eating disorder is that sufferers frequently feel ambivalence
about their illness and may even deny any problem. This means that the
sufferer may manipulate the situation to avoid treatment or tests. The sufferer
may appear to listen and agree with what the doctor says about weight loss,
diet and so on, but have no intention of changing behaviour. This adds to the
stress and distress for a carer who is at a loss as to how to get a professional to
take seriously very real concerns.

Problems with finding medical help are even more difficult when a sufferer is over 18, and therefore legally an adult. A carer may have spent much effort in persuading a sufferer to see a doctor, only to find that they, as parents, are excluded or ignored. Confidentiality may be cited as the reason for this exclusion. Putting up barriers to parental support, however, may prolong the illness. Furthermore, no useful purpose is served by belittling the problems through inappropriate reassurance.

Consideration

Beginnings are very important; they can set a positive scene for professional and family coordinated support efforts – or a negative one. An open and warm approach, a smile and a pleasant greeting from a health professional mean a great deal. Carers appreciate being listened to and being taken seriously. Summary dismissal, such as claims of over-anxiety or over-protectiveness, is unhelpful, as is the reassurance that loss of weight is 'just a passing phase'. It reduces the possibility of building the cooperative approach needed to aid recovery. A watchful waiting approach is more helpful.[6] This involves a regular review of the unfolding course with repeat appointments to monitor nutritional health. Indeed, such an approach can be an effective early intervention and if the weight loss stops, relief all round.

Early diagnosis

The earlier a diagnosis is made in eating disorders and the sooner effective treatment is given, the better the chance of recovery. Often this requires a specialist approach. Precious time is often lost when well-meaning professionals dismiss a parent's concerns rather than accepting that an eating disorder is possibly part of the differential diagnosis. An early effective intervention may help reduce or even avoid the development of chronic illness lasting many years, affecting many lives as well as the sufferer's, and the possibility of early death.

Information

Without information, carers can be helpless. They may inadvertently fall into unhelpful patterns of behaviour that may serve to maintain and prolong the illness (see Chapter 6 and Appendix 1).

Information is needed on the following areas:

- symptoms – what to expect
- how to access services
- overview of possible treatment options – NHS or private, etc.
- funding issues
- support organisations, telephone numbers, e.g. beat (formerly EDA)

- local support information
- if any drugs are prescribed, e.g. for depression, carers need to know of possible side-effects and precautionary measures, as well as frequency and size of dose.

Information about local services and self-help charitable organisations such as the beat/EDA can be a real lifeline for carers.

Honesty

Honesty about the scale of possible problems is valued and required from the beginning. An eating disorder *may* have a relatively short time frame, perhaps a year or two, but the average length of illness is five to seven years. A proportion of sufferers will unfortunately develop a chronic illness lasting for many years. This information can come as a profound shock to carers. Honesty from the beginning is much better than finding out gradually about the most difficult aspects of the illness and being totally unprepared.[7]

Communication and continuity

Without communication and continuity, carers are handicapped. An example of good practice is a service where carers may telephone to report or discuss difficulties. This does not have to be the therapist working with their off-spring. Rather it can be a professional with carer liaison skills or even an expert carer, i.e. someone who has experienced the problem and has some basic skills to impart.

Compassion and support

Hearing difficult information, especially on top of months or even years of struggling at home, cannot be taken in easily. The emotional reaction may vary with the individual. Compassion and support are needed, therefore, to help families absorb and come to terms with the information. It is helpful if carers are given support telephone numbers, e.g. beat and contact numbers of any services in the local area. Carers can be encouraged to seek help for themselves in order to allow them to support their ill family member. An assessment of how a carer is coping (with the offer of help where and when needed) is very important both for carers and those they care for. If carers reach burn-out and can cope no longer because they themselves have become ill with exhaustion and depression, who will then care in the home situation?

No jargon

While doctors and other professionals may understand common medical shorthand terms (e.g. BMI for body mass index), carers without experience sometimes find it difficult to cope with terms that make them feel excluded and patronised, adding further to feelings of helplessness and despair.

It is enormously helpful to avoid any possibility of miscommunication and a divergence of confusion about treatment goals, if the carer is given a time at the end of the session between sufferer and therapist to jointly discuss problems with eating, nutrition and medical risk. It may be helpful to set joint targets for mealtimes and snacks etc. Patient confidentiality need not be breached, but it enables the carer to be a cooperative partner in treatment. If possible, a time should be given between appointments for carers to contact the professional to discuss particular problems that may have arisen. Again, this can be done with the full knowledge of the sufferer.

Workshops

Working in groups with other carers can help to offer insight into difficulties that commonly occur in the face of the illness, e.g. compulsive or 'kangaroo caring', or an overly directive 'rhinoceros response' (see Appendix 1). Practical support addressing how to avoid such traps can have positive benefits. Some of the gains of this type of support include:

- meeting people who have shared similar experiences
- seeing one's own or similar experiences reflected in others lessens feelings of isolation
- finding insight into how best to deal with individual problems
- finding a beneficial discussion forum
- having the opportunity to learn and practise skills such as reflective listening
- making space to focus on carer's own needs and issues, including social activities
- recognising that carers cannot 'save' the sufferer: responsibility for fighting the eating disorder is ultimately in the hands of the individual sufferer.

All of the above means that carers are in a much better position to offer and provide appropriate care for a sufferer. Communication in the daily life of the family is improved.[8]

Family therapy

Family therapy may be offered as part of ongoing treatment and, depending on the individual's experience, can have both positive and negative aspects. Previously stable family relationships may come under severe strain. Poorer relationships will probably have deteriorated rapidly under the pressure of a family member whose behaviour has changed dramatically. The family context may be of a life-threatening condition by the time medical help is found and accepted by a sufferer.

Every family member may try to cope differently, depending on individual personality styles, and may view the offer of therapy in various ways. Some may welcome anything at all which might be helpful in their struggle to offer appropriate support. Others, however, may see therapy in a very different light. 'Therapy' of any kind can be perceived to be 'making better'. Family therapy may be regarded as an attempt by professionals to 'improve' the family and viewed as criticism of the behaviour and beliefs of all its members. This is exacerbated by the constant fear of having somehow failed someone you love, with associated feelings of guilt and helplessness.

A flexible way of working in response to the individual circumstances may be an important key to success. A mix of individual, family, part or whole-family meetings may be more beneficial than rigid insistence on 'individual *only*' or 'family *only*' sessions.

The therapist can have a profound effect on the outcome. On a positive note, if there is warmth and a wish to understand, offering information, support and the possibility of useful strategies and skills appropriate to individual family situations, can be very welcome. Therapy not only may help families through long-term stressful times but also may enhance their coping skills. Families who talk through difficult issues, which may or may not have been openly discussed before, often achieve closer relationships. Negative outcomes can occur, however, when accusation, criticism and blame surfaces and may lead to even deeper deterioration in relationships which are already difficult. Parents may feel completely undermined and the confidence of individual family members may be greatly damaged, especially with parents who already feel they are being judged as failures in terms of their parenting skills. If sessions are regularly fraught and experienced as constantly unconstructive, they may well have an adverse effect on the chances of recovery. Unhelpful behaviours may become further exaggerated, with further fractures in communication and relationships. (Chapters 8–13 discuss therapeutic techniques in greater detail.)

Outpatient care and discharge after hospitalisation

A Transitional Care Plan is needed to allow carers to continue support at home.[9] Without information, guidance or support, carers may inadvertently maintain certain behaviours by falling into less-than-helpful patterns.

The Care Plan should include the following:

- An eating plan, so that carers know what is expected. One of the key aspects of the illness is that sufferers want to avoid eating a health-giving diet, and without information and support, mealtimes may turn into a battlefield. Carers should be taught what is expected at mealtimes, such as appropriate targets to set, possible pitfalls to watch out for and guidance about how to give support. It is likely that sufferers will sometimes attempt to sabotage meals, reducing the amounts eaten and carers should be equipped with strategies to address these issues.
- Information on what is expected in terms of weight gain, weighing etc. It is helpful if there can be some agreed compromise on this.
- Information about possible patterns of unhelpful family behaviour (kangaroo care, rhinoceros response) and which may maintain and prolong the illness (see Appendix 1).
- Information about follow-up appointments for sufferers, so that carers can encourage the individual to keep appointments.
- Appointments to help assess how a carer or family is coping, and to address particular difficulties or concerns.
- Clear communication so that difficulties may be addressed quickly.
- Notes for carers are extremely helpful.

Notes

1 Chapter 3 provides a comprehensive understanding of the carers' perspective with a discussion on specific problems and coping mechanisms utilised when faced with the challenges of the caring role.
2 Until fairly recently, eating disorder specialists would have baulked at the use of the term 'addictive' in the context of eating disorders. However, new animal models of eating disorders, in particular of bulimia nervosa, support the notion that aspects of eating disorders are addiction-like.
3 The mortality rate of 20 per cent for anorexia nervosa comes from a long-term study of patients seen in a specialist unit, i.e. this was a very ill group of people. Other long-term studies of anorexia nervosa quote lower mortality rates. The mortality rate for bulimia nervosa is not elevated.
4 Chapter 4 provides further information on the relationship between carers' and patients' rights.
5 Chapter 11 discusses practical skills-based training. This information is intended to equip the carer with techniques and strategies to use on a daily basis with their loved ones in the hope that it instils a greater sense of mastery and empowerment over their son or daughter's illness.
6 Research by Laura Currin from our group has shown that a GP approach of watchful waiting, with review appointments at close intervals and clear instructions to sufferers and families as to what to do if there is deterioration, is seen as helpful by families, whereas a more ill-defined 'come back and see me if you need to' approach is not.
7 While an honest and realistic discussion about the prognosis will contain some hard-to-swallow facts, it also needs to emphasise that doctors cannot predict the

outcome of any given person and that there are many things carers can do to support a speedy recovery.

8 Chapter 11 provides a comprehensive guide to the aims, format and protocol of the family workshop.

9 Chapter 12 describes an intensive intervention with families in preparation for the transition from inpatient to outpatient care.

Further reading

Smith, G. (2004). *Anorexia and Bulimia in the Family*. Chichester: Wiley.

Smith, G. (2007). *Families, Carers and Professionals: Building Constructive Conversations*. Chichester: Wiley.

www.workingtogethercare.com

Chapter 4

An ethico-legal account of working with carers in eating disorders

Emma Baldock

Introduction

Why an ethico-legal account is needed

As this book makes clear, involving carers in the treatment of eating disorders is of important mutual benefit for the patient and their family. If we are to maximise its benefits, however, then we need an ethico-legal account of its integration into the current health-care system. This is because the western culture of individual autonomy and individual rights is a potential stumbling-block to carer involvement. Professionals have a well-established duty to preserve patient autonomy, which entails respecting the patient's decisions about treatment (consent), including decisions concerning the communication of information about them (confidentiality). More broadly, this culture of respecting individual rights also entails a tendency to treat the individual in varying degrees of isolation from their social context. It is into this individualist culture that the carer involvement initiative has been introduced.

Professionals now not only have a duty to preserve patient autonomy, but also have a duty to address the needs of carers and to consider the carers' potential contribution to the index patient's recovery. The challenge is the ethical and legal integration of these twin duties.

The first purpose of this chapter is to set out in brief the possibilities of integrating these patient-oriented and carer-oriented duties within existing legal boundaries. The second purpose is to set out the possibilities of integrating them in ethical terms. This, I propose, depends on a cultural shift in which respect for autonomy no longer assumes an isolated, independent individual but assumes, instead, individuals who are *socially embedded* and *interdependent*. The third purpose is to argue that this reconceptualisation of autonomy is particularly apposite for anorexia nervosa.

A word about the emphasis of the chapter

This chapter is about the ethico-legal issues of working with carers in eating disorders, but there are some differences of note in the ethical issues raised by anorexia nervosa and bulimia nervosa. First, anorexia nervosa is a highly visible condition and carers are therefore likely to know that something is wrong, even if they have not articulated this formally in the diagnostic term anorexia nervosa. As a consequence, there is no great issue in confidentiality over the diagnosis. Bulimia nervosa does not have this high level of visibility, and it is possible that carers do not know about it (though close family members usually do). If carers do not know about it, it may not always be appropriate to tell them if the patient does not want them to know. Second, anorexia nervosa, as well as being the more visible condition, is also associated with higher medical risk and disability. This means that information sharing with carers is particularly important and some kind of breach of confidentiality is often appropriate. Third, because of the high levels of associated medical risk, anorexia nervosa is more often treated in inpatient settings. This has the consequence that the patient's overall contact with carers is under the control of professionals to a much greater degree than it is in the outpatient setting. If, for example, carers are excluded from an adult inpatient service, the patient may not see their carers for months at a time. In an outpatient service, on the other hand, the consequence of excluding carers would be less far-reaching. Although material in this chapter can be applied to carer involvement in eating disorders as a whole, much of it has special relevance to anorexia nervosa. Finally, the challenge of integrating patient-oriented and carer-oriented duties is particularly salient in the case of adult patients, where an individualist, autonomy-oriented mentality is most likely to take hold. Therefore, the chapter has been written with adult patients in mind. The arguments are still relevant to minors, in so far as the same autonomy-oriented mentality may be applied, but the different legal frameworks which operate for minors are not covered.

Legal boundaries and the integration of duties to patients and carers

Legal and policy guidance on carer involvement

In recent years it has been recognised that carers often have needs which are a direct consequence of the care they provide, and these are now considered an important outcome of treatment programmes (National Collaborating Centre for Mental Health (NCCMH) 2004). It is also recognised that carers need access to certain information to help them to care safely and effectively – at the very least an account of the illness and guidance about how to deal with the patient's problems in so far as they impinge on the carer's life (Bloch et al., 1995). In addition, the NICE guidelines on eating disorders recommend family-based interventions. Legislative measures are now in place which establish the rights of carers to an annual assessment of their needs and to access information concerning the health of the person for whom they are caring (Department of Health, 1999, 2000, 2004a). The Carers UK website at www.carersuk.org provides summaries of and links to all the latest policy and legal documents. Professionals now have a responsibility to offer carers an assessment of their needs, to communicate appropriate information to them and, on the recommendation of the NICE guidelines, to work to involve families in treatment programmes.

Legal and policy guidance on patients' rights

While these developments in carer involvement have been forming, confidentiality and consent have remained foundational principles of ethical health-care. It is a basic right of patients to decide how information about themselves should be shared with others, and this right is a crucial part of the relationship of trust between health professional and patient which facilitates the optimum level of health-care. It is also a basic right of patients to decide whether or not to accept a proposed treatment option.

Confidentiality is a legal obligation derived from case law and is included within NHS employment contracts as a specific requirement linked to disciplinary procedures (Department of Health, 2003). There are four main areas of law which govern its application: Common Law, Data Protection Act 1998, Human Rights Act 1998 and Administrative Law. The NHS Code of Practice (Department of Health, 2003) provides a detailed summary of requirements. Consent, like confidentiality, is a common law principle and the NHS has produced various guidelines on its implications for practice (see for example Department of Health, 2001a).

The integration of duties to carers and patients

Much can be done to integrate these two duty sets by creating a favourable ethos in a service. The patient can be introduced from the start to the idea that carer involvement and information-sharing are part of clinical best practice, and a *modus operandi* for the team. Precisely how that involvement and information-sharing takes shape can then form a routine part of the initial and ongoing dialogue with the patient and their carers. Patient decision-making does not take place in a vacuum, but rather in the context of conversations and relationships with others. Given that carer involvement and information-sharing are part of best practice, patients should be encouraged and facilitated where possible to make decisions in favour of involving their carers.

Carers have a set of rights which exist independently of patient rights, hence there should be no difficulty of integration in this area. Carers have the right to an annual assessment of their needs, to general information concerning the diagnosis, and to advice on how to deal with any associated problems (as, for example, they might glean from the workshops for carers described elsewhere in this book). This kind of information is not personal to the patient and is therefore not governed by confidentiality legislation.

In the following cases, then, the duties to patients and carers need not be in conflict:

- instigating an ethos of carer involvement as part of good practice
- providing carers with general information about the diagnosis
- providing carers with a needs assessment
- providing carers with access to carer workshops where these are available.

Sometimes, even after every effort has been made to encourage and facilitate collaborative care, patients do not consent to the sharing of personal information, or do not wish their carers to be involved in their care.

Conditions justifying carer involvement without patient consent

Szmukler and Bloch (1997) carried out an ethico-legal analysis of issues raised by carer involvement in the treatment of people with schizophrenia and formulated a list of conditions which could justify overriding an adult patient's refusal to have their carers involved. The following is an adapted version of their list, to apply to eating disorders.

- *If the risk of harm (to self or others) is high: sharing information with carers may be necessary in order to practise safely.* This is a necessary condition of overriding a patient's wishes: in other words, without such risk, the patient's wishes should not be overruled.
- *If the patient does not have the capacity to choose.* A lack of capacity is not a *sufficient* condition for overriding a patient's wishes: the action must also be necessary on the grounds of risk. A lack of capacity may not be a *necessary* condition either: see 'A note on capacity' below.
- *If involvement of the family is the least restrictive option* (e.g. if it is an alternative to compulsory inpatient treatment where individual outpatient treatment is not working). This is neither a necessary nor sufficient criterion, but rather a principle to aid clinical decision-making.
- *If there is evidence that communication with the family is reasonable at times when the patient is not acutely ill.* This is neither a necessary nor a sufficient criterion, but rather a principle to aid clinical decision-making.
- *In the case of an inpatient, if there is no history of independent living prior to admission.* This is neither a necessary nor sufficient criterion, but rather a principle to aid clinical decision-making.

A note on capacity

According to the Mental Capacity Act 2005, a person lacks capacity in relation to a matter if, 'at the material time he is unable to make a decision for himself in relation to the matter because of an impairment, or a disturbance in the functioning of, the mind or brain', and the person is unable to make a decision for themselves if they are unable (a) to understand the information relevant to the decision, (b) to retain that information, (c) to use or weigh that information as part of the process of making the decision, or (d) to communicate the decision. The information relevant to a decision includes information about the reasonable foreseeable consequences of (a) deciding one way or another, or (b) failing to make the decision (Department for Constitutional Affairs, 2005: 2–3). In general, a person should not be treated against their will if they have the capacity to refuse treatment. However, there is an exception to this principle under the Mental Health Bill 2007, which amends the Mental Health Act 1983: treatment *can* be given for a mental disorder against the person's will, even when the person has the capacity to refuse the treatment. Nevertheless, there must be sufficient risk to warrant this. Therefore, it may be indicated to override a patient's wishes to exclude their family *even if they have capacity*, if there is sufficient risk (criterion 1).

Two concepts of autonomy and the integration of duties to patients and carers

A culture clash

Many of the difficulties with integrating patient autonomy and carer involvement derive, I argue, from the culture of individual autonomy in western health-care. As witness to this, it is not uncommon for professionals to exclude carers of people with eating disorders, and although in some cases this is because the patient herself does not want contact, sometimes it is because of confusion over the principle of confidentiality. A survey of carers (Scotland, 2000) found that among carers who got no information from professional staff, 40 per cent were given 'confidentiality' as the reason. Sometimes carers were asked to give background information to staff but this was one-way communication only. In other cases, there was no information exchange at all. The Department of Health (2002) identified this issue, stating that

> Confidentiality should not be accepted as an excuse for not listening to carers. Carers should be given sufficient information by mental health services in a way that they can readily understand, to help them provide care effectively.

A culture of carer involvement, which the Department of Health was promoting, was clearly clashing with a predominant culture of individual rights.

A primary reason for these difficulties, I propose, is our individualist concept of autonomy which continues to dominate western bioethics and which has had a profound influence on the policy and legislation governing management in health-care settings. If we are serious about involving carers, then I believe we need to rethink the way we understand autonomy, or else to rethink the emphasis we give to it. I therefore argue for an alternative concept of autonomy which facilitates the integration of duties to patients and carers.

The existing individualist autonomy concept

The English word 'autonomy' is derived from the Greek for 'oneself' (αυτος) and 'law' (νομος) and translates literally as 'self-rule'. This etymo-logical definition captures much of today's meaning of the term, at least in the more restricted sense in which it is often used in western health-care. Autonomy in this context refers to the right of the individual patient to self-rule which in the context of health-care amounts to the right to informed choices concerning their treatment and concerning the disclosure of their personal information to others.

The principle of autonomy in health-care is based on the belief that indi-vidual choice is the most likely mechanism by which to maximise welfare, but it is also considered an end in itself – to be valued even when an individual's autonomous choice does not appear to be maximising their welfare (Grisso & Appelbaum, 1998). Thus in a health-care setting when the principle of promoting the welfare of one's fellow citizens clashes with the principle of autonomy or self-determination then this latter principle normally has the upper hand.

Autonomy is emphasised as a core 'right' and is associated with ideas of the independence of the individual and their freedom from the interference of others. Indeed, the tendency is to equate autonomy with individualism, the movement which according to Dan Callahan (2003) has made auto-nomy so powerful and popular an ethical principle. He writes that autonomy 'is *de facto* given a place of honour because the thrust of individualism, whether from the egalitarian left or the market oriented right, is to give people maximum liberty in devising their own lives and values' (Callahan, 2003: 289).

The existing autonomy concept and carer involvement

That autonomy should be so closely wed to the independence of the indi-vidual and their freedom from the interference of others helps to explain why it is has been difficult to integrate the involvement of carers into our health-care system. It helps to make sense of the reluctance of professionals to share information, and why this reluctance may sometimes present as the *default*. It also helps to make sense of the ethos change in adult services, which may no longer be set up for carer involvement.

An alternative concept of autonomy

The definition of autonomy sketched out above is based on an impoverished view of the human person. It is based on the view of human beings as independent individuals and neglects the fact that human beings are also social creatures who exist in a web of interpersonal relations. George Agich (1993), a health professional working with a population of older adults, was moved to reinterpret autonomy in order to make it applicable to his patients. The older adults under his care are typically dependent to varying degrees on their relatives, but they are still individuals afforded respect. The application of the autonomy principle in this context requires sensitivity to the individual, *in their interrelatedness with others*.

Agich suggests that rethinking autonomy in this way is not only important for the care of those with long-term dependency needs. Those dependent on others are necessarily embedded within a social network, but so are the rest of us – even if with a greater degree of choice. So through the process of rethinking autonomy for the care of his elderly patients, Agich proposes that autonomy should be reinterpreted more generally to accommodate social arrangements such as family, friendship and community associations. He defends this proposal by claiming that this social network not only is a reality for the individual, but also is in fact the very thing that makes possible autonomous human existence in the first place. Autonomous existence, one might say, finds fulfilment in the individual's interaction with others.

The alternative concept of autonomy and carer involvement

The autonomy of the individual thus conceived – in terms of a mutually informative independence and interdependence – need not be in conflict with the practice of involving carers. Real conflicts will still arise in the practical negotiation of varying needs and desires, but the two processes, promoting patient autonomy and involving carers, are at least not antagonistic in principle. It is hoped that this conceptualisation of autonomy might facilitate a collaborative model of patient care in which health professionals can encourage the involvement of carers without fearing that by doing so they are neglecting patient autonomy. If we define autonomy too strictly in terms of independence and non-interference we neglect that the fulfilment of autonomous being lies in the way we live our lives not in isolation but in interdependence with others, in a shared social world.

The integration of duties to patients and carers with special reference to anorexia nervosa

The individualist concept of autonomy is potentially problematic in a wide range of cases, and not just in specific populations like older adults. However, it may be especially problematic for some older adults. Here, I review evidence which suggests that it might also be especially problematic for adults with anorexia nervosa.

Developmental delay and anorexia nervosa

Anorexia nervosa is associated with a delay in the development of inter-personal functioning which is likely to make the individualist autonomy approach particularly challenging for this patient group. This delay has a variety of complex interacting causes and outcomes – social, psychological and neurodevelopmental. Katzman et al. (1997) found evidence for a neuro-developmental delay in anorexia nervosa which they hypothesised to be a consequence of malnutrition on normal brain development over the important developmental period of adolescence. The cognitive and behavioural consequences of such a delay are as yet unspecified, but it is clear that the illness can have severe disruptive effects on psychological development, in particular in the formation of relationships. Whereas during normal adolescence, attachments to parental figures are weakened and new bonds are created with peers, in the case of anorexia nervosa adolescents may become 'institutional-ised' following prolonged admissions and their attachments to parents replaced by attachments to health professionals. They may then be incapable of taking responsibility for their own actions in the way expected of them in adult services, marked by an individualist autonomy ethic. Even if disruptions in attachment processes do not occur in this extreme form, nevertheless patients will often miss out on the usual environment, rich in social inter-actions with peers and with family which most teenagers and young adults experience.

The developmental task of achieving autonomy and anorexia nervosa

Autonomy is a patient right, but a degree of autonomy is also a psychological capacity which is part of being a healthy human being. From our clinical experience, the development of autonomy may be particularly problematic in the eating disorders. First, a sense of powerlessness, or perceived lack of autonomy is characteristic, in combination with a drive for control. Second, anorexia nervosa in particular is associated with high levels of dependence which, if dealt with by over-protective parenting (see 'kangaroo carer' in Appendix 1: Toolkit for Carers), can help to maintain the illness. Third, eating disorders may be associated with a pseudo-autonomous stance in which the sufferer gives the impression of not needing others, yet put themselves at high levels of psychological and physical risk.

Striving for independence is a normal part of growing up and characterises the adolescent developmental period. Eating disorders often develop during this adolescent period and (pseudo-autonomy aside) they may be associated with regression into a childlike state of high dependence. It is extremely difficult for parents in this context to find the balance between protective parenting and promoting autonomy. The regression into high dependence is a feature of the illness and is independent of age, thus in Chapter 16 of this book we hear the following from Julie, an adult who has completed a first degree, has experienced working life, and has now begun a second degree: 'I sort of let Mum make choices all the time for me, I totally relied on her'. Parents can act to maintain this process of dependence and the giving of some independence to their child can be an important step towards their recovery. Julie reflects on this as follows: 'I [previously] spent the entire day with my mother and so when she went out and did her things it meant . . . it was the beginning of me getting better'. The challenge is to find safe ways of giving more independence to patients when the physical and psychological health risks are severe.

Decision-making and anorexia nervosa

Related to these difficulties with the development of interpersonal and independent functioning are difficulties with decision-making. The cognitive skills required for legal capacity tests are generally preserved in people with anorexia nervosa (Tan et al., 2003a), so that it is reasonable to assume that most would have the legal capacity to make decisions about family involvement in treatment. However, human decision-making involves more than the cognitive skills of legal capacity. At least two key factors are not included in legal capacity: the relationship of the person's decision to their values and the person's capacity for emotion processing.

Tan et al. (2003a, 2003b, 2003c) have argued that patients with anorexia nervosa who have preserved legal capacity, nevertheless, have questionable abilities to decide about treatment because of the relationship between their illness and their value systems. In the interviews conducted and recorded by Tan and colleagues, the eating disorder is often described by patients as a central value which displaces other previously valued things. Pertinent to the topic of this book is that some patients cease to value their families when they become ill. If a patient refuses family involvement in treatment when there is evidence that relations were good, and that she valued her family prior to her illness, then it is persuasive to consider whether the refusal is in some sense a part of the illness.

Given the close connection between someone's values and their identity, it is not surprising that the entwining of a person's values and their eating disorder also often entails an entwining of the disorder with their identity (Vitousek et al., 1998; Tan et al., 2003a). This phenomenon, referred to as 'egosyntonicity', makes it difficult for patients to take responsibility for their lives and to make independent, mature decisions about things since they often have a diminished sense of self aside from the eating disorder. Tan and colleagues point out that the identity issue can be particularly problematic for those who develop an eating disorder in early adolescence, since this group may never have established a mature, premorbid, 'preanorexic' identity to function as a clear alternative to the anorexic identity.

As well as these issues surrounding values and identity are related problems with emotion processing. Traditionally, decision-making has been considered the realm of emotion-free cognitive functioning, and this stance is reflected in the definition of legal capacity. However, the latest models of decision-making have started to elucidate the crucial role that emotions have to play – at least with certain kinds of decisions (Damasio, 1994). Damasio and his colleagues have been particularly interested in the role of emotions in everyday life decision-making, which involves balancing various risks and benefits over time. They have designed a laboratory gambling task which is designed to reflect the uncertainty and complexity of everyday life decision-making (Damasio, 1994; Bechara et al., 1997) and have found that it is sensitive to the impairment in everyday life decision-making manifest in neurological patients with lesions of the ventro-medial prefrontal cortex. These patients have difficulty holding down a job and organising their day-to-day lives but perform well on many of the standard cognitive laboratory tasks. Those with anorexia nervosa likewise perform less well than controls on Damasio's gambling task (Cavedini et al., 2004) while having difficulties with day-to-day living, but showing no general impairment in cognitive functioning. There is also evidence of abnormal functioning in the ventro-medial prefrontal cortex in people with eating disorders (Uher et al., 2005).

The case of Carol, described in Chapter 9, may reflect this difficulty with the emotional aspects of decision-making. Carol's therapist advises her mother not to give Carol too much choice, because she has difficulty coping with too many options. In the context of disrupted emotion processing, everyday decision-making can become a problem, even where legal capacity is preserved.

The transition to adult services

These considerations concerning the developmental maturity and decision-making skills of people with anorexia nervosa suggest that an individualist autonomy ethic may be particularly problematic when applied to this population. This becomes a particular concern in the transition to adult services, where the individualist ethic is likely to establish itself most strongly.

Although different local services follow different practices, the transferral of a patient to adult services is often determined by age boundaries, so that a patient reaching adult age (typically 18 in the UK) is likely to be transferred to adult services regardless of their capacities and developmental maturity.

It is a fairly common occurrence for people with eating disorders to experience the transition to adult services since the illness typically arises during adolescence and has a mean progression of about six years (Zipfel et al., 2000). Treasure et al. (2005) report that patients and family members do indeed often find the transition difficult, not only because of confusion over procedures for managing it, but also because of the sudden change in treatment ethos in adult services. The authors comment: 'The increased responsibility placed on the individual for their behaviour that is expected in adult services can be a challenge. Parents can also find they are suddenly excluded from decisions about care' (Treasure et al., 2005: 399).

The clinical severity of anorexia nervosa is an important factor to consider here. Some long-term studies of the illness have suggested that the mortality rate may be as high as 20 per cent, with equal numbers arising through medical complications and suicide (Nielsen et al., 1998; Zipfel et al., 2000). Given this situation, the risks associated with a stressful service transition could be extreme. The NICE guidelines on eating disorders do in fact single out the transition between services in anorexia nervosa as a specific period of increased vulnerability and risk (National Collaborating Centre for Mental Health, 2004).

If we consider the management of adults with anorexia nervosa in the light of these findings concerning their psychological, emotional, social and neurodevelopmental development, there is a strong case for prolonging carer involvement in their management, not only for the sake of carers, nor only so that carers can manage patients more safely at home, but also for the longer term best interests of patients. The crux of the argument here is that these patients may be of adult age but be so defined by their illness, and their general psychosocial and emotional development so disrupted, that they need continued input from others to aid their decision-making.

Conclusion

Agich's (1993) reconceptualisation of autonomy is more apposite then ever in the special context of anorexia nervosa. As with Agich's message, the message of this chapter is that this reconceptualisation of autonomy is appropriate beyond the sphere of eating disorders and into the realm of health-care, in general. We live our lives and make our decisions, not in isolation, but in an interdependent web of human relations. The collaborative care described in this book reflects this fact and our health-care systems, in general, will be all the better for doing the same.

References

Agich, G. J. (1993). *Autonomy and Long-Term Care*. Oxford: Oxford University Press.

Bechara, A., Damasio, H., Tranel, D. & Damasio, A. (1997). Deciding advantageously before knowing the advantageous strategy. *Science* 275: 1293–1295.

Bloch, S., Szmukler, G. I., Herrman, H., Benson, A. & Colussa, S. (1995). Counseling caregivers of relatives with schizophrenia: Themes, interventions, and caveats. *Family Process* 34(4): 413–425.

Callahan, D. (2003). Principlism and communitarianism. *Journal of Medical Ethics* 29(5): 287–291.

Cavedini, P., Bassi, T., Ubbiali, A., Casolari, A., Giordani, S., Zorzi, C. et al. (2004). Neuropsychological investigation of decision-making in anorexia nervosa. *Psychiatry Research* 127(3): 259–266.

Damasio, A. R. (1994). *Descartes' Error: Emotion, Reason, and the Human Brain*. New York: Hayrer Collins.

Department for Constitutional Affairs (2005). *Mental Capacity Act*. London: HMSO.

Department of Health (DH) (1999). *National Service Framework for Mental Health: Modern Standards and Service Models*. London: DH.

Department of Health (2000). *Carers and Disabled Children Act*. London: DH.

Department of Health (2001a). *Consent – What You Have a Right to Expect: A Guide for Relatives and Carers*. London: DH.

Department of Health (2001b). *Consent: A Guide for Children and Young People*. London: DH.

Department of Health (2002). *Developing Services for Carers and Families of People with Mental Illness*. London: DH.

Department of Health (2003). *Confidentiality: NHS Code of Practice*. London: DH.

Department of Health (2004a). *Carers (Equal Opportunities) Act*. London: DH.

Department of Health (2004b). *Draft Mental Health Bill*. London: DH.

Grisso, T. & Appelbaum, P. S. (1998). *MacArthur Competence Assessment Tool for Treatment*. Sarasota, FL: Professional Resource Press.

House of Lords & House of Commons (2005). *Joint Committee on the Draft Mental Health Bill*. London.

Katzman, D. K., Zipursky, R. B., Lambe, E. K. & Mikulis, D. J. (1997). A longitudinal magnetic resonance imaging study of brain changes in adolescents with anorexia nervosa. *Archives of Pediatrics and Adolescent Medicine* 151(8): 793–797.

National Collaborating Centre for Mental Health (NCCMH) (2004). *National Clinical Practice Guideline: Eating Disorders: Core Interventions in the Treatment and Management of Anorexia Nervosa, Bulimia Nervosa, and Related Eating Disorders*. Available www.nice.org.uk

Nielsen, S., Møller-Madsen, S. & Isager, T. (1998). Standardized mortality in eating disorders: A quantitative summary of previously published and new evidence. *Journal of Psychosomatic Research* 44: 413–434.

Richardson, G. (1999). *Review of the Mental Health Act 1983: Report of the Expert Committee*. London: Department of Health.

Scotland, N.F.S. (2000). *'Communication with Carers': The Results of a 1999 Survey into Carers' Experiences*. NFS (Scotland).

Szmukler, G. I. & Bloch, S. (1997). Family involvement in the care of people with psychoses: An ethical argument. *British Journal of Psychiatry* 171: 401–405.

Tan, J., Hope, T. & Stewart, A. (2003a). Competence to refuse treatment in anorexia nervosa. *International Journal of Law and Psychiatry* 26(6): 697–707.

Tan, J., Hope, T. & Stewart, A. (2003b). Anorexia nervosa and personal identity: The accounts of patients and their parents. *International Journal of Law and Psychiatry* 26(5): 533–548.

Tan, J., Hope, T., Stewart, A. & Fitzpatrick, R. (2003c). Control and compulsory treatment in anorexia nervosa: The views of patients and parents. *International Journal of Law and Psychiatry* 26(6): 627–645.

Treasure, J., Schmidt, U. & Hugo, P. (2005). Mind the gap: Service transition and interface problems for patients with eating disorders. *British Journal of Psychiatry* 187: 398–400.

Uher, R., Murphy, T., Brammer, M. J., Dalgleish, T., Phillips, M. L., Ng, V. W. et al. (2005). Medial prefrontal cortex activity associated with symptom provocation in eating disorders. *American Journal of Psychiatry* 161: 1238–1246.

Vitousek, K., Watson, S. & Wilson, G. T. (1998). Enhancing motivation for change in treatment-resistant eating disorders. *Clinical Psychology Review* 18: 391–420.

Zipfel, S., Lowe, B. & Herzog, W. (2000). [Eating behavior, eating disorders and obesity]. *Ther Umsch* 57(8): 504–510.

Part II

Introduction to the theoretical underpinning

In Part II we look at the theoretical foundations behind family skills training interventions.

We begin by examining how families cope when a relative has an eating disorder. Chapter 5 looks at caring responsibilities and specific problems encountered as a result along with those interventions aimed at helping families cope. With its focus on family relationships, it describes the lived experience of day-to-day family functioning in the midst of an eating disorder. It also examines how the responses of close others can influence outcome.

Chapter 6 then follows on this theme by identifying maintaining factors that can foster a maladaptive caregiving pattern. These are illustrated in several diagrams that categorise the key maintaining factors in interpersonal family dynamics and how they operate in either colluding with or accommodating to the eating disorder. The chapter also describes how to utilise these formulations within family skills training, and introduces the reader to techniques that are designed to interrupt maladaptive caregiving patterns by replacing them with more adaptive ways of responding to the symptoms.

The theoretical subject matter continues in Chapter 7 with an introduction to the trans-theoretical model of change. The model is explained in terms of its practical use in working with behaviour change by depicting the importance of matching corresponding techniques to appropriate levels of readiness. The remainder of the chapter offers a 'can-do' approach to the basic principles behind motivational interviewing, in working with people who are either uncertain or not quite ready to change.

Part II ends with a cognitive behavioural approach that illustrates strategies used in working with mistaken beliefs and attributions held by family members in connection with the eating disorder. Chapter 8 reviews some of the behavioural principles that can help families manage these unhelpful or extreme emotional responses. Finally, Part II draws to a close with an introduction to the concept of functional analysis as a first step in modifying behaviours and improving the coping resources of the family.

Chapter 5

How do families cope when a relative has an eating disorder?

Janet Treasure

Introduction

The aim of this chapter is to examine how families adjust when one member develops an eating disorder. In the chapter we develop a stress and coping model of the difficulties that carers encounter in their role. High levels of problems in each of the components that impact on the caregiving role can produce chronic stress, depression and anxiety. These include patient factors, such as the unwillingness to accept the sick role commonly found in anorexia nervosa, and the wide range of symptomatic behaviours associated with an eating disorder. Also the visible nature of anorexia nervosa in particular and the profound impact on a core component of family life produce intense reactions in family members including, attributions about the illness and reorganisation of the family around the illness. The chapter ends with an introduction to those interventions that aim to improve caring coping skills.

Eating disorders can put tremendous demands on the coping abilities of the family members who provide the main support for the patient. The symptoms are interpersonally very challenging and produce a marked disruption in family life. The emaciation of anorexia nervosa is apparent from both within and outside the family. The family are, therefore, drawn into a relationship with the illness. The clearly defined problem, 'not eating', and the apparently simple solution 'to eat' are profoundly frustrating. Bulimic symptoms are usually more secret and there is no overt consequence on weight. Nevertheless, the impact on people who live together can be marked because of the associated mood swings or behaviours that are antisocial and impact on communal living, such as food disappearing from the fridge or larder.

In terms of the responsibilities and difficulties of the caregiving role, the domains on the Experience of Caregiving Inventory (ECI) that were highlighted as difficult included: *difficult behaviours* (e.g. the person with the eating disorder being moody or irritable), *negative symptoms* (e.g. the person being withdrawn), *stigma* (e.g. feeling the stigma of having a mentally ill relative), *problems with services* (e.g. how to deal with mental health professionals), *effect on family* (e.g. how the person gets on with other family members), *need to provide backup* (e.g. having to support the person), *dependency* (e.g. being unable to do the things you want to) and *loss* (e.g. the person's lost opportunities). The highest scores were attained for dependency and loss.

More than half of the carers of young people with bulimia nervosa reported some mental health problems, with a minority (5.4 per cent) experiencing considerable distress (Perkins et al., 2004; Winn et al., 2004). The level of difficulties in most of the general areas of caregiving were comparable to those observed in carers of more chronically ill inpatients with AN and higher than those observed in carers of individuals with psychosis (Treasure et al., 2001). Again, dependency and loss were the subscales with the strongest relationship to carer mental health problems. A negative experience of caregiving predicted the mental health status of carers.

How families cope with problems with their caring responsibilities

Several models have been used to predict how carers cope with their role. Many stem from Lazarus and Folkman's cognitive stress theory (Lazarus & Folkman, 1984). According to this model, an individual's appraisal of their caregiving situation (an evaluation of their ability to cope with the situation) mediates between the problems that they have to contend with as carers, and their own quality of life. This basic model has been extended to include many of the particular difficulties that arise when caring for someone with a chronic illness. Pearlin et al. (1990), for example, have developed a multifaceted model to explain the experience of caring for someone with Alzheimer's disease (Pearlin et al., 1990). The caregiving situation is an amalgam of the intensity of the practical and emotional problems engendered by the patient's illness, buffered by factors such as the quality of the patient–caregiver relationship, the conflict with other roles and the support from others (Pearlin et al., 1990). Carers can develop impaired psychological and physical health and their mental, physical and financial resources may be depleted.

We have developed a model of caregivers' stress in eating disorders based on our research and clinical experience (Kyriacou et al., 2007). We have identified three domains that may be problematic. First, the illness itself, second, the carer's reaction to the illness, and third, the societal context. These are illustrated in Table 5.1.

The illness itself

The multiplicity of eating disorder behaviour and symptoms

Several features of anorexia nervosa make the task of caring particularly taxing. First, there are numerous practical difficulties, for example, every

Table 5.1 An outline of the components of caring for someone with an eating disorder that may be problematic

The illness itself

1   The multiplicity of eating disorder behaviour and symptoms
2   Unwillingness to accept the sick role

The carer's reaction to the illness

1   Carer's beliefs about the illness
2   Accommodation to symptoms
3   Interpersonal relationships
4   Role strain – balancing different roles
5   Parental health
6   Contact time
7   Unmet needs

The societal context

1   Stigma associated with an overt psychiatric illness
2   Service provision: costs and interfaces

meal is disrupted and instead of being a pleasant focus of family life, they are converted into a battlefield. All aspects of the purchase and preparation of food take more time and effort or become subject to strife. The inability to share meals profoundly disrupts many social activities. Often families become very isolated as they avoid all situations that might involve food. Furthermore, it is impossible to disguise the overt signs of the illness.

The behaviours that are associated with anorexia nervosa also pose practical difficulties. Compulsive behaviour, for example, can be irritating and frustrating for other family members. They may include excess activity, rigid timetabling, unreasonable demands over kitchen use and excessive standards of cleanliness and tidiness. The food-related behaviour can be bizarre; for example, one young woman put masking tape on her door to prevent food smells coming into her room as she feared that these might make her gain weight.

Parents are saddened when they notice that their daughter refuses to participate in normal social activities with friends. It is as if the spirit or the joy of living has been sucked out of their daughter. Their daughters may engage in depressive suicidal talk such as being 'better off dead'. Parents feel impotent that they cannot alleviate the low mood. Carers are shocked by the changes in their daughter's temperament. Their daughter may be subject to wild outbursts, which contrast so markedly to the compliant behaviour that was usual before the onset of the illness. Carers often report that they think that their daughter has undergone a personality change. The person with an eating disorder is often angry and hostile. The temper tantrums and violence to themselves or to property can be difficult to manage.

Carers are usually highly anxious about their offspring's physical health. They may have to take special care, such as driving them to school because they are so cold and fragile. The severe starvation causes its own difficulties, such as needing the heating turned up, fatigue, poor muscle power and fainting attacks.

Problems specifically associated with bulimic symptoms

Although bingeing and purging behaviours are hidden, they are usually apparent to close family members living together. These add to carers' difficulties. To begin with, there is the problem of large quantities of food being consumed during binges. Not only can this have a high financial cost, but also there is the inconvenience and embarrassment when food has gone missing. There may be no food left for other family members or visitors, and more time is taken up shopping and preparing food. There can also be unusual behaviours with food, which may be secreted into strange places or hoarded. Furthermore, practical aspects of the purging behaviour can cause problems, such as bathroom use and function (e.g. plumbing problems often arise). The preoccupation with weight and shape leads to prolonged grooming and self-care activities, reassurance seeking and unreliability. Thus, the individual may spend hours checking herself in the mirror, with elaborate rituals to judge her shape and weight. Additional behaviours such as stealing, self-harm, alcohol or drug abuse and other forms of impulsivity add to the palette of difficulties that can arise. People with the bulimic form of an eating disorder can have intense mood swings with temper tantrums and profound depression, often interspersed with dangerous attempts at self-harm.

All of these problems are compounded by the fact that individuals with eating disorders are often ambivalent about their wish to change and to receive help (Blake et al., 1997).

Unwillingness to accept the sick role

It can be difficult to engage people with all forms of eating disorder into treatment, but in particular those with anorexia nervosa find it hard to accept that anything is wrong. One of the most frequently asked questions that caregivers ask of beat (formerly the Eating Disorders Association) is 'How can I get my loved one to accept that she has a problem and needs to go for treatment?' Concerned family members can take children and adolescents for treatment, but once within a treatment setting, they can passively resist. Student or occupational health services, on the other hand, can pressure adult cases into treatment. Thus, even presentation for treatment is not an indication of readiness to change.

When the trans-theoretical model of change was applied to people with eating disorders attending a specialist adult clinic, less than half of the patients with anorexia nervosa were in action, that is were ready to change (for further details see Chapter 7). The majority were in pre-contemplation and contemplation, that is in two minds about change (Blake et al., 1997). More people with bulimia nervosa were in action. A later study found that those people with bulimia nervosa in action showed more symptom change after four weeks (Treasure et al., 1999). Consequently, understanding the process of health behaviour change is necessary to facilitate engagement into treatment and the desire for active change.

There is often a marked discrepancy between the carers' wish for change and that of the person with the disorder. This mismatch is not unique to eating disorders. It is also common in addictions. Indeed, in this field there are various interventions with very different aims and objectives, designed for carers such as Al-Anon groups (based on the principles of Alcoholics Anonymous), which teaches carers to disengage from their relative's problem if they are not ready to accept help, the Johnson intervention, a procedure whereby an individual's social network confronts them with their problem and puts pressure on them to attend for treatment, and Community Reinforcement and Family Training (CRAFT), which is based on behavioural principles and teaches carers skills which are likely to result in facilitating their relative's engagement in treatment. The efficacy of these three very different approaches has been compared in randomised controlled trials (RCTs), in terms of engaging the index case into treatment. The most effective approach in terms of engagement with treatment was CRAFT for index cases with either alcohol abuse (Meyers et al., 1998b; Miller et al., 1999) or drug abuse (Meyers et al., 2002). There were no differences between the approaches in terms of the improvement in caregiver functioning. In the first open study which tested the CRAFT intervention, nearly 90 per cent of the carers took up treatment. In total, three-quarters succeeded in engaging their loved one in treatment. This led to a reduction in drug abuse in the index patients and also a reduction in the level of depression, anxiety, anger and physical symptoms in the carers (Meyers et al., 1998b). In a large and high-quality RCT (involving 130 carers and with 94 per cent follow-up rates) that followed from this preliminary study, the engagement rates of people abusing alcohol in treatment were highest for CRAFT (64 per cent), followed by the Johnson intervention (30 per cent) and Al-Anon facilitation (13 per cent). All three approaches were associated with a similar improvement in carer functioning and relationship quality. Carers who were parents managed to get their offspring with an alcohol problem engaged in treatment more commonly than spouses did (Miller et al., 1999). In a further trial of 90 carers of people abusing drugs, the engagement rate was highest for CRAFT with additional aftercare (77 per cent), followed by CRAFT alone (59 per cent) and Al-Anon or Nar-Anon facilitation therapy (29 per cent) (Meyers et al., 2002). Again, the acceptability of the study procedures and interventions and the interest of the participants were high, with follow-up rates of 96 per cent.

Therapist manuals for CRAFT are available (Meyers & Smith, 1995; Meyers et al., 1998a; Meyers & Miller 2001; Meyers & Wolfe 2004). We use many elements of CRAFT in our work with families of people with eating disorders. Elements of CRAFT include awareness training (information about the negative consequences and benefits of involvement using motivational interviewing (MI) techniques); contingency management training to reinforce non-anorexic behaviours and extinguish anorexic behaviours; communication skills training, including role-play, to increase positive relationship patterns; competing activities planned to interfere with problematic behaviours; outside activities for carers to stop isolation and re-energise.

The carer's reaction to the illness

Carer's beliefs about the illness

Some carers held negative attributions about eating disorders (Haigh et al., 2002). Rather than understanding it as an illness, for example, some carers see it as a facet of their offspring's personality. It follows from this appraisal that the individual herself is seen as being in some way responsible for the problem. This may lead carers to be angry at their offspring for not choosing to take charge of the development of their personality and character and hence their symptoms.

Carers themselves are also likely to experience a wide range of negative emotions, such as intense anxiety relating to the physical risks associated with the illness, feelings of revulsion and disgust about bingeing and purging behaviours as well as feelings of self-reproach and self-blame. Carers are also frequently pessimistic about the future and foresee ominous consequences both for themselves and for the individual with anorexia nervosa (Holliday et al., 2005).

Accommodation to symptoms

Families can often adopt an appeasing stance and organise their behaviour to allow for the eating disorder behaviours (see Chapter 6). Splits within the family can arise as other family members accommodate to these rituals, as they cannot tolerate the pain and distress that arises if or when compulsions are interrupted.

Interpersonal relationships

Communication within the family becomes difficult (Gowers & North, 1999). The outcome of many psychiatric conditions is influenced by the response of close others. One aspect of this response is captured in the construct of expressed emotion (EE) which reflects the amount of criticism, hostility and/or emotional over-involvement expressed by relatives of psychiatric patients toward them. Emotional over-involvement includes behaviours such as self-sacrifice, over-protectiveness, emotional display, over-identifying with the patient, excessive praise and preoccupation with the patient. Warmth appears to be a buffer against the effects of high EE. According to Hooley & Campbell (2002: 1098) 'rather than being a trait or state of relatives, EE in all probability reflects the dynamic interaction between patient and relative factors'. High EE is a well-replicated predictor of relapse across many different psychiatric disorders (Butzlaff & Hooley, 1998). The impact of 'expressed emotion' upon the outcome of anorexia nervosa is summarised in Chapter 2.

Family members with high EE relatives tend to get locked into chains of negative interactions. In contrast, low EE relatives are able to stay out of or withdraw from this cycle. Also, high EE relatives communicate less well with their ill relative, in that they talk more, listen less effectively and spend less time looking at the patient. Low EE relatives are more prepared to listen. This is consistent with the general tendency of high EE relatives to be more socially intrusive and low EE relatives to be more supportive (Kuipers et al., 1983).

High levels of expressed emotion can occur when caregivers and other family members are distressed and anxious. A robust finding from research in children is that there is an association between parental psychopathology and parental EE. It is quite common for mothers of people with eating disorders to have had a clinical or subclinical form of eating disorder themselves. Others have clinical levels of depression, anxiety or obsessive compulsive disorder. In such cases, it is appropriate to encourage the carers to seek help for themselves, as a method to reduce expressed emotion.

Expressed emotion can also arise because of carers' beliefs and attributions about the illness (Tarrier et al., 2002) and how these shape the relationship. The links between a relative's beliefs about schizophrenia and expressed emotion have been studied in most detail. People can become critical and/or over-protective because of how they understand aspects of the illness or the individual with the illness (van Os et al., 2001). Criticism and hostility were secondary reactions to a persistent relapsing course of illness. Relatives high in criticism assumed that the patients had more volitional control and choice over their behaviours and, therefore, attempted to use coercion to change their loved ones' behaviour. In contrast, over-involved relatives assumed that the patient was a passive, impotent victim of the illness. In this case, the parents took over control and responsibility from the patient. In schizophrenia, emotional over-involvement tended to occur when families have been closely involved in caring for their relative. One hypothesis is that relatives' attributions about the illness may be a more reliable predictor of relapse than expressed emotion itself although the evidence for this is limited at the moment (Barrowclough et al., 1994).

High EE relatives experience a higher level of burden of care than low EE relatives (Scazufca & Kuipers, 1996). This subjective burden was not related to the actual number of patient deficits. Thus, interventions to reduce EE may improve carers' coping by reducing some of the difficulties experienced in their role. It follows from the research described above that moderating carers' appraisals about the illness and improving their listening skills may serve to lower their expressed emotion.

There has been some interesting work examining expressed emotion in families of people with an eating disorder. Fathers of people with eating disorders, in general, are less involved and/or become less angry or frustrated, and so a lower threshold of three critical comments (rather than six as in schizophrenia), was used in this group to define high EE. In contrast, a cut-off score of six for criticism was used to define high EE in the mothers. When the threshold for criticism was lowered, as described above, the baseline level was related to outcome (Le Grange et al., 1992; van Furth et al., 1996). Parents of people with bulimia nervosa had higher levels of criticism than those of people with anorexia nervosa (Szmukler et al., 1985).

When families of people with anorexia nervosa were compared to those of people with cystic fibrosis (both groups at minimum had moderate degrees of contact with their families) over one-third of parents, particularly the mothers with ill children, were classified as over-involved. (The norms for control parents of healthy children were 3 per cent.) The level of over-involvement correlated with the severity of the illness and also with the level of distress (Blair et al., 1995).

The level of expressed emotion may be related to the duration of the disorder. In adolescents with an average illness duration of less than a year, only 6 per cent of parents were rated as having high EE using standard cut-off scores (Le Grange et al., 1992). The level of expressed emotion increased in the group with a poor outcome and decreased in those with a good outcome.

Thus, expressed emotion is related in part to the severity and duration of the illness and produces an over-protective response similar to other chronic physical illness. There is a differential impact of the illness on fathers and mothers. Mothers express higher levels of criticism and hostility. Nevertheless, even the lower levels of these behaviours in fathers impact on outcome. The implication from this research is that interventions that reduce the level of expressed emotion, or the amount of patient–carer contact could benefit both patients and carers.

Role strain – balancing different roles

It can be difficult for parents to know how to manage the wider relationships within the family. In addition to their responsibilities for caring for the person with an eating disorder, they usually have to parent other children in the family. Sometimes, their own parents also need to be cared for. Often both parents are working and have other responsibilities and commitments. There is less time and energy for these other demands.

Everyone within the household is affected by these eating disorder symptoms. It is hard to juggle the needs of the person with anorexia nervosa with the needs of other people. Siblings have to make do with less time and attention and often spend more time outside the house. It is common for husbands to throw themselves deeper into work to avoid coming home. Siblings may openly report feeling very left out or isolated from the eating disorder and aspects of its treatment. They often perceive that their own needs, problems and worries are neglected. Other members of the family become angry and resentful about the effects that anorexia nervosa has upon the family.

Parental health

Health worries coupled with all the practical details they have to contend with have a profound impact on the quality of life of the carers. Their sleep may be disrupted. They may, for example, lie awake worrying or wake in the night to check that their daughter is still alive. They can also be wakened by their child, who may choose to have a more nocturnal existence. Carers may have their own nutritional problems. They may, for example, be 'forced' by their child to eat things they do not want or their own appetite may be diminished by stress.

Carers themselves become tired, irritable and depressed. These adverse consequences on the carers' mental health can perpetuate the problem. Moreover, caregivers are plagued by feelings of inadequacy and self-blame.

Contact time

The physical consequences of anorexia nervosa may preclude the individual from attending school or work and so they remain at home. This level of dependency often associated with the need to supervise meals can result in extensive period of face-to-face contact time. In other forms of psychological disorder, high levels of contact are associated with stress for each party.

Unmet needs

Carers acknowledge that they are poorly equipped to meet the demands of their role. The seemingly simple solution to help manage the individual's eating behaviours does not respond to common-sense measures.

The societal context

Stigma associated with an overt psychiatric illness

Every time carers leave home with their offspring, people stop to stare and comment. Thus, the carers are constantly exposed to the shocked reaction and questions from others. Not only is this embarrassing, but also shame is often attached to the stigma. A common public attitude is that people with eating disorders are to blame for their illness and that the difficulties they face are self-inflicted (Crisp et al., 2000).[1]

Service provision: costs and interfaces

In many countries access to services can be problematic. In systems with private care the costs for the family even with insurance can be devastating. Families may lose their homes to pay for expensive inpatient care. In public health systems a form of rationing, which may involve encountering various hurdles on the pathway to care, may be bewildering.

Interventions to improve carer coping

The interventions we have developed for families of people with an eating disorder are aimed at targeting each of these components.

The illness itself

Readiness to change

We teach the family the principles of the trans-theoretical model of change and of motivational interviewing,[2] both as it applies to their daughter and her eating disorder, and to their own behaviours in relationship to the eating disorder (Chapter 7). It is often necessary for members of the family themselves to change either some of their patterns of interacting and responding to the anorexia nervosa or general aspects of functioning. Therefore by reflecting on how difficult change is for themselves, they can learn how change is difficult for their child.

We encourage family members to tailor their approach to their daughter's illness according to her readiness to change. Many parents become frustrated at their daughter's resistance to change and need to be helped to develop ways of interacting and keeping the channels of communication open even when their daughter is less interested in change.

In the stages of contemplation and pre-contemplation, 'LESS is more' is a useful acronym to remind families of how they can be helpful (L = listen, E = empathise, S = share and S = support). This approach can help people move forward from the early stages of change. We teach carers how to listen and to demonstrate that they have heard and understood by paraphrasing or summarising their daughter's point of view. This is reflective listening, a part of the skills base of motivational interviewing. We also encourage parents to empathise with their daughter's underlying difficulties, such as her thoughts and feelings about herself and her relationship to the world rather than being distracted by the superficial issues relating to food, weight and eating. By these means, carers can help the person with an eating disorder develop an overview and reflect on her experiences. Once carers adopt the skills that match their daughter's stage of change, the resistance and tension within the relationship decreases. It can help them remain engaged and actively help, even when their daughter is poorly motivated. This aspect of care is covered in more detail in Chapter 7.

Managing eating disorder behaviour and symptoms

Many symptoms related to eating disorders are difficult to manage. It is common for families to inadvertently reinforce some of the behaviours by giving them attention or by subtly accommodating to them (see Chapter 6). Thus, one aspect of work with the family is to introduce skills to manage these difficult behaviours. In part, this involves practical advice such as strategies to be used for meal planning. Helping with behaviour change involves parents examining their contribution to the behaviours by undertaking a functional analysis of the context (see Chapter 8). It also includes using some of the skills described above to help motivate their daughter. (This is dealt with in more detail in Chapter 7.)

The carer's reaction to the illness

Carer's beliefs about the illness

Education about the eating disorder can be helpful, with due weight being placed on the biological as well as the social aspects of the illness. The forms of intervention that involve some interaction with other carers can be particularly helpful ways to correct common misattributions, as the pattern of behaviours are seen as universal symptoms rather than individual quirks.

Also, any tendency towards self-blame and guilt is moderated by sharing experiences with others. Furthermore, education about the carer's own depression, anxiety and personality traits themselves that can foster unhelpful beliefs can alleviate carer 'burn-out'.

Accommodation to symptoms

The extent to which family members accommodate to the eating disorder can be gently elicited at the assessment interview (see Chapter 9). A semi-structured interview which probes for the key traps is a good way to do this. Carers are then taught the principles of functional analysis and are helped to think of ways to resist falling into these sort of traps.

Interpersonal relationships

Eating disorders have a profound effect on family relationships. This is particularly so with anorexia nervosa, because it is so overt. Carers' emotional and behavioural responses to the illness can inadvertently aggravate or even maintain the symptoms. In the family work, we help families recognise some of their unhelpful patterns of interaction. We use animal metaphors to explain the relationship patterns that often arise: over-protection – kangaroo style care; criticism – rhinoceros care; anxiety and hostility – jellyfish care, disengaged – ostrich care (see Appendix 1). We encourage carers to break free from these traps, which perpetuate anorexic behaviours, and to display gentle guidance – dolphin approach, and warmth – St Bernard care.

Role strain – balancing different roles

Families often have differences of opinion, or at the extreme, polarised strategies about the role that each family member should take in relationship to the anorexia nervosa. This causes conflict and distress. Furthermore, the uncertainty about what to expect at home or from which relationship is stressful for the person with an eating disorder. One of the aims of the work with families is to allow them to reflect and consider these polarised and conflicting approaches and get some balance into the system. This requires the family to meet regularly to review and respect their various perspectives and to come up with joint coherent negotiated solutions. (This is dealt with in Chapter 8.)

Parental health

This involves using strategies to help carers manage their emotional reactions. This can include going for help themselves, possibly with medication or by using CBT strategies, for example, building up positive activities in life and having some time away from the stress. Teaching parents about more advanced emotional regulation strategies such as acceptance, compassionate mind training and mindfulness can also be of value.

Contact time

An important aspect of facilitating carers' coping is to ensure that they have some respite from their caring duties. Carers are encouraged to think about how they can ask friends and family to help. A high level of social support can buffer the difficulties encountered in coping with the challenge of caring for someone with a chronic illness. Unfortunately one of the effects of an eating disorder is to isolate families and cut them off from getting this sort of support. In an effort to reduce contact time, the family have to tolerate taking 'safe risks' whereby they allow their daughter to have increasing responsibility to cope and manage on her own. (This aspect of treatment is described in Chapter 7.)

Unmet needs

The intervention as a whole was designed to address these.

The societal context

Stigma associated with an overt psychiatric illness

The joint family work in workshops or day patient settings enables parents to network with other families. This ability to share and get support can be helpful in reflecting upon unhelpful patterns of family interaction and brainstorming and trying out alternative ways of interacting in a safe environment. This shared experience can turn the emotional tone from one of shame and guilt, to one in which there can be fun and laughter. The sharing of difficulties and ways of coping with them also provides an antidote to the stigma from society.

Service provision: costs and interfaces

The aim of this intervention is to provide a cost-effective way of optimising care and collaboration by sharing information and skills.

Conclusion and outlook

This chapter has illustrated how various aspects of eating disorders as well as the family's strengths, weaknesses and resources can determine the carer's ability to cope. The aim of the intervention described in this book is to help the carers attain a better quality of life with less distress, and yet at the same time, be more effective and engaged in their caring role.

Notes

1 Indeed carers themselves may hold some of those stigmatising views about the illness of their loved one.

2 The transdiagnostic model of change and its application to eating disorders has come under criticism on conceptual and empirical grounds (for a review, see Wilson & Schlam, 2004). Nonetheless, it is a helpful way of describing why it is hard for some people to change.

References

Barrowclough, C., Tarrier, N. & Johnston, M. (1994). Attributions, expressed emotion and patient relapse: An attributional model of relatives' response to schizophrenic illness. *Behaviour Therapy* 25: 67–88.

Blair, C., Freeman, C. & Cull, A. (1995). The families of anorexia nervosa and cystic fibrosis patients. *Psychological Medicine* 25: 985–993.

Blake, W., Turnbull, S. & Treasure, J. (1997). Stages and processes of change in eating disorders: Implications for therapy. *Clinical Psychology and Psychotherapy* 4: 186–191.

Butzlaff, R. L. & Hooley, J. M. (1998). Expressed emotion and psychiatric relapse: A meta-analysis. *Archives of General Psychiatry* 55: 547–552.

Crisp, A. H., Gelder, M. G., Rix, S., Meltzer, H. I. & Rowlands, O. J. (2000). Stigmatisation of people with mental illnesses. *British Journal of Psychiatry* 177: 4–7.

Gowers, S. & North, C. (1999). Difficulties in family functioning and adolescent anorexia nervosa. *British Journal of Psychiatry* 174: 63–66.

Haigh, R., Whitney, J., Weinman, J. & Treasure, J. (2002). Caring for someone with an eating disorder: An exploration of carers' illness perceptions, distress, experience of caregiving, and unmet needs. Personal communication.

Holliday, J., Wall, E., Treasure, J. & Weinman, J. (2005). Perceptions of illness in individuals with anorexia nervosa. A comparison with lay men and women. *International Journal of Eating Disorders* 37(1): 50–56.

Hooley, J. M. & Campbell, C. (2002). Control and controllability: Beliefs and behaviour in high and low expressed emotion relatives. *Psychological Medicine* 32(6): 1091–1099.

Kuipers, L., Sturgeon, D., Berkowitz, R. & Leff, J. (1983). Characteristics of expressed emotion: Its relationship to speech and looking in schizophrenic patients and their relatives. *British Journal of Clinical Psychology* 22(4): 257–264.

Kyriacou, O., Treasure, J. & Schmidt, U. (2007). Understanding how parents cope with living with someone with anorexia nervosa: Modelling the factors that are associated with carer distress. *International Journal of Eating Disorders* 41: 233–242.

Lazarus, R. S. & Folkman, S. (1984). *Stress Appraisal and Coping*. New York: Springer.

Le Grange, D., Eisler, I. D. C. & Hodes, M. (1992). Family criticism and self starvation: A study of expressed emotion. *Journal of Family Therapy* 14: 177–192.

Meyers, R. J. & Miller, W. R. (2001). *A Community Reinforcement Approach to the Treatment of Addiction*. Cambridge: Cambridge University Press.

Meyers, R. J. & Smith, J. E. (1995). *Clinical Guide to Alcohol Treatment: The Community Reinforcement Approach*. New York: Guilford.

Meyers, R. J. & Wolfe, B. L. (2004). *Get Your Loved One Sober: Alternatives to Nagging, Pleading, and Threatening*. Center City, MN: Hazelden Press.

Meyers, R. J., Smith, J. E. & Miller, E. J. (1998a). Working through the concerned significant other. In W. R. Miller & N. Heather (eds) *Treating Addictive Behaviours*, 2nd edn. New York: Plenum.

Meyers, R. J., Miller, W. R., Hill, D. E. & Tonigan, J. S. (1998b). Community reinforcement and family training (CRAFT): Engaging unmotivated drug users in treatment. *Journal of Substance Abuse* 10: 291–308.

Meyers, R. J., Miller, W. R., Smith, J. E. & Tonigan, J. S. (2002). A randomized trial of two methods for engaging treatment-refusing drug users through concerned significant others. *Journal of Consulting and Clinical Psychology* 70: 1182–1185.

Miller, W. R., Meyers, R. J. & Tonigan, J. S. (1999). Engaging the unmotivated in treatment for alcohol problems: A comparison of three strategies for intervention through family members. *Journal of Consulting and Clinical Psychology* 67: 688–697.

Pearlin, L. I., Mullan, J. T., Semple, S. J. & Skaff, M. M. (1990). Caregiving and the stress process: An overview of concepts and their measures. *Gerontologist* 30: 583–594.

Perkins, S., Winn, S., Murray, J., Murphy, R. & Schmidt, U. (2004). A qualitative study of the experience of caring for a person with bulimia nervosa. Part 1: The emotional impact of caring. *International Journal of Eating Disorders* 36: 256–268.

Scazufca, M. & Kuipers, E. (1996). Links between expressed emotion and burden of care in relatives of patients with schizophrenia. *British Journal of Psychiatry* 168: 580–587.

Szmukler, G. I., Eisler, I., Russell, G. F. & Dare, C. (1985). Anorexia nervosa, parental 'expressed emotion' and dropping out of treatment. *British Journal of Psychiatry* 147: 265–271.

Tarrier, N., Barrowclough, C., Ward, J., Donaldson, C., Burns, A. & Gregg, L. (2002). Expressed emotion and attributions in the carers of patients with Alzheimer's disease: The effect on carer burden. *Journal of Abnormal Psychology* 111: 340–349.

Treasure, J. L., Katzman, M., Schmidt, U., Troop, N., Todd, G. & de Silva, P. (1999). Engagement and outcome in the treatment of bulimia nervosa: First phase of a sequential design comparing motivation enhancement therapy and cognitive behavioural therapy. *Behaviour Research and Therapy* 37: 405–418.

Treasure, J., Murphy, T., Todd, G., Gavan, K., Schmidt, U., James, J. et al. (2001). The experience of caregiving for severe mental illness: A comparison between anorexia nervosa and psychosis. *Social Psychiatry and Psychiatric Epidemiology* 36: 343–347.

van Furth, E. F., van Strien, D. C., Martina, L. M., van Son, M. J., Hendrickx, J. J. & van Engeland, H. (1996). Expressed emotion and the prediction of outcome in adolescent eating disorders. *International Journal of Eating Disorders* 20: 19–31.

van Os, J., Marcelis, M., Germeys, I., Graven, S. & Delespaul, P. (2001). High expressed emotion: Marker for a caring family? *Comprehensive Psychiatry* 42: 504–507.

Wilson, G. T. & Schlam, T. R. (2004). The transtheoretical model and motivational interviewing in the treatment of eating and weight disorders. *Clinical Psychology Review* 24: 361–378.

Winn, S., Perkins, S., Murray, J., Murphy, R. & Schmidt, U. (2004). A qualitative study of the experience of caring for a person with bulimia nervosa. Part 2: Carers' needs and experiences of services and other support. *International Journal of Eating Disorders* 36: 269–279.

Chapter 6

Family processes as maintaining factors for eating disorders

Janet Treasure, Christopher Williams and Ulrike Schmidt

Introduction

We do not know the exact cause of eating disorders. As in other psychiatric problems there is not just one cause; rather there is a combination of interacting factors. One way to clarify thinking about what starts an eating disorder and what keeps it going is to divide the risk factors into three broad categories – predisposing, precipitating and perpetuating. *Predisposing factors* are present before the onset of the problem and increase the vulnerability to develop an eating disorder. These include genetic factors, birth trauma, childhood temperament and personality factors, and aspects of upbringing or childhood environment (e.g. childhood abuse or neglect or high parental expectations). *Precipitating factors* occur around or just before onset such as stressful events or going on a diet. *Perpetuating factors* are mechanisms (both internal and external) that cause the problem to persist. These are also known as *maintaining factors*. In this chapter we discuss maintaining factors in particular in relation to anorexia nervosa, although many of the considerations that follow are also relevant to bulimia nervosa and other eating disorders.

As discussed in Chapter 2, the most plausible explanation to account for the development of anorexia nervosa is that a mixture of factors, including a genetic variation in neurotransmitter function and patterns of information processing, mean that the reaction to life experiences during the critical phase of puberty and consolidation of adult development is anomalous.

It is probable that some of the predisposing factors also contribute to keeping the disorder going, thus accounting for the variation in the prognosis of eating disorders (discussed earlier in Chapter 1). Other maintaining factors relevant to the prognosis, however, occur strictly as a consequence of the illness. Consequently, a mixture of predisposing factors (or vulnerability traits) and secondary consequences may cause the poor outcome in those people with a long duration of illness. Some maintaining factors may be biological, a consequence of prolonged starvation and interruption of the maturation of the social brain as described in our model (Southgate et al., 2005) but further psychological or social impairments accrue.

It is beyond the scope of this book to discuss predisposing and precipitating aetiological factors and biological maintaining factors in any more detail. There have been two excellent systematic reviews which condense much of the research evidence (Stice, 2002; Jacobi et al., 2004).

This chapter, then, looks at the maintaining factors in anorexia nervosa, in particular family-related factors. We discuss how in the context of family skills training, using simple user-friendly cognitive behavioural formulations can help to identify family-related maintaining factors and which techniques to use to interrupt maladaptive caregiving patterns. We also examine relationships with siblings and peers along with their resulting effects.

Maintaining factors in anorexia nervosa

Historical approaches

Many clinical conceptualisations of anorexia nervosa emphasise maintaining factors. This is because of their potential accessibility to interventions, which can interrupt these processes. A common idea is that anorexia nervosa is valued by the sufferer because it serves as a *coping mechanism* in the face of perceived difficulties. In his historical summary, Gerald Russell (1995) argued that the essence of anorexia nervosa is that

> the patient avoids food and induces weight loss by virtue of a range of psychosocial conflicts whose resolution she perceives to be within her reach through the achievement of thinness and/or the avoidance of fatness. These conflicts include the dread of fatness, but may need to embrace the fear of sexuality and fertility, or the reluctance to acquire independence from the family or some as yet unpredictable issue.
>
> (Russell, 1995)

It is noteworthy that this conceptualisation is broad and does not merely focus on weight and shape concerns as the sole maintaining factor.

An introduction to the concept of maintaining factors in anorexia nervosa

Two criteria have to be fulfilled in order to confirm that a given factor has a role in maintaining an illness (Stice, 2002):

- It is necessary to show that the relevant factor has an effect on outcome.
- Any intervention that changes the relevant factor, modifies the process of change and the eventual outcome.

This second level of proof, of course, can be applied only to those risk factors that are modifiable. The interventions described in this book are aimed at changing those family processes that we think are important as maintaining factors.

A maintenance model for anorexia nervosa

We have developed a maintenance model for anorexia nervosa (Schmidt & Treasure, 2005) which follows from the model of Russell (1995), in that it is not culture bound and has a focus beyond weight and shape issues alone. In brief, the model suggests that the core maintaining factors of AN are:

- the response of the individual to her anorexia nervosa (including altered thinking, feelings, physical symptoms and behaviour), and in particular the positive beliefs that the person comes to develop about the utility of anorexia in her life (pro-anorexia beliefs)
- the response of others such as family members to the anorexia nervosa
- underpinned by obsessive compulsive traits (such as perfectionism, attention to detail at the expense of the bigger picture and rigidity)
- anxiety traits with high threat sensitivity and with cognitive and emotional avoidance (see Figure 6.1).

The basic tenet of the model is that whatever the individual predisposing and precipitating factors, once the symptoms of anorexia nervosa are established, they are kept going by these key maintaining factors. Different maintaining mechanisms may come into play in different phases of the illness.

Carers and other family members can get caught up and become a part of the unhelpful patterns of behaviour that perpetuate anorexic behaviours. Drawing up a formulation in which carers and patients consider the impact of their responses to the anorexic behaviours themselves or various safety

Predisposing traits	Perpetuating consequences
Emotional avoidance	Interpersonal relationships
Obsessive compulsive traits	Beliefs about the value of AN in the person's life

Figure 6.1 A schematic diagram illustrating the key maintaining factors for anorexia nervosa.

behaviours that surround them,[1] on keeping the illness going, can form the basis of a plan to reduce any such unhelpful behaviours.

Family maintaining factors

The reaction of close family members can have a marked effect on the outcome of an eating disorder. In Chapters 2 and 5 we introduced the concept of 'expressed emotion' and how this can have a profound effect on the outcome of anorexia nervosa. If close others express even mild levels of criticism and hostility towards the sufferer, it adversely affects the outcome. Importantly, bulimic symptoms seem to arouse particularly high levels of criticism and hostility. Furthermore, over-concern and wrapping the person in cotton wool in a bid to protect them from every upset or challenge leads to emotional over-involvement, another form of emotional response that adversely moderates the outcome. These emotional and behaviour styles have been found to be key factors that predict relapse in all psychiatric disorders, but the size of the effect in anorexia nervosa appears to be large (Butzlaff & Hooley, 1998).

In Chapter 2 we reviewed how high expressed emotion in close others not only has a role in outcome but also is differentially modifiable by the types of intervention used (Szmukler et al., 1985). In conclusion, therefore, expressed emotion fulfils the two criteria required for it to be considered a maintaining factor in anorexia nervosa. The effects of high expressed emotion are even further pronounced when there are high levels of contact between the person with the eating disorder and her parent.

Broader types of emotional reactions and behaviours of family members towards each other can also have an effect on outcome in other psychiatric disorders. In bipolar disorder, for example, an increase in emotionally positive behaviour among family members, rather than a decrease in negative expressed emotion, was found to be an important mediator of change (Miklowitz et al., 2003). Maternal warmth was also found to be a predictor of outcome in early onset bipolar disorder (Geller et al., 2002). Thus, either a decrease in negative comments or an increase in positive comments within the home environment can improve the outcome of severe psychiatric illness. As yet, family warmth has not been specifically looked at as a moderator of outcome in anorexia nervosa, although the overall quality of family function is an important prognostic factor.

In developing our model of interpersonal maintaining factors in anorexia nervosa, we have used a cognitive behaviour therapy perspective. What is identified here as 'maintaining factors' is a range of extreme and unhelpful altered behaviours or emotional displays by parents and carers.

Anorexia nervosa as a form of communication to others

*   It's not about food, it is about feelings.

The symptoms and weight loss of anorexia nervosa are particularly visible to others and the illness becomes a powerful, indirect, non-verbal form of communication. One of the positive themes that emerged from our qualitative analysis of the therapeutic letters that patients in our clinic write to anorexia nervosa as a friend was 'anorexia nervosa helps me communicate' (Serpell et al., 1999). This was replicated in our quantitative study using a scale designed to measure the pros and cons of anorexia nervosa (Serpell et al., 2004). It is often unclear to all parties, however, exactly what it is that is being communicated. In the early stages, it may be that the person with anorexia nervosa is trying to be good by displaying a focused striving for goals and increasing her sense of power in relationship to the world.

The reactions of other people may initially encourage weight loss. There may be compliments about the changed appearance, or some of the associated features such as an increased focus on school work, or an interest in fitness. Indeed, in competitive environments in which schools are judged on their test results or coaches are judged by their trainee's performance, the early eating disorder behaviours can be actively encouraged. The striving for perfection and to please others, characteristic of the personality of people with anorexia nervosa, matches these environments. This reinforces the efforts of the person with anorexia nervosa to persist with their behaviours such as dieting and exercise.

Nevertheless, the anorexic behaviour will persist over time, even when some of the initial functions, such as being special or perfect in some way, are no longer relevant. It is possible that the cognitive rigidity associated with anorexia nervosa, which in neuropsychological tasks manifests as a difficulty in shifting set,[2] plays a role in the persistence of the behaviours. The interpersonal message from the person with anorexia nervosa to the people around her now changes. The syndrome provides a non-verbal way of signalling that something is profoundly wrong. The emaciation of anorexia nervosa becomes an implicit marker of distress. It mobilises others to help.

The following examples are from letters or interviews with people with anorexia nervosa where they describe their relationship with the illness and how it serves to communicate with others:

If I'm feeling really depressed ... I've realised I've got to make it physically obvious that something is wrong. By losing weight.

I think in a way when I am showing that there's something wrong, Mum and Dad pay a bit more attention to me, they understand that I am finding it hard and they try and talk to me and everything like that, I don't know whether they'd be so sensitive or whatever if I didn't have it.

In this way, the symptoms of anorexic behaviour can be seen as a form of somatisation – where the language of physical symptoms is used to communicate emotional distress.

Impact of anorexia nervosa on emotional functioning of parents

Anorexia nervosa in the family will hugely impact on several domains in the carer's life. In this chapter, we use Williams' (2001) Five Areas Assessment Model to exemplify some of the vicious reciprocal cycles that can develop between carers and their loved one with anorexia nervosa (Figure 6.2).

The template underpinning the formulation diagrams is simple and user friendly and can be drawn up collaboratively with carers to understand with them how their response to particular life situation and practical problems posed by their child's anorexia can help keep things stuck. The same template can also be used to map out what the same event would look like from their daughter's perspective. Below we discuss each of the components of the formulation diagram in turn.

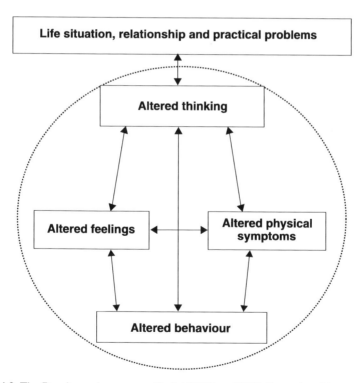

Figure 6.2 The Five Areas Assessment Model (Williams 2001). Reproduced by permission of the author and publisher (Hodder Arnold).

Life situation, relationship and practical problems

This box is a hold-all for specific 'trigger situations' that elicit unhelpful thoughts, feelings and behaviours in the carer, such as mealtimes or points of obvious deterioration in anorexia. What can also usefully be included here are important background factors that might colour the other aspects of the formulation, such as other pressures on the family, affecting emotional or practical resources, or the parents' own personality. One such background factor that deserves special mentioning is that of poor emotional intelligence.

Poor emotional intelligence

Difficulties with direct emotional communication and emotional processing may be part of the family culture. This 'stiff upper lip approach' to emotions often leads to weak and insecure attachments. Parents may have always found it difficult to tolerate distress in their child and so negative emotions may have been suppressed or ignored during development. Thus, losses, hurts and traumas may not have been acknowledged or may have been labelled as invalid or bad. In most cases, anorexia nervosa occurs as a response to a stressful event. If the emotional reaction to such an event is indirectly ignored or is expressed in a muted way, it is impossible to take the final steps of reparation and forgiveness. Consequently, problems persist and fester. In families which have a culture of avoiding emotions, logical reasoning is often highly valued and 'gut feelings' are ignored and shunned. This means that their daughters do not have the skills or confidence to listen to their own emotional responses and may make bad choices because of this, reinforcing the idea that having or listening to and expressing emotions is somehow weak, dangerous or bad and that it is safer to suppress them with the help of anorexia nervosa.

Altered thinking

Loss, self-blame and stigma are all major themes in the thought process of carers: 'I have lost my healthy daughter', 'I have failed', 'Where did I go wrong?', 'Others will blame me'. Other thoughts are to do with catastrophic outcomes, such as: 'She will never get better', 'She is going to die'.

Altered feelings

As a result, carers often experience a wide variety of negative emotions including depression, anxiety, guilt and shame, often alternating with irrita-tion, anger and disgust. Parents are often angry and irritated by their children who refuse to eat, or binge and purge. This is an entirely understandable response. However, such angry reactions can be counterproductive. This anger may lead to altered behaviours (see also below), such as shouting, swearing or occasional violence. It can lead to verbal threats ('Eat it or else!') and sometimes parents may try to force their children to eat or prevent them from leaving a room until food is taken. A vicious circle can develop because the person with anorexia nervosa is not able to change her behaviour and feels even worse. Intense emotional reactions to the illness, such as becoming too sad or too mad, are maladaptive. We have labelled this response with the jellyfish metaphor (Treasure et al., 2007), that is the emotion is too transparent and that the individual is too ruled by this and 'drifts around at sea'.

Altered physical symptoms

Altered emotions such as sadness, depression and accompanying hopeless, self-blaming thoughts are often associated with physical unease and a lack of energy. Anxiety and anger are related with high arousal, tension, being unable to relax or sleep.

Altered behaviour

We have already mentioned above how anger can lead to unhelpful parental behaviours such as verbal or physical coercion of the person with anorexia nervosa. Alternatively parents may try overly hard to accommodate all the whims and wishes of the person with anorexia to get them to eat or to reduce conflict.

Sadness and self-blame often leads to families withdrawing from taking part in pleasurable activities, spending less time on things they themselves enjoy – such as going for walks or doing a hobby. Parents may alter their behaviours with others. The family may avoid contact with others due to shame and embarrassment because their daughter has a psychiatric illness. They may experience stigmatisation from others and withdraw. They may 'mind-read' that others will think that the anorexia is caused by 'bad parenting'. This leads to an unhelpful vicious circle where they become increasingly isolated and more depressed. The problem is that this avoidance isolates the parents from possible sources of support such as friends and health-care practitioners. It means that they do not expose themselves to experiences that make them feel that they have a sense of mastery in relation to the problem. It also saps confidence and may leave the parent feeling they lack the resources to cope and make helpful responses that might otherwise have led to positive change. We have called these withdrawing or avoiding behaviours *ostrich* tendencies (see Treasure et al., 2007). If this ostrich tendency is taken to an extreme, the parents may be unwilling to accept that something is wrong and completely withdraw themselves from the issue by, for example, throwing themselves into their work.

Figure 6.3 gives a sample formulation of a parent that demonstrates the reciprocal negative cycle of loss, blame and stigma.

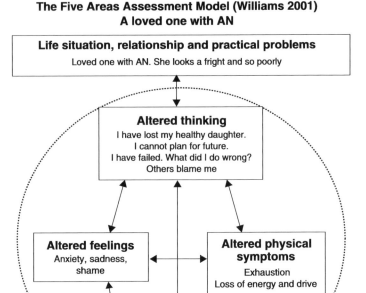

The Five Areas Assessment Model (Williams 2001)
A loved one with AN

Life situation, relationship and practical problems
Loved one with AN. She looks a fright and so poorly

Altered thinking
I have lost my healthy daughter.
I cannot plan for future.
I have failed. What did I do wrong?
Others blame me

Altered feelings
Anxiety, sadness, shame

Altered physical symptoms
Exhaustion
Loss of energy and drive

Altered behaviour
Isolate family
Avoid pleasurable activites
Avoid get help: intrusive into privacy
They will blame me

Figure 6.3 The reaction of a parent to their child with an eating disorder including loss, self-blame and stigma.

Figure 6.4 illustrates how the emotional reaction of the parents can lead to a reciprocal negative response in the person with anorexia nervosa. They observe the effects of their behaviour on their parents and feel intensely guilty but this merely serves to increase behaviours which help distract them from this emotional reaction, that is safety behaviours such as over-exercise and food rules.

How to utilise these formulations in family skills training

It follows from this that a focus on the work we do with parents is to help them to develop a 'just right' emotional position, whereby they recognise and acknowledge their emotional response, but can be reflective rather than impulsive about it. They can analyse what an emotional reaction means and use it to shape their plans and behaviour rather than either being overwhelmed by their

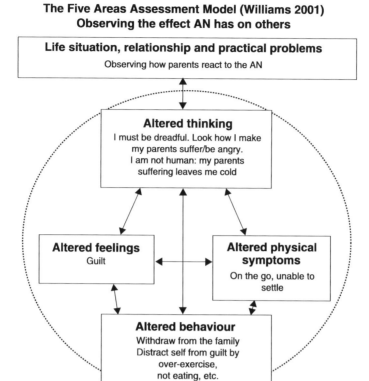

Figure 6.4 The reaction of the individual with an eating disorder to her parents' concerns.

response, or ignoring it. One of the key difficulties in people with eating disorders is that they are unable to regulate and reflect on their emotional response. Thus, any intervention for carers related to emotions can have the advantage of a knock-on effect by modelling good emotional processing.

Basic cognitive behavioural techniques such as planning and goal setting can help overcome the vicious circle that develops when parents have a dysregulated emotional reaction to the anorexia nervosa. One of the first steps is to identify activities that have been reduced or stopped, as a result of caring for the person with anorexia nervosa, and to reintroduce them back into life in a planned step-by-step way. We encourage carers, for example, to restart hobbies and interests, to plan pleasant activities and to increase their social connections. The carer is encouraged to build in some time each day just for themselves. It is hard to persuade carers to do this. Our skills-based training serves the function of starting to help carers take a step back and reflect upon their own needs for a few hours a week.

Carers may also share some of the same perfectionist beliefs with the person with anorexia nervosa, for example, 'I must be a perfect caregiver' or 'Failure to leave a meal unsupervised to care for myself is a catastrophe'. Parents can also share similar rigid, black-and-white beliefs as their daughter or son with an eating disorder: 'Either I give no supervision over meals at all and leave it up to them or I have to be there micro-managing every detail'. Identifying these beliefs with the help of the formulation can be the starting point for helping parents develop a more balanced approach to caregiving, aiming for 'good enough' rather than 'perfect'.

One of the first tasks is for the family to acknowledge the problems and difficulties of the current situation. In our intensive day workshops, for example, we use letter writing to vent and explore emotions and to encourage a reflective response that can help to defuse the situation. Writing a letter describing what it is like to live with AN, for example, allows the carer the opportunity to express their frustrations. 'What my daughter means to me' increases warmth and positive feelings. This accesses the love within the relationship. This use of writing may act as the first step towards processing the emotion, leaving behind the grief for the loss of their cherished aspirations for their child and developing a new relationship with their child in the present.

Another focus of the family workshops is to help the family to break the cycle of avoidance and start to reach out to others to get help. Carers' groups facilitated by the EDA can also offer help and support. Here are comments from two different carers demonstrating new self-reflective discoveries on their emotional reactions to their loved one's illness.

> It was very easy for me to shout, not to lose my temper in a rage physically, 'cause I am not an abuser in that way, but I did not realise that I would abuse them in another way, in that if someone upset me I would shout extremely loudly and I have big lungs and I can shout extremely loudly and that actually has an effect on my wife, not so much my other daughter, but it affects all of my family. This got pointed out to me at family sessions by my family. I just realised the futility of it. What I was doing was releasing my anxiety by shouting at other people when actually it was making matters worse. I used to think that to blow off is a good thing, but actually by keeping calm and discussing things the atmosphere at home improved.
>
> (Carer 1)

This example illustrates how this family recognised that their intense emotional reaction to their daughter's illness was unhelpful and took steps to modify it. Both mother and father were upset and distressed by each other's emotional response (the father became angry and more controlling, and the mother was depressed). They recognised how this led to a vicious circle and merely served to increase anorexia nervosa behaviours. They were able to change their behaviours based upon what they had learnt from the family workshops when their daughter had a further relapse of her anorexia nervosa.

> Last time I just didn't want to do anything. I was a nervous wreck and I thought I was going to have a breakdown. I just kept crying all the time. That is one of the major things that I did. I cried because I was upset. You cry because of the frustration as well but you get into the habit of it and you get slowed down. She's seen me cry a lot. Obviously that doesn't serve any purpose. We've learnt either that makes it worse because it makes her feel . . . they feel bad about themselves, and they feel bad about themselves so she says that she despises herself. She says that she loses weight because she is taking up too much space on this earth. So if you kind of cry and get upset, it makes her feel worse 'cause the last thing she wants to do is to upset us. Equally it didn't do me any good 'cause when the waterworks start you just carry on and on. I do still cry but it's not a continuous thing and not really in front of her because it doesn't help her in any way.
>
> (Carer 2)

These parents came to realise how negative emotional expression, letting their emotions show through like a jellyfish, not only led to an increase in anorexia nervosa behaviour but also resulted in distress in other family members.

It is important to point out that we are not asking carers to suppress or deny emotions. Rather, we want them to be aware of the emotion, learning lessons from it as opposed to being controlled and overwhelmed by it, possibly responding in an aggressive manner. We want them to reflect on what the emotion means and to think of ways of assertively responding to the situation. We want them to recognise when frustration is pushing their anger buttons. Instead of flying into a rage, we encourage our carers to take a step back and think, 'What are my options?' 'Are there any alternative responses that will relieve my frustration?' 'Can I ask others to change some of their behaviours to remove some of the factors that are triggering this?'

Common parental responses to anorexia nervosa and how to deal with them

Controlling reactions and over-directive tendencies

Some families engage in protracted arguments about food and weight in order to logically argue or 'shout down' the anorexia nervosa beliefs. In the carer manual (Treasure et al., 2007), we have termed this over-directive parental behaviour *rhinoceros* response (see Appendix 1 for full explanation of 'animal responses'). Our research suggests that the use of logical argument and debate in relationship to anorexia nervosa beliefs is ineffectual. We have examined the beliefs held by people with anorexia nervosa by using a measure developed to assess delusional thinking. People with AN had scores on this measure that were between those obtained from people who were severely deluded with a psychotic illness and the comparison population. The following examples illustrate some of these 'wacky' beliefs. These are very much akin to 'magical thinking'.

- A medical student with anorexia nervosa admitted after trust was gained late in therapy that she had the belief that if she smelt food that she would gain weight. She therefore tried to hold her breath when she detected food aromas.
- A young man with anorexia nervosa would avoid touching food items with his bare hands as he thought that he would absorb calories.
- A young student described how when she ate something she had the experience of it becoming morphed into fat on her body.

Ideas such as these are often held secretly as the individuals themselves recognise them to be unusual. However, anorexic beliefs are held with rigid, unshakeable conviction with a strong emotional component. Once trust is attained in therapy, people with anorexia nervosa admit to these beliefs. They fear that if they voiced them, they would be labelled 'mad' and locked away. Any attempt to argue with these beliefs merely gives the person with anorexia nervosa the opportunity to rehearse them and increase their salience by validating them as a justifiable point of view. The person with anorexia nervosa can argue about weight, shape and food for hours. Family members who start this process are usually defeated (lose control or face). They experience their daughter as holding alien ideas and being 'weird'. The lack of reward in terms of change in eating disorder behaviours, set against the effort put into argument is intensively frustrating. It is a common reaction to become angry in such a situation. These unhelpful interactions can increase feelings of helplessness and self-blame for 'failing to help their daughter'.

These arguments are also counterproductive, as they focus attention onto the anorexia nervosa beliefs and serve to maintain them. Furthermore, any victory over parental authority can be reinforcing, particularly in this age group. The lesson the person with anorexia nervosa learns is that anorexia nervosa beliefs enable them to become powerful in interpersonal situations. Low power over the world is thought to be a risk factor for anorexia nervosa (Dalgleish et al., 2001) and so arguing for anorexia nervosa becomes reinforcing. As discussed above, we use the *rhinoceros* metaphor to illustrate the vicious circle of maladaptive behavioural patterns that can arise. Attempts to control the anorexia nervosa behaviours are met with resistance. This leads the carer to use ever more threatening or coercive methods of control such as shouting, arguing or punishment.

Parental rhinoceros behaviour, however, has a tendency to backfire, because the sufferer becomes more rebellious and determined not to be bullied. Often people with anorexia nervosa have been sensitised to being overruled. Their usual role in life is to be subservient and to try to please and so this is one area in which they can be powerful. Consequently, the person with anorexia nervosa becomes more obstinately determined to cling to her anorexic identity. Rhinoceros behaviour is construed as indicating that her parents do not love or understand her. She loses trust in her parents and so there is more of a drive to retreat to the 'safety' of anorexia nervosa. If, for example, a family member is in tears and using this as emotional blackmail or uses other instrumental methods of control, there may an angry backlash ('How dare s/he tell me what to do!'). In response, she may withdraw still further from them and punish herself by reducing her eating even more.

The reciprocal reaction to rhinoceros behaviour, from both the carer's and the sufferer's perspective, is shown in Figures 6.5 and 6.6.

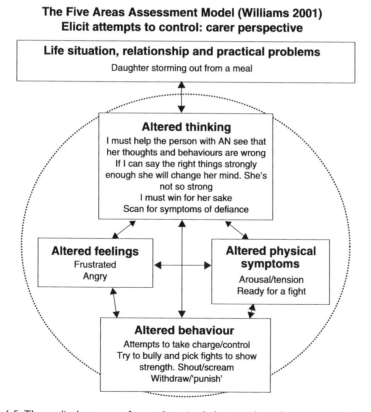

**The Five Areas Assessment Model (Williams 2001)
Elicit attempts to control: carer perspective**

Life situation, relationship and practical problems
Daughter storming out from a meal

Altered thinking
I must help the person with AN see that her thoughts and behaviours are wrong
If I can say the right things strongly enough she will change her mind. She's not so strong
I must win for her sake
Scan for symptoms of defiance

Altered feelings
Frustrated
Angry

Altered physical symptoms
Arousal/tension
Ready for a fight

Altered behaviour
Attempts to take charge/control
Try to bully and pick fights to show strength. Shout/scream
Withdraw/'punish'

Figure 6.5 The cyclical process of over-directive behaviour (carer's perspective).

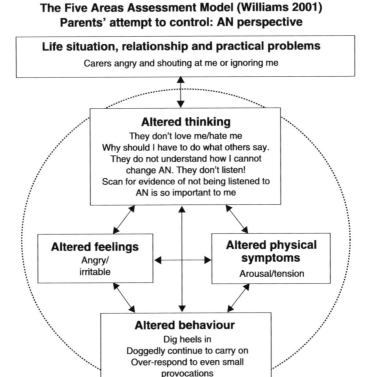

The Five Areas Assessment Model (Williams 2001)
Parents' attempt to control: AN perspective

Life situation, relationship and practical problems
Carers angry and shouting at me or ignoring me

Altered thinking
They don't love me/hate me
Why should I have to do what others say.
They do not understand how I cannot
change AN. They don't listen!
Scan for evidence of not being listened to
AN is so important to me

Altered feelings
Angry/
irritable

**Altered physical
symptoms**
Arousal/tension

Altered behaviour
Dig heels in
Doggedly continue to carry on
Over-respond to even small
provocations

Figure 6.6 The cyclical process of over-directive behaviour (sufferer's perspective).

Over-protective reactions: excessive caregiving

When a child (or anyone else) is ill, those around them expect to alter what they do to provide support. When someone has flu, for example, warm drinks will be brought. Knowing how to respond to a long-term illness, such as anorexia nervosa, can be very difficult. The overt signs of distress and anxiety in the person with anorexia nervosa can draw carers in to provide excessive comfort and reassurance. The person with anorexia nervosa becomes special, dominating family routines and is treated with kid gloves. Mothers may drive for miles to get special food and give inordinate amounts of time to the preparation and consumption of a meal. Mothers can feel that their prowess at being a mother is being tested and found wanting. This can merely fuel their attempts to try harder and a vicious cycle develops. We have called this type of response the *kangaroo* approach because it is as if the person with an eating disorder is put into a pouch of maternal or paternal care, protecting them from the outside world.

There are two dangers from this parental over-protection. First, it reinforces the anorexic behaviour, and second, it causes the child to become suffocated and unable to accomplish tasks that foster self-efficacy. The person with anorexia nervosa becomes isolated and is unprepared to face challenges unaided. Robbed of the chance to master challenges, core beliefs that the world outside is indeed a dangerous place, are exaggerated. This, in turn, makes the sufferer feel more anxious and with more of a need to cling on to her parents, leading to a vicious circle of co-dependency. This response has been labelled 'compulsive caregiving' and is similar to the co-dependency described in behaviours of families of alcoholics. Over-protection is one of the emotional responses that contribute to a toxic aspect of expressed emotion, with an adverse effect on outcome.

This style of compulsive care can lead to negative effects on the person giving it. They become exhausted and trapped into the eating disorder universe. Other family members deprived of care and attention become resentful and negative interactions arise. Tensions and conflict within the family merely serves to reinforce the anorexia nervosa behaviours. As a result, another cycle of interaction maintaining anorexia nervosa symptom develops. The mutually reinforcing care eliciting and caregiving circle from both the carer and the sufferer's perspectives are illustrated in Figures 6.7 and 6.8.

Techniques designed to interrupt maladaptive caregiving patterns

Externalisation

Externalising the anorexia nervosa behaviours into an independent concept such as the 'anorexia nervosa minx' or 'the anorexic voice' serves to separate the source of the negative emotion onto the illness rather than from their daughter. This facilitates better communication within the family (for more details, see Chapter 7).

We coach family members to use this strategy when trying to modify eating disorder behaviours, for example:

- I get very frustrated when your anorexic voice makes the meals stretch out for over an hour. [explanation of distress]
- Is there any way we could help you make the mealtimes less protracted? [offer to help]
- What about if we let you know at ten minute intervals how much time has gone? [suggest helpful strategy]

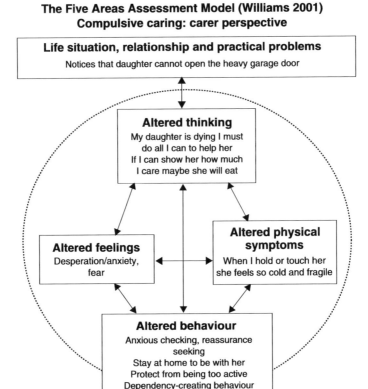

The Five Areas Assessment Model (Williams 2001)
Compulsive caring: carer perspective

Life situation, relationship and practical problems
Notices that daughter cannot open the heavy garage door

Altered thinking
My daughter is dying I must
do all I can to help her
If I can show her how much
I care maybe she will eat

Altered feelings
Desperation/anxiety,
fear

**Altered physical
symptoms**
When I hold or touch her
she feels so cold and fragile

Altered behaviour
Anxious checking, reassurance
seeking
Stay at home to be with her
Protect from being too active
Dependency-creating behaviour

Figure 6.7 The cyclical process of over-protective behaviour (carer's perspective).

Reflective listening

Sometimes difficulties in the family make the need for closer attachments more relevant. The person with anorexia nervosa, for example, may have high levels of anxiety because she is concerned that her parents' marriage is in trouble. Alternatively, she may be uncertain whether she is unconditionally loved and cared for. Some of the genetic findings suggest that people with anorexia nervosa have a higher sensitivity to anxiety than the rest of the population and so minor threats and hassles can be profoundly stressful. This uncertainty about these core attachments makes the pseudo safety and security of anorexia nervosa reassuring.

One of the interventions used to break this cycle of unhelpful behaviour is for the family to show support and care but *not just* in relation to food and other anorexia nervosa behaviours. Whenever possible, the family should try to schedule pleasant non-AN activities together. We encourage parents to spend time listening to their daughter, using the skills of reflective listening.

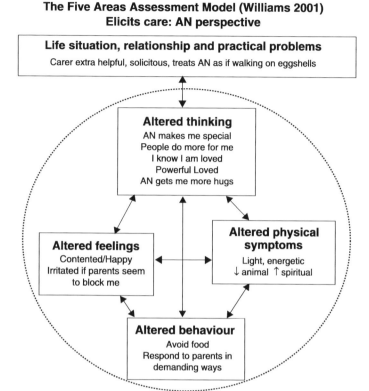

Figure 6.8 The cyclical process of over-protective behaviour (sufferer's perspective).

The experience of attentively being listened to helps to strengthen the attachment bonds. This encourages a shift from non-verbal to verbal strategies in seeking help and getting noticed and attended to.

Overcoming the vicious circle of parental over-control

In order to change maladaptive patterns of interpersonal relationships, it is helpful to recognise when and how they occur. We find that the animal metaphors make it safe and fun to discuss these patterns. Consequently, we ask carers to monitor *rhinoceros* behaviour by using a diary sheet to note any critical or controlling actions. Having established a baseline of when they occur and how they are triggered, the next step is to plan a step-by-step reduction in these behaviours.

A functional analysis of the times when an escalation of confrontation occurs may highlight triggers that can act as warning bells. It may be possible to develop plans and strategies to consider how these can be circumvented.

At the same time, communication skills training can give parents alternative ways of responding. It is useful to practise with role-play, that is how to react in situations where an over-controlling or critical reaction would usually have occurred. To begin with, this might include leaving a situation rather than shouting or hitting. The eventual goal should be to allow the parent to assertively (rather than aggressively) deal with the situation. The skills of motivational interviewing in which people 'roll with resistance' rather than attempt to counter and correct are useful tools for parents to learn.

Carers find it a great relief to realise that there are ways to interrupt these negative confrontational interactions by using reflective listening (Chapter 5). This skill involves listening to the feeling behind the food, weight and shape talk rather than arguing with the overt content. We teach carers to empathise with the underlying emotional distress and confusion and to sidestep an argument rather than confronting and challenging the anorexic beliefs with logic. The sufferer then experiences being carefully listened to. This does not mean that there is not a bottom-line fixed boundary about eating that can still be applied. In the following excerpt this mother describes how she was able to withdraw from confronting the anorexia nervosa behaviour head on all the time.

> I think that was one of the main things that family work taught us that you are not actually arguing with T, you are arguing with the anorexia. I think of it as if there is a monster in the head talking. If you start arguing with a monster, there is no reason, no logic at all. Of course we didn't know that to start with. We just thought she was coming out with so much silliness that we just ended up arguing and getting cross. Bearing in mind she was only 14/15 at the time you kind of treat it in a way as if it was just being a teenager misbehaving and you tell her to stop doing it but of course that's no good either.
>
> (Mother of anorexic daughter)

The notion of 'safe risks'

One strategy is to ensure that only a 'good enough' amount of care is offered. We encourage both parents to spend time discussing with each other, how to manage the anorexia nervosa so that they can realistically appraise whether the amount of care they are giving is warranted or whether it is excessive and suffocating. Parents need to be able to communicate effectively between themselves about this. Each parent needs to listen and also be heard. The skills of reflective listening can help with this dialogue. Often in any relationship there is a tendency for one person to be more dominant and to jump in with opinions without listening to their partner. This opens the way for the more passive partner to get on with what they think is the correct approach when the other partner's back is turned. Anorexia nervosa thrives on such inconsistency. It is easy to fall into the trap of becoming a super carer because they dismiss their husband (it is often mothers) as not listening or understanding. This is a dangerous strategy that undermines the relationship. Such splitting is also very damaging as it accentuates the imbalance in the type of care given. The person with anorexia nervosa is given confused mixed messages from her parents. This lack of coherence allows the anorexia nervosa behaviours to flourish. It is critically important for the parental couple to be able to communicate effectively with each other and work as a team.

The following quote from a father illustrates how this process of splitting, caused by extremes of temperament and behaviour, worked in their family. One of the effects of the family intervention was for the couple to recognise this process.

> K and I had totally different approaches with M. She was protecting her and I was trying to snap her out of it. . . . I still think K is too easy on her. I tend to go overboard, K is a bit too far the other way. We need someone in the middle. I can drive people mad, I go over and over and over things and I drive me and other people mad. Whereas K, I don't think, does it enough.
>
> (Father of anorexic daughter)

Ideally parents should jointly appraise the risk and their daughter's level of motivation. It can be a useful exercise for them both to make a judgement about these issues on a 0–10 scale (with 0 meaning no risk and 10 meaning high risk) and, if there is a marked discrepancy, explain to each other the reasons for their judgement. Once the severity of the risk has been agreed upon, the next step is to make a plan to come up with a 'safe enough' solution. This means taking safe risks in order to reduce over-protection.

It is not easy to decide about how and when to withdraw support. A problem-solving approach can be useful to work through this process. Often it is helpful if these discussions can take place with someone outside the family, a therapist, the general practitioner, a beat support person or a family friend. This is particularly important if the main carer is a single parent.

Other relationships: relationships with siblings and peers

Although we have focused so far on the parent–child relationship, other types of relationships with siblings, peers and friends can have an impact on the illness and serve as maintaining factors.

People with anorexia nervosa have a tendency to judge themselves negatively in comparison to others. If the person with anorexia has a sister, she is likely to consider her to be more attractive, intelligent and favoured by their parents than they themselves are. This can give rise to intense feelings of jealousy. It is not considered appropriate to have jealous feelings in our society, so often these feelings are dismissed and ignored. They can interfere, however, with the development of a supportive relationship with siblings. People with anorexia nervosa also often have a high level of fear and anxiety and are acutely sensitive to any negative comment. This can make them more sensitive to bullying and teasing. They are perfect victim fodder as they respond to the bully by cowering and reacting submissively.

One of the driving forces behind some of the anorexia nervosa behaviours is a striving for perfection. The extreme extent that this is taken to when anorexia nervosa takes hold, however, can make the sufferer appear alien and odd. Furthermore, their attention to detail, at the expense of being able to respond to the gist of a situation, can make them seem not 'with it'. As the anorexia nervosa behaviour takes hold, their peers withdraw from them as they become rigid, unidimensional in their interests and lacking in fun. Friends no longer know what to say to them.

In addition to being shunned by their peers and siblings because of their behaviours, the person with anorexia nervosa tends to isolate herself so that she can focus exclusively on anorexia nervosa. Starvation means that she has less working memory free to concentrate on complex social interactions and so she will appear distracted and uninterested. She will have lost her sense of humour as her mood falls. She has little in common with her friends and they serve only to distract her from her chosen focus. These cycles of unhelpful behaviour, both from the friends/peers perspective as well as the sufferer's perspective are illustrated in Figures 6.9 and 6.10.

Interventions to improve peer–sibling relationship

Whenever possible it is helpful to include siblings in treatment. This allows them the opportunity to express their own feelings about the situation and to describe their own experiences. The family work can give them a chance to listen to and understand the feelings that underlie the 'obnoxious' behaviours of their sister with anorexia nervosa. Often siblings are excluded or withdraw themselves from the battlefield. This is a resource that must not be squandered if at all possible. Siblings can offer helpful support and provide a bridge for reconnection to the world outside of anorexia nervosa and promote engagement with non-anorexic behaviours. It is sometimes helpful to have separate meetings with the siblings alone, in order to build upon these relationships.

Conclusion

In this chapter, we have focused on the patterns of relationships within families and peers, which act as maintaining factors in anorexia nervosa. We have shown how a cognitive behavioural analysis of these patterns of

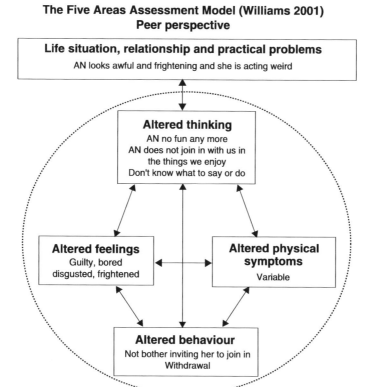

The Five Areas Assessment Model (Williams 2001)
Peer perspective

Life situation, relationship and practical problems
AN looks awful and frightening and she is acting weird

Altered thinking
AN no fun any more
AN does not join in with us in
the things we enjoy
Don't know what to say or do

Altered feelings
Guilty, bored
disgusted, frightened

**Altered physical
symptoms**
Variable

Altered behaviour
Not bother inviting her to join in
Withdrawal

Figure 6.9 The unhelpful pattern of peer withdrawal from the peer's perspective.

relationships can be helpful, not only to illustrate to family members the traps that they fall into but also as templates against which to construct exits from these traps. These less than helpful interactions between the person with anorexia nervosa and their carers are of course not unique to this disorder. Much of what has been described also applies to bulimia nervosa and other eating disorders. Similar patterns can also occur in the alcohol and substance abuse area where some of them are called pejoratively co-dependency. In our approach, we have used humour to defuse any defensiveness, using animal metaphors to label the various interactive styles, such as jellyfish, ostrich, rhinoceros and kangaroo. In our experience we have found that such an approach provides a light-hearted way of addressing deeper issues. It adds a more playful attitude to which carers respond well.

Chapter 7 will introduce the concept of motivational enhancement and its role in working with models of health behaviour, specifically that of stages of change. This chapter explains the stages of change typical in eating disorders and provides practical case studies and skills that may be useful when working

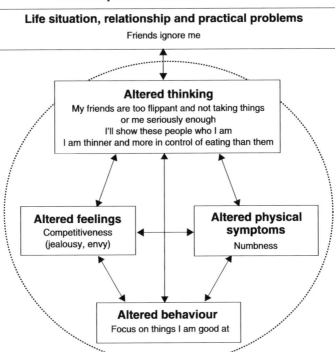

The Five Areas Assessment Model (Williams 2001)
AN: Response to friends' withdrawal

Life situation, relationship and practical problems
Friends ignore me

Altered thinking
My friends are too flippant and not taking things
or me seriously enough
I'll show these people who I am
I am thinner and more in control of eating than them

Altered feelings
Competitiveness
(jealousy, envy)

Altered physical symptoms
Numbness

Altered behaviour
Focus on things I am good at

Figure 6.10 The unhelpful pattern of peer withdrawal from the sufferer's perspective.

through these stages. The central principles of motivational interviewing are described along with examples of styles of interaction that are consistent with motivational interviewing techniques.

Notes

1 The term safety behaviour was coined by Professor Paul Salkovskis from the Institute of Psychiatry to describe a range of behaviours that a person employs to reduce a sense of threat, e.g. a person with a fear of contamination may carry with them a large range of cleaning materials, tissues and wipes or avoid certain situations altogether.
2 Set-shifting is the ability to switch between different tasks or task demands.

References

Butzlaff, R. L. & Hooley, J. M. (1998). Expressed emotion and psychiatric relapse: A meta-analysis. *Archives of General Psychiatry*, 55: 547–552.

Dalgleish, T., Tchanturia, K., Serpell, L., Hems, S., De Silva, P. & Treasure, J. (2001). Perceived control over events in the world in patients with eating disorders: A preliminary study in personality and individual differences. *Personality and Individual Differences* 31: 453–460.

Geller, B., Craney, J. L., Bolhofner, K., Nickelsburg, M. J., Williams, M. & Zimerman, B. (2002). Two-year prospective follow-up of children with a prepubertal and early adolescent bipolar disorder phenotype. *American Journal of Psychiatry* 159: 927–933.

Jacobi, C., Hayward, C., de Zwaan, M., Kraemer, H. C. & Agras, W. S. (2004). Coming to terms with risk factors for eating disorders: Application of risk terminology and suggestions for a general taxonomy. *Psychological Bulletin* 130(1): 19–65.

Miklowitz, D. J., George, E. L., Richards, J. A., Simoneau, T. L. & Suddath, R. L. (2003). A randomized study of family-focused psychoeducation and pharmacotherapy in the outpatient management of bipolar disorder. *Archives of General Psychiatry*, 60: 904–912.

Russell, G. F. M. (1995). Anorexia nervosa through time. In G. Szmukler, C. Dare & J. Treasure (eds) *Handbook of Eating Disorders: Theory, Treatment and Research.* Chichester: Wiley.

Schmidt, U. & Treasure, J. (2005). Anorexia nervosa: Valued and visible. A cognitive-interpersonal maintenance model and its implications for research and practice. *British Journal of Clinical Psychology* 45(3): 343–366.

Serpell, L., Treasure, J., Teasdale, J. & Sullivan, V. (1999). Anorexia nervosa: Friend or foe? *International Journal of Eating Disorders* 25: 177–186.

Serpell, L., Teasdale, J., Troop, N. & Treasure, J. (2004). The development of the P-CAN: A scale to operationalise the pros and cons of anorexia nervosa. *International Journal of Eating Disorders* 36: 416–433.

Southgate, L., Tchanturia, K. & Treasure, J. (2005). Building a model of the aetiology of eating disorders by translating experimental neuroscience into clinical practice. *Journal of Mental Health* 14: 553–566.

Stice, E. (2002). Risk and maintenance factors for eating pathology: A meta-analytic reveiw. Personal communication.

Szmukler, G. I., Eisler, I., Russell, G. F. & Dare, C. (1985). Anorexia nervosa, parental 'expressed emotion' and dropping out of treatment. *British Journal of Psychiatry* 147: 265–271.

Treasure, J., Smith, G. & Crane, A. (2007). *Skills-based Learning for Caring for a Loved One with an Eating Disorder: The New Maudsley Method.* London: Routledge.

Williams, C. (2001). *Overcoming Depression: A Five Areas Approach.* London: Hodder Arnold.

Understanding models of health behaviours and the processes used to facilitate change

Janet Treasure

Introduction

The syllabus to address carers' needs is similar to that required for any health professional working in the area of eating disorders. There are direct parallels between managing anorexia nervosa on an inpatient unit and what happens at home. Both professional and non-professional carers alike need to be armed with knowledge about the illness and skills that help rather then hinder change. Models of health behaviour change can be helpful in structuring knowledge about behaviour change and motivation. One of the many processes used to facilitate change is motivational interviewing. We discuss these in this chapter as well as some of the concepts and mechanisms that explain human drives and motivation.

The trans-theoretical model of change is easily understood and suitable for sharing with families (Prochaska & DiClimente, 1984). It enables families to judge how committed their loved one is to change and to understand why change might be difficult. Furthermore the model predicts what sort of interaction is most suited for each level of readiness.

Motivational interviewing is a style of working which may be particularly helpful for people who are uncertain about or not ready to change (Miller & Rollnick, 1991, 2002; Treasure & Schmidt, 2008). It is designed to help people think about changing problematic behaviours. We have found that it is particularly useful in working with people with anorexia nervosa, as the majority of this group are not ready to actively change (Blake et al., 1997). We also use this approach to work with family members so that they are willing and able to implement some of the cognitive and behavioural changes that are necessary to break vicious circles of unhelpful behaviour (Treasure & Schmidt, 2008). The therapist encourages the family to use these concepts and skills to engage productively with their loved one, in order to instigate change (see Chapter 12).

Health behaviour change

All of us have behaviours that we know are unhelpful. We may, however, have mixed feelings about how and/or whether we want, or are able, to change these behaviours. There are several psychological theories that have been proposed to explain behaviour change. The theory of reasoned action and the theory of planned behaviour have been studied most often (see Figure 7.1).

Three core variables are thought to influence the strength of an intention to change: the importance of change in terms of the expected value that will accrue from change, subjective norms and a measure of self-efficacy, perceived behavioural control.

The first factor, the importance or expected value, refers to an individual's perceptions about the advantages and disadvantages of performing a particular behaviour and includes the expected perceived outcomes that will follow from performing the behaviour. These are termed the behavioural beliefs.

The second factor, subjective norms, is made up of two components. The first component relates to the normative beliefs about the behaviour, that is, what are the expectations of society or important others, in relation to this behaviour. The second aspect is the individual's willingness to fall in with these expectations.

The third factor relates to self-efficacy beliefs. Perceived behavioural control refers to the individual's perception that he or she can carry out the behaviour and overcome the obstacles that stand in the way of implementing it. Figure 7.1 is a schematic outline of the various concepts that have been used to describe behaviour change.

Trans-theoretical model of change

In our work with families we have found that the trans-theoretical model of change is a model that is easy to understand and the concept of stages has

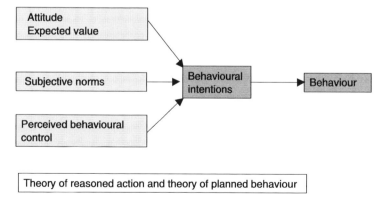

Figure 7.1 Theories of behaviour change.

some practical utility. The trans-theoretical model of change breaks down the concept of readiness to change into five stages: *pre-contemplation*, not even ready to think about change seriously; *contemplation*, ready to think about change; *preparation*, preparing to make plans for change; *action*, implementing change; and *maintenance*, ensuring that the change in behaviour becomes habitual (Prochaska & DiClemente, 1984; Prochaska & Norcross, 1994). One of the predictions from this model is that for each stage, certain behaviours to facilitate change can be particularly constructive or destructive. Figure 7.2 illustrates how this concept can be applied to eating disorders.

An individual's position on the cycle of change – what stage of change they are at – is dependent upon how important it is for them to change their behaviours and how confident they feel that they can do it. The steps illustrate some of the processes of health behaviour change that are most helpful at each stage.

In the pre-contemplative state the focus of work is reflection upon the desire and ability for change. The process involves helping the patient step back from the here and now to take a more global perspective on their life and their cherished values and beliefs about their life. Warmth and a non-judgemental attitude and respectful attitude allow the individual to drop some of their guard. The use of affirmation and reframing and reflections on positive aspects of the individual and their environment increases self-efficacy. Reflective listening allows the individual the opportunity to see themselves as others see them. The therapist uses a bias to focus on the good within an individual. A useful metaphor of the therapeutic stance is for the therapist to be a bee working with nectar and pollen rather than a fly looking

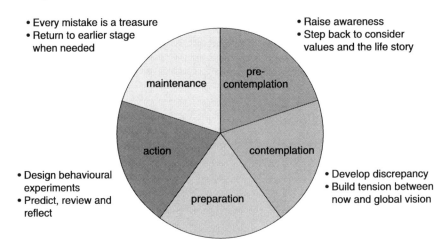

Figure 7.2 Model of health change.

for rot and decay. The individual is encouraged to reflect on themselves across the timeline of life from the present to the past and future.

In the stage of contemplation the individual faces the tension between where they are now and where they would like to be. The therapist can hold and reflect back this discrepancy and works to increase dissonance. The resolution of this ambivalence may be associated with a sudden change in the patient's mind set. This has been referred to as the 'click' moment when there is a perceptual shift. This is the point at which the patient suddenly recognises the inherent contradictions in their current pattern of behaviour and commits to making the change. It should be noted, however, that this is not necessarily a sudden stage jump or even a slow gradual linear process. Different patients will respond in different ways, sometimes going back to previous positions, and some patients may get stuck in a particular pattern of responses. This is where the therapist may have to use a range of different approaches to help patients move forward and start talking about and committing to change. The drivers for adopting change can vary between individuals. These may not always be based on logic; they may be emotional in origin. Resolving the ambivalence is often associated with an increase in the importance of change with a shift in the decisional balance between the factors that promote or inhibit change. However, logic alone cannot produce change and there needs to be the energy from emotional commitment added to the process. Fear of failure or of the unknown and a lack of sense of mastery and competence and disconnection from the current social context can sabotage change. The bedrock of a good therapeutic alliance can alleviate these blocks' affirmation to foster self-efficacy and/or recall of successful change events in the past, and planning for social support can help foster change.

Once an individual is committed to change, then using standard behaviour change principles such as setting goals, designing behavioural experiments planning their implementation, predicting and preventing obstacles derailing the process are helpful. This includes many of the standard techniques of cognitive behavioural therapy.

Working with the concepts of health behaviour change with the family

Families find the trans-theoretical model useful and they move from the simple concepts underpinning readiness and motivation to change into thinking about where they are on the circle of change and what stage they think their daughter is in. This is useful to help people move from polarised extreme positions. Asking their daughter questions such as 'Do you want to get better or not?' merely leads to frustration and anger.

Movement around the circle is fired by the balance between the perceived costs and benefits of both the status quo and change. We encourage family members to have conversations with their offspring which elicit and open up discussions relating to their mixed feelings about change. The topics can be structured around two dimensions: how important it is for them to change, and how much confidence and trust they have in both themselves and their carers (professional and family) that they can achieve change. We do not expect the families to undertake the detailed work understanding their off-spring's ambivalence about change, but it is helpful if they have a broad understanding and are able to help set appropriate goals and offer to help. No matter how deep the regression of behaviour, it is helpful if the family remain optimistic, albeit with modest goals. Both the therapist and family have an important role to play by retaining a positive disposition and increasing the individual's confidence by highlighting any positive features or green shoots of change that they detect. Within this model relapse is seen as part of the circle of growth and an opportunity for new reflection and learning. We find the adage that every mistake is a treasure useful for this.

Concepts from models of health behaviour change are used to plan and negotiate the type and level of support that is needed. Thus, in terms of the core symptoms of eating and nutritional health, there needs to be a balance between how much the individual can change her anorexia nervosa behaviours and how much active help carers need to give to maintain safety.

The advantage of this model is that it is clearly dynamic with activities prescribed to build momentum and facilitate movement. This ensures that carers do not merely withdraw as an extreme reaction when they understand that active change is impossible (e.g. 'Talk to me when you are ready to change') but they can keep connection and communication at all stages. It helps carers find the middle ground between being overly coercive or per-missive in relation to the behaviour.

What is a stage of change?

Carers are usually the first people to detect and recognise the illness and want change. This means that the agenda of the person with the illness (who, in the case of someone with anorexia nervosa, values rather than decries her symptoms) and her carers are at cross-purposes. This can lead to conflict and distress. One of the first tasks is for the carers to consider the concept of stage of change for both themselves and for the person with anorexia nervosa. In our work with the individual with anorexia nervosa we ask them to self-rate their motivation to change. We have transferred this approach to our work with families. We use linear scales to measure the dimensions of readiness to change. We ask each family member to rate themselves, each other and the person with anorexia nervosa on these scales.

It is common for both carers and the person with anorexia nervosa to be situated in different positions in terms of their 'stage of change' (pre-contemplation, contemplation, preparation, action, maintenance) in relationship both to the anorexia nervosa behaviours and to other behaviours within the family. Family members, for example, will want their daughter to be in action in regards to changing the anorexia nervosa. They may not recognise, however, that some family behaviours and interactions are problematic and may need to be changed.

In contrast, the person with anorexia nervosa may be unmotivated to change their anorexia nervosa and may have come into hospital to please her parents but may want to be able to talk and relate to her family in a different way. One of the tasks of the therapeutic work is for carers and the person with anorexia nervosa to negotiate a plan whereby they are in more similar positions in terms of readiness to change both anorexia nervosa and family behaviours. Readiness to change and motivation is a fluid concept and carers need to regularly adjust their judgements. We find that some carers find this concept is one that they can usefully adopt when talking to their offspring about problematic behaviours. It allows the interaction to be playful rather than confrontational.

Occasionally carers may be less certain about the status of the symptoms. Family and friends may value some of the symptoms for some of the time. In such cases, carers can be drawn in as an advocate negotiating with professionals about aspects of their loved one's care. Carers can be drawn into the debate about an appropriate target weight and argue on their daughter's side for inadequate weight gain. Similarly carers for people with bulimia nervosa may want them to stop bingeing and being sick but they may not want their daughter or girlfriend to gain weight and lift the restrictions on their diet. It is important to be able to manage and understand all these different agendas.

What processes might be useful?

The next step is to consider what help is best suited to their daughter's readiness to change and level of motivation. Figure 7.3 depicts the readiness

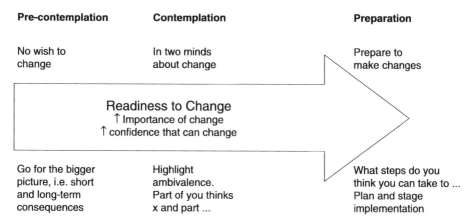

Figure 7.3 A dimensional model of change with suggestions about interventions suitable for each stage that can be used with families.

to change as a linear variable, with some of the processes and types of help that are best matched for the stage.

The level of support will need to move back and forth to follow their daughter as she oscillates between stages. We ask families to guess where their daughter is in terms of the stages of change, for each AN behaviour, such as feeding. If the daughter is in pre-contemplation about changing her feeding pattern and her physical state is at high risk, then carers will have to take more responsibility for feeding and be more active. Once there is movement towards more readiness to change, then the carer can relinquish some of this control.

The therapist needs to ensure that the family do not get stuck in one stage. When anorexia nervosa is severe, there is regression to a childlike state, in which parents often need to step in to take responsibility for feeding and many aspects of life. In some cases this regression can be mutually reinforcing. It can create an extreme variant of the unhelpful caregiving and care-eliciting (kangaroo) pattern of behaviour (Appendix 1). In order to get out of this trap, the therapist and family need to work with that part of the person with anorexia nervosa, who wants a healthier outcome, gradually handing back nutritional care to the index patient. The following example illustrates how this pattern can develop.

Case study: Yvonne

Yvonne was a 19-year-old patient with severe anorexia nervosa, who had required a prolonged admission. Yvonne was very ambivalent about change. She recognised that part of her wanted to be a child, with her parents taking responsibility for her. She also talked about not wanting to keep coming back into hospital. The therapist had spoken to Yvonne about plans for her next leave and she anticipated a childlike passive position, 'Oh my Dad will force me to eat'. While she allowed her father to keep forcing her to eat, she did not learn to take responsibility for her nutritional health. This meant that the parent–child relationship remained very dependent and immature. (This level of dependence can be rewarding for those with avoidant personality traits, especially if both patient and parents are anxious and avoidant and so there is little momentum to change.)

The therapist suggested that Yvonne needed to work out how much responsibility she would take for herself in terms of her eating, and how much she wanted her parents to do. The therapist encouraged her to be open and to clearly communicate her needs and how much she wanted her parents to help. The therapist used a line scaled 1–10, with 1 anchored at 'I cannot have any responsibility to care for my own body, i.e. feed it' to 10 'I can take full responsibility to care for my body. I can feed it so that it remains healthy'. Yvonne gave herself a score of 3. The therapist asked why she had given herself this score rather than 0. She said it was because before, her father would automatically spoon-feed her, whereas she now felt that if her parents served her, she would be able to eat. The therapist asked what would help her move to a higher score; she said that once she took one or two first steps of feeding herself it would probably get to be a habit. Yvonne was able to set herself some small goals and make future plans using this method.

The therapist worked with Yvonne with the family present so that the family could also learn a new way of interacting rather than reverting to these polarised extremes. Although her father was keeping her alive with his approach of spoon-feeding her, this regressive pattern did not allow her to become more competent. Thus, the therapist was able to coax Yvonne step by step towards breaking the pattern in which she perpetually took the role of a passive childlike victim. This modelling of a new relationship with food paved the way for Yvonne to start to think of herself as someone who could conceptualise herself as a survivor of the traumatic experience that precipitated her anorexia nervosa.

A similar thing can happen on inpatient units. In this context nurses take control, which means that the person with anorexia nervosa may never have to take responsibility for attending to her nutritional needs and, unless she is given the opportunity for home leave, will have no confidence that she is able to make changes. We find that some patients can easily become institutionalised and welcome the security of the ward.

Feeding is not the only aspect of self-care that the family may have to take over if the patient is in pre-contemplation. Often there are other aspects of self-neglect, wearing the same clothes day after day, not washing etc.

Although parents may need to step in to take control in these areas it is important that they re-evaluate their position regularly. Using simple linear scales at intervals with a focus on outcomes and solutions can be a useful monitoring tool. Debriefing, following small behavioural experiments in which the level of responsibility between parent and child is varied, can be very informative. Such practical experiments need to be reviewed and revised as necessary. It does no harm to take a step back if the experiment fails. Indeed, such an experience is to be valued as it is possible to learn what went wrong and take preventative action to remedy it.

Motivational interviewing and motivational enhancement

Motivational interviewing was developed as an intervention for working with people with behaviours that are difficult to change, such as addictions, because people are often in pre-contemplation about change. It is often used when concerned others or society wants action and change to take place. It is beyond the scope of this book to discuss the background and breadth of motivational interviewing in more detail. For more information there are standard texts (Miller & Rollnick, 1991, 2002), a website (www.motivationalinterviewing.org) and a systematic review of the evidence base of its efficacy (Dunn et al., 2001). Motivational interviewing combines elements of style (warmth and empathy), which improves self-confidence that change can occur, with techniques (e.g. key questions and focused reflective listening) that examine the importance and ambivalence about change. Figure 7.4 illustrates some of the principles of a motivational approach.

A core tenet of the technique is that the individual's motivation to change is enhanced if it is the patient, not the practitioner (or parent), who talks about change. Thus, this model stands in contrast to one in which a dominant, more powerful or expert other gives advice. Once there is commitment to change, the individual is encouraged to make and implement a plan. This approach helps foster a sense of mastery to implement change. A strong principle of this approach is that conflict is unhelpful. Warmth, with a collaborative relationship where the person with anorexia nervosa is given the time and space to reflect on the problem, is essential. The five central principles of motivational interviewing are shown in Table 7.1.

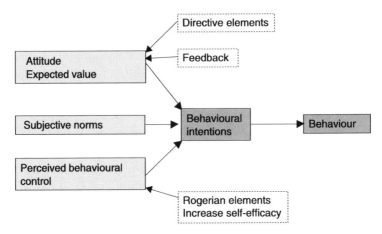

Figure 7.4 An outline of the processes used in motivational interviewing: the various aspects of the techniques are shown in the dotted boxes, which map onto the core elements involved in behaviour change.

Table 7.1 Central principles of motivational interviewing

1   Express empathy by using reflective listening (the therapist uses a minimum number of questions and focuses on summarising the patient's thoughts and underlying feelings) to convey that they understand and are interested in the client's point of view.

2   Develop discrepancy between the client's most deeply held values and ambitions from their life story, and their current behaviour. (Explore within the past, future and present to find a position when the patient would not want to be in the current state.) Ask open questions – following the 'DARN' principle (D = desire for change, A = ability to change, R = reasons for change, N = need for change).

3   Sidestep resistance (do not get into arguments) by reflecting their position and emphasising their ambivalence 'part of you thinks' and so on.

4   Support self-efficacy, by building confidence that change is possible by warmth and affirmative feedback.

5   Elicit commitment to change statements and use reflection to encourage the client to speak about change. Once commitment to change is reached, encourage the individual to make small steps and develop a plan in small stages. Ask them to construct a storyboard of how they would make a film detailing them in a new role as someone taking up the challenge of change. Focus on the outcome: how would they know they were succeeding, what other resources might they need to get there.

Rollnick & Miller (1995) defined specific and trainable therapist behaviours that lead to a better therapeutic alliance and better outcome. These are shown in Table 7.2.

The first four items fit well with the trans-theoretical model of change, in that they explore the reasons that sustain the behaviour and aim to help the client shift the decisional balance of *pros* and *cons* into the direction of change. The last two items cover the interpersonal aspects of the relationship. The therapist provides warmth and optimism and takes a subordinate,

Table 7.2 Good motivational therapist behaviours

1   Understanding the patient's frame of reference.

2   Filtering the patient's thoughts so that for-change statements are amplified and counter-change statements dampened down.

3   Eliciting for-change statements from the client, i.e. expressions of problem recognition, concern, desire, intention to change and ability to change.

4   Matching the processes of the intervention with the stage of change of the client. Do not jump ahead of the client, i.e. expecting action when the patient is in pre-contemplation.

5   Expressing acceptance and affirmation.

6   Affirming the client's freedom of choice and self-direction.

non-powerful position, which emphasises the client's autonomy and their right to choose whether to use the therapist's knowledge and skills. The fable about the sun and the wind is a rather nice metaphor about the spirit of motivational interviewing:

> The sun and the wind were having a dispute as to who was the most powerful. They saw a man walking along and they challenged each other about which of them would be most successful at getting the man to remove his coat. The wind started first and blew up a huge gale, the coat flapped but the man only closed all his buttons and tightened up his belt. The sun tried next and shone brightly making the man sweat. He proceeded to take off his coat.

Motivational therapists need to model themselves on the sun! They have to be able to suppress any propensity they might have to show the 'Righting Reflex', that is to help solve problems and set things right. They have to be flexible and meticulously monitor the patient's movement in readiness to change and mirror this with an appropriate balance of acceptance and drive for change and at the same time to be able to show warmth and respect.

Using a motivational interviewing approach with the family

In this approach with families, we use motivational interviewing skills and demonstrate and model the principles in action. The therapist is, therefore, warm and accepting of the family and listens to them with respect. The aim is to increase their sense of efficacy by reflecting on the positive aspects of their life together. The therapist listens and summarises what members of the family are trying to say. The principles of this approach with families are outlined next.

Examples of the interviewing style consistent with motivational interviewing

Ask open-ended questions

- What are you expecting to happen in this meeting?
- What do different family members think about that?

Listen reflectively

Make an educated guess about the emotion or thought behind each family member's contributions. Paraphrase and put yourself in that person's shoes. Here are some examples of reflective listening:

- There seems to be some difference in opinion between Dad and Jane. Can you tell me more about this?
- Mum, you've noticed that your family tends to . . .
- You're concerned that . . .
- You've noticed that . . .
- Mum, you are terrified because you have watched TV programmes showing people who have been admitted to hospital for life-threatening AN and Sally looks worse than them.
- Sue, you have noticed that since your mother has stepped back from helping you plan out your meals in advance, it has been harder for you to fight for your nutritional health . . .

Summarise

Therapists include important points that they want to reinforce in the summary such as:

- Let me see if I got this right. You are saying . . .

The summary is used to clarify issues and, if possible, to emphasise positive aspects.

- You are a family who reflect on what people have said, are eager to contribute etc.

Try to synthesise different members' points of view in a way that makes sense to everyone and in a way that has a focus on good intentions.

- All in all, this family is saying . . .

Affirm

Show respect for the family and appreciation for their skills and troubles. Know and use everyone's name. Acknowledge everyone in the room within the first few minutes, including children. Find positive things to say about the family:

- It is impressive how willing to help everyone is.
- I am impressed with how inventive you have been.
- You are a close family who want to help each other.

Therapists model the type of behaviours that they want the family to develop. They will ensure that there is a low level of criticism and hostility within the sessions by using interventions that do not engender resistance and backing down, and curtailing any confrontation if it arises. Whenever possible, positive features should be emphasised. There should be a warm atmosphere with no scope for victimisation and blame.

Therapists use reflective listening with the family and show respect and curiosity for the family's values and beliefs and to understanding the difficulties the family face:

- Help me to understand that better.
- I don't think I quite understand, could you tell me a little bit more about that?
- That sounds awful. I wonder how you have coped with all that?
- Tell us what it's like when you feel blamed.
- How are you able to stop fretting about blaming yourself?

Therapists use motivational interviewing skills to help resolve ambivalence about change. This includes strategies such as double-sided reflection, in which both sides of a dilemma are articulated:

- You would like to be able to step back from having such an intense involvement with J's meals and you are terrified that unless you are in control that she will start to lose weight [a double-sided reflection].

At times you may want to overplay or make a black-and-white approach even more extreme in your reflection. This often has the effect of releasing a more moderate approach.

- J's behaviour makes her so dependent on you that you get drawn into treating her like an infant, preparing and controlling her meals, controlling her activities etc. [overshooting].

It is important to use affirmation as much as possible to foster the warm atmosphere:

- I feel I am really going to enjoy working with you.
- I can see that you have coped with some really difficult issues in your family.

Deal with resistance

Sometimes the family will show resistance. It is important to roll with this: let it pass you by and do not enter into any form of argument or defensive strategy:

Mother: Well, I read your handout and it said we should not focus on food all of the time, so I have withdrawn. I have not been spending time helping S plan her food for the week. Since I have stopped doing that, her weight has fallen.

Therapist: Great, you have made an experiment and tested out whether your involvement with S in relationship to her nutritional health was helpful or not so helpful. You have come to the conclusion that the advice in our booklet was wrong. It's fantastic that you now have evidence about what works in your hands. Will you be able to start helping more with meal planning again? [Sidestep hostile comment about therapist expertise and highlight the approach which fostered change]

Examples of styles of interaction that are inconsistent with motivational interviewing

Confrontation and denial cycle

If family members are defensive, don't push them or confront them. Think of ways to gently go around the defensiveness:

- I appreciate it was difficult for you all to make time to come to this meeting. Thank you for coming to work with us on trying to make a life without anorexia nervosa.

Labelling

Do not label anyone in the family.

- We see families as the solution rather than the problem.
- Every member of the family has knowledge or skills that are helpful to us.

Blame

Do not blame anyone in the family. If necessary, say something like:

- We are not here to figure out who is to blame. We are not interested in the factors that cause the illness. They are unknowns within a black box. Most of the strongest causes of AN, that we do know about, are things we cannot change such as genes, being female etc. What we want to work on is trying to minimise any factors that maintain the illness. We can modify some of these if we work hard together and focus on what can go right rather then try to ruminate and recriminate about what can go wrong.
- Guilt, blame and criticism are depleting and stoke up the fires on anorexia nervosa. We need to look for the good and celebrate that.

Question and answer cycle

The therapist tries not to ask a battery of questions. If this pattern starts to emerge, the therapist summarises what has been said after about three questions and tries to get the family actively involved in a conversation.

Sidestepping resistance

One of the most important aspects of motivational interviewing is learning how to avoid generating resistance. If and when resistance comes, it is essential to have strategies to sidestep it and defuse conflict in both its active and passive forms. The resistance in family settings can be complex. It can be between a family member and the therapist, or between individuals within and between families, if a group of families are together. Resistance may be overt with arguments or covert with passive aggressive strategies such as sarcasm or avoidance.

Resistance may occur in the following ways:

- outright disagreement (between therapist and family member, or between two family members)
- one or more family members looking bored, switching off and not paying attention
- 'denial' where one or more family members are saying: 'I don't have a problem, *she* has the problem', 'I don't have to make any changes; she needs to do . . .'

When the therapist sees resistance it is important to be matter-of-fact and avoid using sarcasm or irony themselves and also avoid getting dragged into an escalating argument.

The types of responses that the therapist can make if there is anger and hostility between family members include the following.

Simple reflection

- It sounds like Janet is unhappy with the number of hours you work, because she wants to see more of you. However, Tom, you are under a lot of pressure at work and you cannot let your team down and this may mean promotion and a better standard of life for the family. Therefore, you are locked in a struggle that neither of you can win.

Amplified reflection

- You are such individualists that it is impossible for you two to find anything that you are in one mind about.

Undershoot reflection

- OK you don't feel you have a problem. At the moment you do not think that the quality of your family life can be improved at all.

Double-sided reflection

- On the one hand, you find the need to go for perfection irresistible and you both hate fighting.

Shifting focus

For example, if a couple is arguing:

- At this point, I'm going to stop you because I know you've had this argument many times before. We need to move on to . . .

Reframing

- It sounds like your mother is terrified about your illness and worries about you because she loves you, and that is why she puts pressure on you to eat.

Dealing with family resistance

Family members can also be resistant to the therapist themselves and be angry and confrontational, as the following examples illustrate.

Mother:	I am very unhappy about the ward's management of Y. Everyone says something different. We had made a plan and now you want to change it.
Therapist:	It sounds as if you feel anxious and confused that there is no one clear answer and way to do things. [Reflect the emotion]
Mother:	I have been taking J to school. She comes and has lunch with me in the car. She had told me that she was eating snacks. However, we found out that her weight had not been accurate as she had been water loading. So all the progress I thought we had made was false and we were back where we started.
Therapist:	You must been terrified at how powerful the anorexia nervosa force has been. It sounds as if you have gone to extreme lengths to help fight the AN. What must add to your difficulty is that you must have to be constantly vigilant and not trust or feel safe about anything. [Reflect the emotion]

| Mother: | It has been like living in a nightmare. I have done my best. |
| Therapist: | You must be exhausted. Have you been able to get any support and respite? [Reflect the emotion] |

Father:	You have asked us to come here. It is not easy to have time off work. It is S that is the problem, not us. I am not sure why you want us here.
Therapist:	We really appreciate you coming to try to work with us to think about how we can help S get a bigger life despite her AN.
Father:	I am not sure I will be able to get any more time off work. It has been difficult. My wife Mary has had to have prolonged compassionate leave. Someone has to keep the household going.
Therapist:	It is not easy is it? We could write a letter to work for you if you like, explaining you need time off on medical grounds. In Germany the doctors give the parents sick notes so that they can get benefits. They are justified, as this is a health issue. Could we help in this way?
Father:	No, it is OK. Carry on.
Therapist:	OK. We appreciate you coming to spend time so that we can all work together collaboratively caring for S. We find that all carers, and I mean professional nursing teams as well as family, can get burn-out from the stress and strain of helping people with anorexia nervosa care for their nutritional health. We have a list of key areas of difficulty. Is there any one of these that might be relevant to you and cause you and the family any difficulty in your caregiving role?

The therapist's job is to set the scene so that family members themselves voice the reasons they want to change, discuss their problems (a cognitive acknowledgement of the difficulties), and express concern about them (an emotional response to the problem). An important milestone is when families commit themselves to change. The therapist's job then is to provide the skills and knowledge for them to feel confident that they can implement changes (i.e. self-efficacy).

Teaching the family the skills of motivational listening

In addition to using the skills of motivational interviewing to help motivate the family, in turn, the therapist teaches the family some of the basic elements of motivational interviewing so that the family can interact with their daughter more effectively.

The skills that the therapist wants the family to gain include general communication and listening skills, which can improve warmth in the family. Family members are taught some of the principles of motivational interviewing to use in their interactions with the person with anorexia nervosa. In particular, the core foundation of motivational interviewing, how to listen reflectively, is a critical skill. The essence of what we teach parents is summarised in the aphorism 'LESS is more'. The letters of 'LESS' spell out the type of style of interaction that we want the family to try to adopt. 'LESS' is an easy way to keep the principle in mind and also it reminds people that a motivational approach involves them being less active, that is not too much talking and telling.

- *Listen:* Ensure that the person with AN is given time to talk. Show by your body language that you are willing to listen and by your ability to summarise that you have listened.
- *Empathise:* Not sympathise – understand the perspective of the person with AN, do not pity her.
- *Share*: Non-AN life – be interested in the bigger picture. Aim to join in with life outside anorexia nervosa.
- *Support:* Increase the confidence of the person with anorexia nervosa.

We help parents take less of a powerful, dominating approach so that their daughter can become an active partner. We want parents to be like a mentor to their offspring with AN. Thus, they need to treat their daughter as someone who is worthy of respect, who can hold the attention of someone else, and who has views and thoughts that are worthy of consideration. This is essential as one of the core features of anorexia nervosa is a sense of powerlessness. In order to make the person with anorexia nervosa feel more powerful, it is critical that she is treated as a person who is an equal to be respected. The task for those listening is to try to understand the emotions and core beliefs about self, that is those beliefs that lie under the camouflage of food, weight and shape talk, or compulsive safety, vomiting and reassurance seeking.

In our more intensive interventions such as workshops (Chapter 11) or the work with day patients (Chapter 12), we coach family members themselves in the skills of reflective listening. One task is for them to discuss in pairs something they are in two minds about, such as how much they are willing to change their behaviour in relationship to the anorexia nervosa, what colour to paint the bathroom, or where to go on holiday. This is to enable parents to develop their listening skills and capture the essence of what they have heard in the form of a short summary. We also model and give practice in using open, outcome-orientated questions. Many parents can pick up these skills after only a short demonstration.

We sometimes use more extended role-play, in which one parent plays a person with anorexia nervosa. Ideally, this feedback should focus on the emotional aspect of what is said – i.e. the feelings that underpin all the talk about food and weight.

The following quote illustrates a sister's description of learning the skills of reflective listening:

Yeah, just like practising reflective listening, I came out of that and went, wow, that's going to change how I'm going to talk to Jane. And when I've really tried to consciously use it, it had. And it's worked and I think, I mean, I think that's what it was. It wasn't like trying to be like an analyst or anything like that, it was just listening and not feeling like I had to solve Jane's problems in one conversation. And just kind of, it's OK that everything isn't OK, and just accepting. I think that's a lot of it just accepting the situation as it is now and um, and not constantly feeling guilty about it. That was quite a revelation!

(Sister of anorexic woman)

This suggests that this skill can be useful, but as in clinical work with motivational interviewing, it is necessary to have lots of practice and supervision before people are able to put this into practice. Bill Miller teaches that one of the best gifts that you can give someone is to listen to them for five minutes, and so this skill has widespread generalisability.

Conclusion

The spirit of motivational interviewing permeates through all the work we do with families. We use this approach with carers to help them change their behaviour with the person with anorexia nervosa and ultimately, so that they can also use this sort of approach with their loved one with an eating disorder.

In Chapter 8, we look at working with families from a different theoretical stance, whereby cognitive behavioural strategies are used for working with families on maladaptive attitudes and beliefs about the illness. We examine some of the issues that arise from the carer's perspective along with a range of skills that can improve the coping resources of the family.

References

Blake, W., Turnbull, S. & Treasure, J. (1997) Stages and processes of change in eating disorders: Implications for therapy. *Clinical Psychology and Psychotherapy* 4: 186–191.

Dunn, C., Deroo, L. & Rivara, F. P. (2001). The use of brief interventions adapted from motivational interviewing across behavioral domains: A systematic review. *Addiction* 96: 1725–1742.

Miller, W. R. & Rollnick, S. (1991). *Motivational Interviewing: Preparing People to Change Addictive Behaviour*. New York: Guilford.

Miller, W. R. & Rollnick, S. (2002). *Motivational Interviewing*, 2nd edn. New York: Guilford.

Prochaska, J. & DiClemente, C. (1984). *The Transtheoretical Approach: Crossing the Traditional Boundaries of Therapy*. Homewood, IL: Dow Jones Irwen.

Prochaska, J. & Norcross, J. (1994). *Systems of Psychotherapy: A Transtheoretical Analysis*, 3rd edn. Pacific Grove, CA: Brooks/Cole.

Rollnick, S. & Miller, W. R. (1995). What is motivational interviewing? *Behavioural and Cognitive Psychotherapy* 23, 325–335.

Treasure, J. & Schmidt, U. (2008). Motivational interviewing in the management of eating disorders. In H. Arkowitz, H. A. Westra, W. R. Miller & S. Rollnick (eds) *Motivational Interviewing in the Treatment of Psychological Problems*. New York: Guilford.

Chapter 8

Changing behaviours in the family

Janet Treasure

Introduction

In this chapter we discuss some of the cognitive and behavioural strategies we use in our work with family members, both on their assumptions about and reactions to anorexia nervosa. We start by identifying the underlying model of anorexia nervosa held by family members. Often their conceptual framework contains inaccurate assumptions about the illness. These can fuel unhelpful emotional reactions such as anger, shame or guilt. Education and cognitive restructuring can help build a more realistic parental model of the illness that can, in turn, improve the emotional atmosphere in the family.

We review some of the behavioural principles that can help families manage the key symptoms. We then describe how families can undertake a functional analysis of anorexia nervosa behaviours within the home and plan interventions. Finally, we illustrate how families can recognise and interrupt unhelpful cycles of interactions and replace them with more adaptive strategies.

Models of health and illness

It is part of human nature for symptomatic individuals, and those who care about them, to develop a model of their illness. This helps them to understand and grapple with the problem (Leventhal et al., 1984, 1992). These models are shaped by many factors, such as an individual's psychological characteristics, the features of the illness and external factors, such as the information available to them. In most models, there are usually five domains: identity, cause, timeline, illness consequences and controllability. These resemble the clinical domains, diagnosis, aetiology, clinical features, treatment and prognosis.

The *identity* component consists of ideas about the label and nature (symptoms) of the condition; the *causal* component refers to ideas about the likely causes; the *timeline* is concerned with perceptions of the duration of the condition (acute, short lasting, chronic, cyclical or episodic); the *consequences* reflect the perception of illness severity and likely impact on functioning, and the *controllability* component indicates the extent to which the person believes the condition to be amenable to cure or control. Leventhal's theory about models of illness and health predicts that the carers' model shapes their cognitive and emotional response and their ability to cope.

Attitudes about the illness not only affect how people behave and cope, but also can influence the outcome. The *consequences* component, for example, reflects an individual's beliefs about the severity of an illness. These impact on functioning and relate to the levels of distress, disability and the number of times they visit the doctor (Weinman et al., 1996). The *timeline* and *perceived control over symptoms* is associated with medication compliance (Meyer et al., 1985). The adjustment to the illness becomes more complex once the illness runs a chronic course and if it draws in family members. We discussed some of the effects on carers in Chapter 5. In schizophrenia, carers' cognitive appraisals about their loved one's symptoms, for instance, colour their interaction with the index patient (Barrowclough & Parle, 1997). In part, this is mediated by expressed emotion (e.g. Brewin et al., 1991; Barrowclough et al., 1994; Lopez et al., 1999). Carers' beliefs about the illness impact on the course of the illness (Barrowclough et al., 1994). Moreover, the well-being of carers is linked to their beliefs about the patient's symptoms (Barrowclough et al., 1996).

Living with anorexia nervosa over time leads to a reorganisation of family life. Routines start to revolve around the illness (Eisler & Asen, 2003) and families accommodate to the unusual behaviours. Although different families respond in different ways, for some these secondary effects can have a paralysing effect and serve to maintain the illness (Chapter 2).

First impressions: the meaning of an eating disorder for carers

Eating disorder symptoms are unusual in that many of them are overt. This is especially true for anorexia nervosa, which means that carers may have developed their own model of the illness with their own opinions as to the importance of change and whether recovery is feasible before seeing a clinician. This can cause a clash and conflict, especially if the primary care doctor minimises the problem. It is preferable if health professionals can expose and integrate the carer's models of the illness into treatment (Treasure et al., 2002, 2005).

The meaning of the symptoms to the family may be idiosyncratic with resonances within the history of the family. A mother, for example, may have had a secret period of anorexia nervosa herself when she was young (see Chapter 14). This can cause an intense emotional reaction to aspects of treatment. Once such an emotional response is clarified and acknowledged, it can clear the stage for the next task, which is to seek out strategies that will help to manage the emotion. Not only is this process important for the carer's well-being but also it is a useful opportunity to model mature emotional processing for the person with an eating disorder.

This use of emotional intelligence is a two-stage process. The first stage is to be able to name and recognise the emotional state. The second is to find strategies to buffer that state. Thus, if carers are terrified about the medical consequences of their loved one's illness, they may secure some safety by asking for some practical measures to be agreed upon to reduce their anxiety. Consequently, they may request that the person with anorexia nervosa goes to the practice nurse each week to get weighed and has a medical risk assessment carried out at regular intervals.

Developing a shared eating disorder model: the carer's perspective

Listening to and making sense of the relatives' model of anorexia nervosa is a useful starting point in any intervention with carers. Within the therapeutic environment there may be a minimum of three different perspectives on the illness, those of the sufferer, the carer and the professionals. It is helpful if these models can be made as compatible as possible. The aim for any intervention is for carers, patient and therapist to respect each other's perspective and to weave a common, evidence-based understanding. In the following section we examine the various domains within the illness perception model and consider the common misperceptions that can arise.

Symptoms

Sometimes parents interpret the symptoms of anorexia nervosa (e.g. food restriction, underweight, physical and emotional frailty) as markers of their failure to nurture their child. This can lead to shame and stigma. In bulimia nervosa, the mix of parental negative emotions differs. The symptoms of bingeing, vomiting and purging and associated impulsive behaviours (e.g. drinking, drug-taking, stealing) result in carer reactions of anger, disgust and shame.

The following quotations illustrate some common themes in areas that families found difficult:

> X has become an ungrateful, rude, manipulative and totally self-controlled individual who is subject to violent mood swings. She has always been a quiet, introverted individual who worries about everything but was very low . . . This change has been very difficult for us to come to terms with.

> It seems to me that anorexia is an incredibly selfish disease. Y apparently has no interest in or concern for anyone else. I know that's part of the illness but I

find it hard to bite my lip when I see her basically being rude. These days she rarely says thank you no matter what we do or how hard we try.

Before her admission the stress of meals, her abnormal sleep pattern — sometimes she would only sleep during daylight — and her fear of dying were obviously difficult to cope with.

The attendant comorbidity of eating disorders, such as emotional lability, compulsive behaviours and reversing behaviours, is difficult for the family to comprehend. A common reaction is to feel as if their daughter has been transformed into someone with an alien personality.

Causation

Most people try to make sense of the illness. It is common for people to want to find a clear and simple answer to the question of what has caused the eating disorder. It is less satisfying to think that there may be several interacting factors, some of which may always remain mysterious that resulted in the development of an individual's anorexia. It is rarely helpful to try to pinpoint causal factors. A more useful strategy is to search for factors that can contribute to maintenance. These should be the targets of scrutiny and problem solving.

Families often blame themselves for causing the anorexia nervosa although they may be uncertain what they may have done. They can live in fear of getting it wrong again. One parent may believe that the person with anorexia nervosa is deliberately choosing not to eat in order to punish them. This results in a variety of negative emotions such as guilt; loss and fear or they may be angry, ashamed and disgusted. They may blame the child and retaliate or withdraw. Some parents may believe that it is easy for the person with anorexia nervosa to choose to eat and cure herself and others may conceptualise the symptoms to be part of the index patient's personality and thus to be controllable.

- You are doing this because you are vain. [e.g. personality trait or value system]
- If you tried harder / ignored it / loved us [controllable] more you would stop.
- On some level you must really dislike us with what you are doing to us. [controllable and wilful]

These types of beliefs engender criticism and hostility and/or helpless and hopeless interactions and can lead to rhinoceros or kangaroo behaviours and jellyfish or ostrich emotional reactions (see Appendix 1). An aim of work with carers is to construct a balanced model of the illness in which there are realistic expectations for change.

Here are some of the common causal misperceptions parents have shared with us:

- She must have had a poor upbringing. Was I away from home and at work too often? Were there too many nannies or helpers? Has there been any abuse?
- I know I feel I am not a very good father. Have I failed to give her enough encouragement? Does she think – wrongly – that her younger sister is favoured?
- I became more aware how my behaviour might be impacting on her causing the condition, contributing, desperate that I didn't know how to change.
- Did I push Y too hard at school? Was it because I was always on diets, encouraging her to eat healthy foods? Was I in any way to blame?

Perhaps the most common misperception is the idea that the person with anorexia nervosa has wilfully chosen the problem. This conceptualisation includes the unexpressed idea that they could just as easily choose *not* to have it. It is also common for parents (and also the lay public and professionals) to assume that the behaviours of anorexia nervosa are goal driven, such as not wanting to grow up, wanting to die etc. Our understanding is that it is difficult for someone with anorexia nervosa to know *what* they want in relationship to the world or to other people. They are only certain in their relationship with food. These assumptions of wilful intent are wrong and fuel a variety of negative emotions such as anger, frustration, shame and sadness.

Education can help put these initial conceptualisations of the illness into context so that the family hold more realistic beliefs. The information in many books or websites may be flawed, however, and based on idiosyncratic clinical understandings, rather than the scientifically accumulated evidence. One carer, for example, told us how distraught she was when she read a variety of books on anorexia nervosa that appeared to blame the parent.

Health consequences

Carers are terrified about the dangers to physical health and safety. Aside from these consequences for the sufferer, the family are affected. Their child will continue to be dependent upon them and they will experience high levels of stress and strain. Carers may believe that their own physical or psychological health is put at risk and become angry or fearful. Here are some examples of catastrophic thinking about negative consequences that we have heard:

- Her tendency to escape from hospital or wander off from home could result in her becoming a long-term missing person and/or a sufferer from hypothermia.
- I approached the house at the end of the day, my heart pounding, very agitated, wondering what I would find when I opened the front door.

These quotations illustrate how parents have a highly active sense of threat and worry about the anorexia nervosa. There is no doubt that it is terrifying to live with someone with anorexia nervosa, because the mortality rates are high. This fear may be exaggerated, however, as parents often share the trait of anxiety or nervousness with their daughters. Everyone in the family may be a born worrier. This depletes the family's resilience and parents develop clinical levels of depression and anxiety. The negative emotions (the jellyfish response) or emotional avoidance (the ostrich response) feed into anorexia nervosa. When clinical levels of depression and anxiety arise we encourage parents to get support from carers groups, counselling and for themselves from their general practitioner.

Loss

The losses that accumulate by the arrest of social and emotional development are also distressing. Examples of lost aspirations that many carers experience can be as follows:

- At these times I indulge myself in thinking of what he could be now if he was not anorexic. And at these times I grieve for the brother I think I have lost.
- Watching N change from a happy-go-lucky little girl to a very disturbed young woman has been very distressing. There are so many occasions when I've thought 'if only', but try not to dwell on them too much as I get extremely upset.

The theme of loss of the person they used to know is something that has to be accepted and worked through. The therapist needs to help the family process this loss and to counterbalance it by hope and optimism with a new form of attachment. We work to help carers rekindle their relationship with the person with anorexia nervosa and increase their social network. Cherished imagined goals from the past are replaced with realistic goals set within a readjusted time frame. We use techniques such as writing to each other about the meaning of the relationship (see Chapter 10) to re-evoke the love they shared. We raise their efficacy and esteem by reflecting on positive aspects of their function.

Effect on the family and siblings

Anorexia nervosa becomes the focus of the family. All other family relation-ships and activities are put on hold. In part, this is a result of a caregiving and over-protective kangaroo response. This usually involves the mother as it fits with the traditional role of mothers. This means that most of the mother's time and attention is taken up by trying to support or worrying about the person with anorexia nervosa.

Also, many practical aspects of family living may be changed to fit in with the anorexia nervosa rules and rituals. Parents may agree not to use their kitchen at certain times of the day. The family may drive for miles to get certain items of family shopping. The family may stop inviting friends to come in because they interrupt anorexic routines.

The family need to review how much their lifestyle revolves around the anorexia nervosa and not be bullied or emotionally blackmailed into supporting the obsessional rituals and routines or drawn into reassurance seeking that bolsters anorexic beliefs. There is less time and attention for other family members. Time management techniques to plan non-anorexia nervosa periods, with a focus on other relationships, within the family are helpful.

Siblings have a different set of difficulties. They can feel neglected by their parents, causing them to feel angry. One reaction is to prematurely develop and become independent or leave home early because the home environment is tense. Others may have a form of survivor guilt. They may feel guilty and embarrassed that they are successful in attaining the normal developmental milestones, degrees, marriage etc. Anorexia nervosa casts a shadow over their celebrations. Such quotations are common:

- I feel guilty for doing normal young adult activities and long for her to enjoy life as she once did.
- I feel very protective of Y, almost like a big sister, and will not allow anyone to put her down – especially not herself.

Others may welcome the chance to take a role in caring and feel pride in their nurturing activities. We illustrated how peer relationship with the sibling can be distorted in Chapter 6. Often siblings are excluded from treatment and they may be deprived about information of the illness. This can lead to them distancing themselves from the problem.

In work with the family it is helpful to unpick or clarify some of these maladaptive emotional reactions and if possible bring siblings closer. The sibling relationship can be invaluable in helping overcome some of the social isolation and the avoidance, which is a key symptom in anorexia nervosa. Consequently, a major role that a sibling can offer is to support and mentor a return to peer-related activities. Sometimes it can be helpful if the therapist offers time for work with siblings to help improve the sibling relationship and to ensure that this relationship is used to good effect to promote behaviour change.

The response of other people

We go to the shops and people turn round. Sadly, they do not turn round for any other reason than the desire to have another look. I get hurt, angry and

> embarrassed. S doesn't. She thinks she is getting well when people cease to turn round. She doesn't want to be well. When people don't know S or myself, like new work colleagues, I want to explain that she looks like she does because she has a problem. I don't know why I feel the necessity to have to explain.

Carers are often very sensitive to the response of other people. One common reaction is avoidance, i.e. to not participate in social events and to isolate the family from friends and relatives. This can often be a secondary response to feelings of shame and guilt, which arise because people either feel responsible for their daughter's ill health or they assume that others will implicate them in the cause. Sensitivity to this sort of perceived or real injustice and stigmatisation often leads to anger. The Royal College of Psychiatrists' stigma campaign (Cowan & Hart, 1998) reported on a survey of the general public which revealed that stigmatising attitudes were based on four beliefs about those with mental health problems, namely:

- Sufferers are thought to be dangerous to others.
- The disorders are thought to be self-inflicted.
- The outcome is thought to be poor.
- It is difficult to communicate with sufferers.

Gowers and Shore (1999) reviewed the part played by these factors in stigmatising those with eating disorders. They argued for improved training of health service staff and greater public education. One of the major advantages of working with more than one family is that it helps to reduce shame and can be an antidote to feeling stigmatised. Carers themselves can be the best advocates to fight stigma by being open about their daughter's difficulties.

Timescale

- It never occurred to me that S would not get better.

Often in the early stages of anorexia nervosa, the severity and prognosis of the illness are underestimated. Parents and professionals can underplay the problem and dismiss it as a passing phase. It is surprising, frustrating and disappointing when these expectations are proved to be incorrect. This may lead to frustration and anger when the illness is seen to persist into a chronic form. It may mean that people do not take appropriate precautionary steps to maximise changes of recovery or avoid relapse.

Controllability

- I think Mum can do something to make her illness go away and be able to do nothing. I know that Y is beyond my help. I was powerless to do anything about it.

These helpless cognitions illustrate the paralysing sense of ineffectiveness that carers develop. Research has shown that one of the most intensely stressful aspects of life is when you have to cope with an uncontrollable threat. This is the relentless pressure which carers of people with eating disorders have to face every day. (A similar frustration can cause burn-out among staff on inpatient units.) The aim of the intervention is to remove that feeling of helplessness and to give the parents a sense of self-efficacy. On the face of it, the symptoms of an eating disorder seem so simple to be overcome and it is difficult for carers to understand how it cannot be simply cured or treated. 'Why don't they just eat?' is a common lament and one that leads to exasperation and frustration.

The brain as part of the causal process

Research into biological processes within the environmental context indicates that many of the mechanisms that underlie eating disorders may be not under conscious control. The high levels of heritability found in genetically informative studies is evidence that genetic variation contributes to the illness (Bulik et al., 2000). The intermediate mechanisms, which lie between genes and behaviour, are unknown at the present time. One possibility is that part of the risk may be caused by a particular pattern of information processing characterised by sensitivity to appraisals of threat, or a difficulty in extinguishing a learnt reaction once it is formed and also a tendency to show rigidity and inflexibility in the way that perceptual information and ideas are processed (Tchanturia et al., 2001, 2004).

The activation of the brain to food cues differs in people with eating disorders from healthy controls (Uher et al., 2002). Parts of the front of the brain that are involved in decision-making and emotional regulation become activated, rather than the areas normally activated by food. Even after recovery, these same brain areas remain abnormally activated by food. It is possible that this abnormal pattern of activation contributes to the maintenance of the disorder. At the present time it is uncertain whether the pattern of activation seen in people who have recovered from anorexia nervosa represent changes that have occurred during the process of therapy, or if they were markers that predict a better outcome and were there at the onset of the illness. Brain scanning has revealed tangible proof of how the reaction to food and weight cues is entangled with other brain processes such as emotional regulation and the synthesis of drives, motivation and planning of behaviours.

A different type of scanning technology suggests that the neurochemical matrix in those with anorexia nervosa differs from that of healthy controls. The level of serotonin receptors in the parts of the brain activated by food cues is unusual in people with anorexia nervosa. This neurochemical difference remains after recovery (Frank et al., 2002). In conclusion, this neuroscience evidence suggests that anorexia nervosa cannot merely be explained by wilful stubbornness on the part of the sufferer. A specific biological template is clearly associated with the illness.

The results from risk modelling studies suggest that most of the risk for developing an eating disorder comes from genetic factors. There is very little that comes from general environmental factors that are shared within the family. Nevertheless, because it is human nature to try to explain or understand what is happening, parents tend to blame themselves. It is helpful to have information about research into the aetiology of eating behaviour available for family members. We encourage carers to join our volunteer database so that they can get recent information about research findings. We also encourage carers to go to our website www.eatingresearch.com, which also contains information abut research in progress.

Skills to improve the coping resources of the family

Emotional coping

The assessment interview is the first opportunity to exchange information and examine for these parental misperceptions. A more detailed exploration is undertaken in the day treatment by asking family members to write about their experiences of living with anorexia nervosa (see Chapters 10 and 12). If maladaptive appraisals about the illness are elicited, the therapist offers information or constructs behavioural experiments to help parents develop more adaptive beliefs. This lessens emotional responses. Anger is defused, for example, if difficult behaviours are seen as part of the illness and not as their daughter being awkward, naughty or trying to punish them. Externalisation is a useful technique, framing the difficulties they experience, as a function of the anorexia nervosa, rather than deliberate wilfulness on their daughter's part. This can extend to talking about the illness as an objective entity (e.g. anorexic minx, bulimic boa constrictor) as a device to develop a shared model with less blame.

The meaning of the symptom to the family may be idiosyncratic. Sharing the emotional response and unpicking some of the cognitions that underpin it produces a new perspective. The aim is for family members to develop a new, flexible perspective over their mental world, and to be no longer overwhelmed by intense emotions fuelled by maladaptive cognitions.

The therapist encourages family members to be reflective about their emotional well-being and to consider their needs. It may be necessary, for example, to put safety measures in place if they are anxious, to provide opportunities for comfort and joy if they are sad and depressed, and to identify new strategies or goals if they are angry or frustrated. If they are consumed by jealousy and envy of others who may appear to be problem free, they may need to be brave enough to enter into a conversation and have the opportunity to share in the good fortune.

Increasing validation

We teach carers to validate their daughter's experience by construing the problem as an illness of the emotions (feelings rather than food). It follows from this that logical arguments about weight and shape issues (rhinoceros behaviour) are rarely helpful. Other general behaviours that carers need to avoid are:

- dismissing or criticising the person with an eating disorder
- failing to take the concerns of other family members seriously
- insisting on the correctness of the parents' view of the problem which the daughter does not accept
- not listening and attending to other people's points of view
- not providing support
- not recognising areas of competence.

Practical coping

Practical coping responses can also be counterproductive. Common beliefs and assumptions about how to react when faced with an acute illness in the family are less adaptive when the illness runs a protracted course. Social rules change when someone is ill and excused from their usual responsibilities, becoming regarded by others as indulged and spoilt. Nonetheless, this type of adaptation is less appropriate with an illness that can last many years such as an eating disorder. It can be all too easy for carers to fall into the trap of pandering to the obsessive rituals and compulsive routines of their daughter's illness. This serves only to maintain the rigid strait-jacket of the illness. The whole family may be subjugated by the power and inflexibility of the eating disorder symptoms and live their life as if walking on eggshells. Carers need to be able to agree on a consistent approach to these symptoms, which is fair for the rest of the family. They may have to live with these over time as change may be slow and difficult.

Positive communication

Parents need to provide a safe home for all family members, and rules are necessary to achieve that aim. In all homes this can become particularly problematic when children reach adolescence and want to exert their own identity. Rules change and adapt with the child's striving for autonomy. This is a difficult task as many of the rules that parents grew up with no longer apply. The world in general is more liberated. There is the perception that things have become more dangerous, there is more violence on the streets and drugs are more easily accessible. In addition, there are more tools that can help provide safety, for example mobile phones and access to information. More choice leads to complexity. More families are breaking up as parents divorce. It is more common for both parents to work. Although this freedom has its good aspects, the not so good aspects are that it is difficult to rely on the rules and limits that have been laid down over time. Each family circumstance is different and so generating fair home rules, which can be applied consistently, is problematic.

Anorexia nervosa develops within the context of this phase of maturation but adds complexity as it produces a form of regression. The person with anorexia nervosa becomes more dependent as exemplified by the inability to care for her nutritional needs. The safety behaviours (over-exercise, vomiting, compulsions) may produce further risk. As a result, parents have to readjust and set limits.

This general difficulty in coping with the changing needs and demands of adolescent children is made much worse when anorexia nervosa enters. It can be hard to find a balance between these two opposing tendencies (the granting of autonomy and the need for parenting). The decisions about what and how to prioritise risks and unwanted behaviours are not easy and a joint approach, if possible, is essential. The ability to communicate effectively is needed to navigate this phase. A degree of negotiation and fluidity is helpful but with a clear bottom line. The rules cannot be set in stone but should be experimental and flexible, adapting to the changing needs of someone with anorexia nervosa.

Rule setting using positive communication

The rules of positive communication themselves should be honoured in order to negotiate this phase. The elements of this are for people to:

- be brief
- be positive
- be specific and clear
- label their feelings
- offer an understanding statement by accepting the different perspective of someone with anorexia nervosa
- accept partial responsibility (if appropriate)
- offer to help.

In essence, this style of communication uses many of the skills of assertiveness training. It helps parents to find the balance between being a doormat and being a bully or, using our animal metaphors, a kangaroo or a rhinoceros. These behaviours are taught to parents didactically and practically, shaping and modelling these interactions. An example of remodelling unhelpful interactions is given below.

NOT:

> You are always taking our food [*criticism*]. It makes me so angry that I can never rely on anything to be in the fridge [*hostility*].

BUT:

> I get upset that I cannot make plans for meals for the household [*label feelings*]. I know that the cravings get overwhelming [*understanding statement*]. Are there any ways that I can organise things so that all my plans are not scuppered? [*offer to help*]

NOT:

> Whenever I can get in the bathroom it stinks [*hostility*]. I am disgusted with you [*criticism*].

BUT:

> I find it difficult to come to terms with your purging behaviour [*label feelings*]. Is there any way that I can help you make it less obvious to the rest of the family? [*offer to help*]

Completing a functional analysis with the family

The vicious circles of unhelpful behaviours that carers themselves fall into (described in Chapter 6) can be a useful starting point to illustrate how to think about the triggers and consequences of behaviours. The concept of a functional analysis with an ABC (antecedents, behaviours and consequences) structure is then introduced. It is possible to move from a personally relevant analysis and the variety of triggers and consequences onto the anorexic behaviours (restricting, slow, picky, selective, rule driven and ritualised eating, binge eating) or the safety behaviours (vomiting, over-exercise, laxatives, diuretics, body weight, shape checking, self-harm).

These are difficult constructs to teach. In the worksheets in Appendix 1, we give some illustrations of these processes. The overall aim is try to reinforce non-anorexia nervosa behaviours and extinguish (withdrawing attention from) anorexia nervosa behaviours. We warn the parents that they have to be patient since it may take five exposures to new contingents to change any behaviour. Our research into anorexia nervosa, however, suggests that any 'un'-learning may take longer. There may be a rebound with more excessive behaviour before it gets better.

Family interactions can inadvertently reinforce or reward or precipitate these behaviours but these can give useful opportunities to shape new reactions.

The choice of which behaviour to start with can be difficult. One obvious strategy is to focus on the behaviour that seems the most important to change. The most important behaviour, however, may also be the most difficult. Hence, as a compromise it might be worth trying to find a different area where it would be easier to produce change. Success early on can generate a sense of self-efficacy and increased confidence that this type of approach works. Trying to intervene in the excessive rule-driven eating of anorexia nervosa can be very difficult. It might be easier to think about a simpler behaviour to start on, such as 'reducing laxative or diuretic misuse or multiple weighing'. It will also be important to help parents think about what they see as monolithic difficult behaviours that they simply want to stop into more manageable components. The general approach is similar.

Using Figure 8.1 to structure the analysis can be helpful. The first step is to consider those external triggers that we refer to as 'the antecedents', i.e. the context in which the unwanted eating or safety behaviour occurs. We break it into steps:

- Column 1 is when we compare situations where (a) there is no likelihood that the problematic behaviour would occur, with (b) situations where it would inevitably be evoked. A series of 'who, what, why and how' questions can help define the context. The first question can be 'who' is your loved one with, or who is not there when the unwanted eating or safety behaviour occurs? 'Where' are they when the behaviour happens, are they at home, outside of the house, at school, at work etc? 'When' does it occur? 'What' time of day?
- Column 1b asks the carer to use empathy to speculate about internal

Antecedents	Behaviour	Consequence
External When, what with who, how		Positive
Internal Thoughts, feelings, sensation, memory		Negative

Figure 8.1 ABC analysis.

triggers. 'What' thoughts might be going through the person's head? 'What' are they feeling?

- Column 2 describes the behaviour. Here specify the exact behaviour, what happens, how intense is it, how long does it go on for etc.
- Column 3a looks at the positive consequences. Again, we ask the family member to do some mind reading and use their skills of empathy to imagine what happens when their loved one carries out the behaviour.
- Column 3b details the negative consequences. Some of these are usually self-evident and so there is no need to belabour the point.

Reducing unwanted behaviours

Punishing eating disorder behaviours usually does not work. If the punishment is too mild, it may reinforce the behaviour; if it is too severe, it can cause rebellion and reactance. Nagging, threatening, pleading, crying, lecturing or throwing food down the toilet also usually do not work.

Family members can sometimes inadvertently collude with the eating disorder by covering up the consequences such as making excuses to other family members, cleaning the bathroom etc. This particularly occurs if there are 'kangaroo' behaviours. Consequently, the therapist encourages the family to question their own assumptions and behaviours and be open and curious about what would happen without their intercession.

- What would happen if you did not step in to care and cover up for your daughter's eating disorder behaviours?
- What would be the repercussions and consequences of not doing it?

It may take several conversations before individual family members can get to the stage when they want to change their pattern of interaction. (The skills of motivational enhancement are useful to work on these issues.) Before any plans for implementation are set in place, it is important that the implications and possible barriers to change are discussed with all family members. Will everyone be able to follow through and be consistent with this approach? It may be helpful to practise, through role-play, how they will explain why and how the house rules are going to change. It is useful to frame any change as an experiment. Ask the parents to make notes and observations throughout the process.

Rather than forcing the family to change, suggest that they might want to try doing things a different way over a period of time (remember that a minimum of ten consistent repetitions with the new contingencies are usually required). Warn the parents that if they are inconsistent, it will take much longer and may even cause the behaviours to persist more, as this would produce a pattern of intermittent reinforcement. It is also important to emphasise that the behaviours are likely to get worse before they get better.

It will take a great deal of courage, trust and commitment to instigate any new approach.

Reinforcing non-anorexia nervosa behaviours

In parallel with a functional analysis of problematic behaviour is a reciprocal procedure with non-eating disorder behaviours, that is pleasurable and enjoyable activities in the family or fun with the offspring's peer group. These might include having a normal conversation, going out to the cinema, playing a game, watching a television programme, going out with friends, visiting a museum. These behaviours are analysed in exactly the same way as the eating disorder behaviours. Once again, we define the antecedents, that is the external triggers that foster these behaviours. Who is it that helps promote these behaviours? Where can they take place and when? The empathy and mind reading column defines the thoughts and feelings that precede these non-anorexic and normal family or peer-related activities. What, if any, are the negative consequences that may follow from connecting with the non-eating disordered world and what are the positive consequences of strengthening these activities in other domains of life.

Can the family generate a portfolio of alternative behaviours and positive activities, which can substitute for the anorexia nervosa behaviours and give a similar type of reward? If possible, include a wide variety of activities ranging from those that are short and simple, such as watching a television pro-gramme together for ten minutes, playing a board game, brushing her hair, giving her a foot massage, going for a short walk, having a conversation relating to their daughter's favourite topic, to the more complex, such as trips out, going to a film. Family members may want to consider obtaining skills by joining a class in some of the physical, alternative therapies such as yoga, aromatherapy or reflexology. These can be used to give positive reinforcement for non-eating disorder behaviours and such rewards could be withdrawn when eating disorder behaviours occur. Also these are activities that could be done together.

Conclusion

This chapter concludes Part II and has considered how carers may have mistaken beliefs about the illness and how these can lead to unhelpful and/or extreme emotional responses. We have also introduced the concept of a func-tional analysis as the first step in modifying behaviours along with other skills aimed at improving the coping resources of the family.

In Part III we will look at the different models of interventions and their practical elements.

References

Barrowclough, C. & Parle, M. (1997). Appraisal, psychological adjustment and expressed emotion in relatives of patients suffering from schizophrenia. *British Journal of Psychiatry*, 171: 26–30.

Barrowclough, C., Tarrier, N. & Johnston, M. (1994). Attributions, expressed emotion and patient relapse: An attributional model of relatives' response to schizophrenic illness. *Behaviour Therapy* 25: 67–88.

Barrowclough, C., Tarrier, N. & Johnston, M. (1996). Distress, expressed emotion, and attributions in relatives of schizophrenia patients. *Schizophrenia Bulletin* 22: 691–702.

Brewin, C. R., MacCarthy, B., Duda, K. & Vaughn, C. E. (1991). Attribution and expressed emotion in the relatives of patients with schizophrenia. *Journal of Abnormal Psychology* 100: 546–554.

Bulik, C. M., Sullivan, P. F., Wade, T. D. & Kendler, K. S. (2000). Twin studies of eating disorders: A review. *International Journal of Eating Disorders* 27: 1–20.

Cowan, L. & Hart, D. (1998). Changing minds: Every family in the land. A new challenge for the future (editorial). *Psychiatric Bulletin* 22: 593–594.

Eisler, I., Le Grange, D. & Asen, E. (2003). Family interventions. In J. Treasure, U. Schmidt & E. Van Furth (eds) *Handbook of Eating Disorders*, 2nd edn. Chichester: Wiley.

Frank, G. K., Kaye, W. H., Meltzer, C. C., Price, J. C., Greer, P., McConaha, C. et al. (2002). Reduced 5-HT2A receptor binding after recovery from anorexia nervosa. *Biological Psychiatry* 52: 896–906.

Gowers, S. G. & Shore, A. (1999). The stigma of eating disorders. *International Journal of Clinical Practice* 53: 386–388.

Leventhal, H., Nerentz, D. R. & Steel, D. J. (1984). Illness representations and coping with health threats. In A. Baum (ed.) *Handbook of Psychology and Health, Volume 4*. Hillsdale, NJ: Erlbaum.

Leventhal, H., Leventhal, E. & Diefenbach, M. (1992). Illness cognition: Using common sense to understand treatment adherence and affect cognition interactions. *Cognitive Therapy and Research* 16(2): 143–163.

Lopez, S. R., Nelson, K. A., Snyder, K. S. & Mintz, J. (1999). Attributions and affective reactions of family members and course of schizophrenia. *Journal of Abnormal Psychology* 108: 307–314.

Meyer, D., Leventhal, H. & Gutmann, M. (1985). Common-sense models of illness: The example of hypertension. *Health Psychology* 4: 115–135.

Tchanturia, K., Serpell, L., Troop, N. & Treasure, J. (2001). Perceptual illusions in eating disorders: Rigid and fluctuating styles. *Journal of Behaviour Therapy and Experimental Psychiatry* 32: 107–115.

Tchanturia, K., Morris, R. G., Brecelj Anderluh, M., Collier, D. A., Nikolaou, V. & Treasure, J. (2004). Set shifting in anorexia nervosa: An examination before and after weight gain, in full recovery and relationship to childhood and adult OCPD traits. *Journal of Psychiatric Research* 38(5): 545–552.

Treasure, J., Gavan, K., Todd, G. & Schmidt, U. (2002). Changing the environment in eating disorders: Working with carers/families to improve motivation and facilitate change. *European Eating Disorders Review* 11(1): 25–37.

Treasure, J., Whitaker, W., Whitney, J. & Schmidt, U. (2005). Working with families of adults with anorexia nervosa. *Journal of Family Therapy* 27: 158–170.

Uher, R., Murphy, T., Brammer, M., Dalgleish, T., Phillips, M., Ng, V. et al. (2002). Functional neural correlates of eating disorders. Personal communication.

Weinman, J., Petrie, K., Moss-Morris, R. & Horn, R. (1996). The illness perception questionnaire: A new method for assessing the cognitive representation of illness. *Psychology and Health* 11: 431–445.

Part III

Different forms of intervention

The book now takes a turn from a more theoretical perspective to a more practical stance. It begins with an assessment of the family in Chapter 9. The chapter begins by listing the process for initial planning of information sharing and joint working opportunities as well as citing several important reasons for developing a family-focused formulation. It then takes the reader through the all-important first meeting with the carer as well as providing illustrative case studies of those various models of familial attributions to the illness and treatment programme, that the carer may bring with them. The chapter offers ideas and suggestions as to how the therapist might work with these varied models.

Chapter 10 demonstrates how to use writing as a reflective tool in the therapeutic process. The chapter offers some theoretical background before presenting a list of themes that have emanated out of recent qualitative research. Themes are endorsed by ideas and suggestions as to how the therapist can work with these narratives, by using them as a vehicle for emotional processing, whereby emotions and misattributions are observed in an attempt to build stronger foundations on which to build warmer, empathic relationships.

In Chapter 11 the reader is guided through a series of skills-based training workshops. These workshops that are offered to carers are similar to those undertaken by health-care professionals in the management of eating disorders. The format and protocol of the six workshop sessions are described in the chapter, along with a brief discussion of the results of a small randomised control trial, designed to assess their impact and acceptability. Chapter 12 continues the theme of skills-based training workshops but specialises instead on families that require a more intensive intervention, that is those individuals who are preparing for the transition of their loved ones from inpatient to outpatient care and where there may be a greater risk of relapse. Although similar to the workshops described in Chapter 11, this intervention adopts a more individualised approach and is tailored to working with only two families. The chapter outlines the structure and timetable of an intensive three-day intervention.

Part III closes with a portrayal of two more recent skills-based learning interventions, designed to deliver training to an even wider audience. Chapter 13 describes two interventions that are aimed at addressing issues of high demand, scarce resources and geographical time constraints. Two forms of intervention are illustrated: a series of DVDs, manuals and telephone coaching, and an internet-based intervention with telephone or email support. The chapter takes the reader through the format and process of each intervention.

Chapter 9

Working with carers on an outpatient basis

The assessment of the family

Janet Treasure

Introduction

The NICE guidelines suggested that the needs of the family and other carers should be considered in addition to those of the individual with anorexia nervosa. The needs of the families of people with binge eating forms of disorders were not considered. The focus of this chapter, therefore, is mainly on the carers of individuals with anorexia nervosa, although we do highlight some of the issues that are pertinent to the wider spectrum of people with eating disorders. The service at the Maudsley gives all carers access to a variety of sources of information. The carers' section of our website www.eatingresearch.com is an up-to-date source of information. We have a book specifically written for carers (Treasure et al. 2007b) and we are actively researching the use of a web-based programme and DVDs which offer more skills-based information. We also give carers the opportunity to join carers' workshops (Chapter 11). Some carers are offered individual work (Chapter 12). This specific work for carers runs in parallel to other interventions.

In this chapter, we begin by outlining the processes involved in the individual treatment for anorexia nervosa and how this is complemented with carers' involvement. We then discuss the process of planning and providing opportunities for information sharing and collaborative caring. A family-focused formulation is discussed that, first of all, looks at the model of the family as a source for maintaining eating disorder symptoms, before moving on to practical strategies in addressing these issues. Case studies, for example, illustrate the manner in which the family can organise themselves around the eating disorder and offer tips and suggestions on how therapists can work with the family to disentangle established dynamics within the family unit.

Carer involvement in individual treatment for anorexia nervosa

An outline of the individual treatment used for adults with anorexia nervosa at the Maudsley is shown in Figure 9.1.

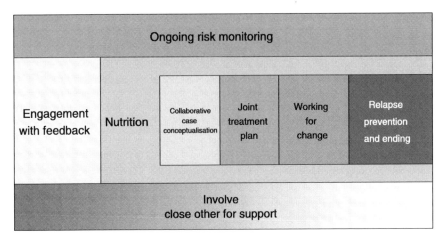

Figure 9.1 Maudsley anorexia nervosa treatment.

Figure 9.1 is based on our model of treatment, which is tailored to match the core maintaining processes in anorexia nervosa. We have summarised this model in several reviews (Schmidt & Treasure, 2006; Southgate et al., 2005; Treasure et al., 2005). The key elements of this model include:

1   Engagement and feedback: feedback from the nutritional, medical, psychosocial, family and neuropsychological assessment is given in a motivational manner over the first two engagement sessions.
2   Medical monitoring and a focus on nutrition are present during the whole course of treatment. The detail and time taken by this aspect of treatment varies with the level of risk and the response to treatment.
3   The collaborative case conceptualisation includes a review both of pre-disposing and perpetuating factors (Schmidt & Treasure, 2006).
4   Treatment involves several goals:

  • moving from subservience to eating disorder rules (focusing on details of food, weight and shape) towards more broadly defined nutritional goals (i.e. the ability to eat sufficiently, socially, with adequate variety and a regular form)
  • moderating the impact of this extremely inflexible and overly analytical detail-focused way of viewing the world (which contributes to an obsessive compulsive personality) and how it impacts on other domains of life
  • learning how to express and manage difficult emotions without avoidance
  • developing a more balanced relationship with the world, other people and the self (e.g. being 'good enough' rather than perfect,

being open to new experiences and opportunities, and tolerating the uncertainty that is associated with this, allowing yourself to make mistakes, not neglecting your own needs at the expense of others).

5 The work with carers has three broad aims within this context. First, an examination of possible predisposing factors is considered. The context in which learning about relationships with the world, other people and the self, emerged is considered. The second aim is to examine possible perpetuating factors such as high expressed emotion in interpersonal relationships and accommodation to the symptoms. The third aim is to develop a relationship that can work to moderate eating disorder behaviours.

Planning and providing opportunities for information sharing and joint working

In our initial letter to the referred individual, we invite the person to offer his or her carer(s) the opportunity to attend the first assessment. Carers of adults with anorexia nervosa (usually parents) often take up this opportunity, whereas even the use of the term 'carer' may not be relevant for adults with bulimia nervosa, who tend to keep their symptoms hidden. A joint approach to treatment (or, indeed, separate help for carers) very much depends on the results of the assessment as well as the inclination of the sufferer and her family. In adult patients, this should be handled flexibly and with an individualised tailored approach, as illustrated by some of the case examples given later in this chapter.

If the individual is in close contact with her family or living at home, a more detailed assessment of family maintaining factors is of value (Treasure et al., 2008). Also, if the acute risk is high or the response to individual treatment has been poor, then including the family as an adjunct to individual therapy can be an effective and necessary step before considering more intensive interventions.

In adults, the first meeting with the parents to discuss collaborative care may come much later during the process of treatment. In some cases, where patients have mixed feelings about involving a close other and are able to make progress with individual treatment alone, there may be no need for such an intervention. If therapy is stuck or failing (i.e. weight loss continues), then meeting with others is an important supplement to treatment, as it opens the possibility to consider this facet of maintenance. In this context, patient and therapist would jointly set the agenda. In all work with the family, the barriers of confidentiality (Chapter 4) have to be balanced with the need for information sharing and work on interpersonal maintaining factors.

Who is the relevant carer?

If there are major concerns about medical risk, it is wise to involve the responsible next of kin as soon as possible, in case decisions about compulsory treatment need to be made. Outside of this medical crisis framework, it is possible to be much more flexible.

Sometimes in older patients it may not be obvious who should be regarded as the primary caregiver or supporter. In our workbook that accompanies individual treatment, we have a questionnaire which we ask people to complete, 'Who should I get to help?' It is usually possible to judge from the results of the completed questionnaire who is the person best suited to this role. This exercise may also serve those interpersonal interactions that are less than ideal. Question 2 on the worksheet, for example, asks about those interactions that have high levels of expressed emotion, such as criticism and hostility. As discussed earlier (Chapters 2 and 5) this type of emotional reaction fuels the continuation of the problem. Consequently, the decision needs to be made whether it makes sense to work with this person and spend time reducing the negative emotional experience or whether the plan should be that contact with this person be limited. Either of these options could be satisfactory. It is possible to change whoever is involved in individual treatment, depending on the phase of treatment. Pragmatic reasons may determine who is involved. Friends may be more accessible, whereas the distance from family members will make joint work difficult. Nevertheless, whatever the distance, we recommend meeting the family some time during the course of therapy. If there is resistance and low risk then the need to involve the carer can be delayed. Later on in treatment, when there is more trust and confidence, it may then be possible to set up a meeting. Here the focus will be on emotional and interpersonal coaching and siblings or peers may be of particular help. An effort should also be made to include fathers (see Chapter 15).

Resistance to the involvement of carers

In Chapter 4 we discuss some of the ethical and legal aspects of working with carers. If your patient is resistant to the idea of involving the family, it is helpful to spend time understanding the reasons for this. It is usually possible to work around the roadblocks and come to some form of compromise. You need to explain what, why and how you want to involve the family, as well as whether a joint treatment approach or one that runs parallel to an individual approach, is appropriate. Table 9.1 outlines some of the reasons why involving the family is important.

Table 9.1 Reasons for inducting carers and parents into the therapeutic setting

Reasons for the carer

1 The UK government recognises that carers have rights. Hence, anyone who cares for someone with a severe illness, such as anorexia nervosa, is entitled to have information about the illness and an assessment to determine if they have unmet needs.

2 Carers often have high levels of anxiety and depression, in part caused by misunderstanding about the condition. If they are given the correct information, they will be more effective.

3 Carers want to help but can inadvertently fall into unhelpful patterns of responding. If they have some guidance about what strategies work, the atmosphere at home improves for everyone.

Reasons for the person with the eating disorder

1 Some of the evidence-based guidelines recommend that families are involved in treatment (in particular for people aged less than 20).

2 The atmosphere at home will be improved.

3 Carers will be less stressed.

The goals of including the family in the assessment process

The goals of the family assessment are, first, to offer carers the opportunity to obtain information. Second, the family are a resource to complete the case conceptualisation with the different perspective they have to offer about the lifetime context in which the illness emerged. This includes an assessment of how interpersonal features might play a role in maintaining the disorder by reinforcing the illness behaviours. The preliminary discussion covers the concept of expressed emotion using the animal metaphors (see Appendix 1) and then an assessment of how the family have organised themselves around the eating disorder. This is particularly relevant to those cases in which the individual still lives at home or is in receipt of continuing parenting because of the overt signs of the illness. The aim of this joint assessment is to ensure that the family are not pulling in a different direction to the therapeutic team. Finally, carers may be offered specific extra help with practical skills to adapt their own behaviours and manage the eating disorder symptoms.

In addition to the standard description of the illness, the following is a list of information-sharing aims and skills that are useful for carers. The latter can also be demonstrated by the therapist within the session.

Information

- Strengthen the family's belief in the importance of their contribution in facilitating change. Families can play a large part in giving help and support and can help to ensure that any maintaining factor is kept to the minimum.

- Develop a shared evidence-based model, which gives the family the opportunity to express their concerns about the causes and effects of the anorexia nervosa and moderate their level of guilt etc. We do not know what causes anorexia nervosa and it is wrong to pinpoint one factor as the cause.
- Understand that if they are left untreated, eating disorders can lead to a chronic and destructive illness. The individual with the eating disorder may not be able to help herself as she is trapped and confused by the illness.
- Understand the basic elements of health behaviour change, that is the stage and dimensional-based models of stage of change.
- Discuss the basic principles of behaviour change, that is reinforcement to foster positive behaviours and a functional analysis to identify the triggers to problematic behaviours.

Skills

- Use modelling, affirmation, coaching and a solution-focused approach.
- Model the use of externalising to reduce the level of criticism.
- Develop a functional analysis of family interactions.
- Teach good communication skills (the ability to listen and to elicit, express and process emotions).
- Promote respect, cohesiveness and satisfaction within the family relationship.
- Learn the skills of facilitating problem solving with their offspring.
- Maximise parenting skills (warmth with limits and boundaries, i.e. authoritative parenting).
- Produce a shift in the environmental context to attenuate factors, which maintain the problem such as confrontation, collusion, high expressed emotion, criticism, hostility, or a dieting culture.

Developing a family-focused formulation

The family often become organised around the eating disorder. We have used an antecedents-meaning-consequences (AMC) framework in order to structure this part of the assessment. The components of this include: **A** for antecedents within the family that may both act as predisposing and maintaining factors, **M** for meaning or how the eating disorder can have particular connotations for some families, and **C** for consequences, in other words, accommodating, allowing and inadvertently supporting eating disorder behaviours (see Figure 9.2). These will now be considered in greater detail.

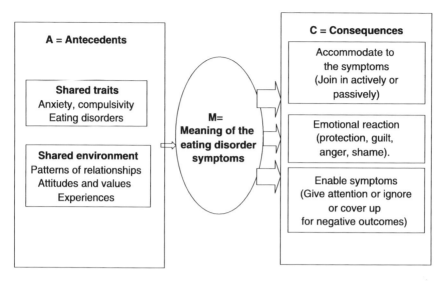

Figure 9.2 A model of the family as a source of maintenance of ED symptoms.

Antecedents: shared vulnerabilities (the familial pattern of anxiety, compulsivity and eating disorders)

In the original version of the Maudsley model of anorexia nervosa, we suggested that anxiety, avoidance and compulsivity are both predisposing and perpetuating factors for eating disorders (Schmidt & Treasure J, 2006). We have been able to establish empirical evidence for this model and found that some of the concepts, such as compulsivity which is linked to weak central coherence, are transdiagnostic and are also found in the binge forms of eating disorder (Treasure et al., 2007a; Lopez et al., 2008a, 2008c). We have expanded this model to consider the familial element of eating disorders (this is further explored in Chapters 11 and 12). In the assessment it is helpful to explore for these shared elements within the family as they can explain some of the reactions to the illness. Some of these elements may be shared biological traits (anxiety, compulsivity and eating disorders), whereas others are learned attitudes and behaviours resulting from a shared environment.

Anxiety

The negative consequences of the illness will be more salient and threatening to those family members with high trait anxiety (Whitney et al., 2007). High levels of anxiety are associated with an over-protective response (Kyriacou et al., 2008). Both parent and child can find it hard to tolerate uncertainty, a key component of anxiety (Dugas et al., 1998; Dugas & Ladouceur, 2000) and want simple rules and solutions and so find the process of therapy difficult.

The combination of a sensitive disposition and the difficult situation of living with someone with an eating disorder may overwhelm coping resources and clinical levels of anxiety and depression emerge. A cascade of unhelpful behaviours can then arise ranging from impulsive, ill-considered attempts to alleviate the negative mood (alcohol, risk taking, etc.), to avoidance of situations which require initiative and drive (social opportunities and healthy lifestyle behaviours, etc.) and withdrawal from the family itself (ostrich response). Irritability, avoidance and inaction resonate unhelpfully through all interpersonal interactions. Anxiety is highly contagious. When individuals with eating disorders sense anxiety in others, they become more anxious and their eating disorder symptoms escalate. Defeated, helpless, hopeless and guilt-ridden appraisals paralyse action and mutual cycles of criticism and hostility spin out of control.

Compulsivity, rigidity and a focus on detail

Compulsive traits are linked to a cognitive style characterised by inflexibility, and a bias to detail at the expense of the bigger picture (Lopez et al., 2008a, 2008b, 2008c). During childhood these traits may have contributed to a controlling somewhat authoritarian style of parenting (Enten & Golan, 2008). This style of parenting is most evident in the fathers of people with bulimia nervosa (Soenens et al., 2008). High expectations from parents and perfectionism in response to parental demands are commonly seen in eating disorders (Bardone-Cone et al., 2007; Sassaroli et al., 2008).

These traits may also have a role as perpetuating factors and jeopardise the ability to adapt to changing circumstances and synthesise new information and generate alternative behaviours. This can interfere with effective problem solving. Indeed, poor problem solving has been observed in eating disorder families (Blair et al., 1995). Carers with an overly analytical focus are easily seduced into discussions about the minutiae of eating symptoms and find it difficult not to fall into the trap of reassurance, as both partners find it difficult to tolerate uncertainty. This gives an opportunity for the individual with an eating disorder to rehearse and articulate her beliefs, which unfortunately merely serves to validate and reinforce them.

Eating symptoms

Family members often have clinical and subclinical eating problems themselves (see Chapters 11 and 12). These shared characteristics lead to guilt, competition, jealousy and envy. The family are already primed to accommodate to these symptoms.

Attachment history

Interpersonal issues form a key component of the formulation. The relationships between family members form a template for wider interpersonal issues. Anorexia nervosa persists because of an imbalance between the relationship to food and their relationship to friends, family and the world. Attachment issues such as the pattern of relationships over the lifetime are a critical part of the developmental formulation. The relationships in anorexia nervosa can be highly polarised. Thus, they can be overly dependent on close others and/ or may be over solicitous in their care for others. Often an individual can oscillate between these two poles. Others will avoid close relationships with people and become solitary and isolated figures, forming an intense relationship with their work. Atypical patterns of attachments can cascade through the generation. We found, for example, that the mothers of people with eating disorders have insecure attachments as do their daughter with anorexia nervosa (Ward et al., 2001).

We have reviewed the attachment patterns of people with eating disorders in some of our previous research (Ward et al., 2000a, 2000b, 2001). The relationship with the therapist will mirror some of these patterns. Additional information from carers can help to complete the conceptualisation (e.g. events around birth and early childhood which suggest high stress, early illness, the pattern of the relationship with food and others, temperamental traits).

Meaning and behaviour: the meaning of the eating disorder

In Chapter 8 we discuss how misattributions about the eating disorder can impact on meaning and the emotion reaction of family members. The behaviours associated with an eating disorder are particularly challenging as they strike the core of family life. Also, much of the content of the psychopathology merely echoes a general cultural concern about weight and shape. The form of the problem, however, sets it aside from normative discontent. Obsessive thinking patterns and highly ritualised and regulated behaviours, interspersed in some cases with impulsive, destructive episodes of dysregulated behaviour damage brain, body and society. The individual becomes more deeply swallowed up by the illness. Bystanders look on impotently, paralysed by the paradox of abusive, controlling behaviours from an individual that appears to be physically and/or mentally fragile.

Consequences: enabling and accommodating to the illness

The reactions and behaviours of family members can inadvertently reinforce eating disorder symptoms. We discuss how the emotional reactions of parents produce this effect in Chapter 6. Family members may give attention or credence to the eating disorder 'voice' or they may mop up negative consequences that arise from the eating disorder behaviour. The family may accept that eating disorders symptoms dominate the household: becoming subservient to eating disorder food rules (where, why, how, when and with whom, etc.), safety behaviours (exercise, vomiting, body checking, fasting or cutting back) and obsessive compulsive behaviours (reassurance seeking, counting, checking and control). The individual with an eating disorder controls those around him or her by explicit or implicit emotional blackmail. If eating disorder rules are disobeyed, for example, then patients may threaten not to eat at all, to harm themselves or to act destructively in other ways.

In addition individuals with an eating disorder may control, compete, compare or calibrate themselves with other family members (often siblings) in terms of what and how much to eat or exercise. Again, this behaviour is tolerated in an effort to keep the peace and because there is fear about resisting. Finally, family members may be drawn into enabling the eating disorder by covering up, or removing or buffering the natural negative consequences that would accrue from the behaviour, turning a blind eye.

We have developed an instrument that measures aspects of this behaviour. The Accommodation and Enabling Scale for Eating Disorders (AESED) (Sepúlveda et al. 2009) consists of five factors: Avoidance and Modifying Routine, Reassurance Seeking, Meal Context Ritual, Control of Family and Turning a Blind Eye.

Phase 1: Sharing information – exploring models of illness

The first meeting with carers

Younger people with an eating disorder may prefer to have the initial interview with their parents present. It is good practice to ask the individual for his or her preference. In joint sessions it is helpful if you try to engage with the child to elicit their point of view and show that they will be listened to and heard. In the NICE guidelines the recommendation is that some part of the assessment should be conducted with the child alone so that they can discuss things privately (National Collaborating Centre for Mental Health (NCCMH), 2004). Often this can be arranged around the physical examination.

In cases in which the level of risk is high at baseline, it is important to set out ground rules about how physical health and other aspects of risk will be measured and monitored. It is helpful to make a plan about what the parents should do if they have worries about risk and whom they should contact. Similarly the therapist should outline who he or she would contact in the event of increasing levels of risk.

Once plans about the management of risk have been covered, it is usually clearer as to what part of therapy or family life is to be set aside as private and confidential, unless there is a joint agreement that an open discussion would be of benefit.

The structure of treatment should also be outlined. How many sessions would be involved? Are there opportunities for carers to get help, e.g. to see a dietician? Often carers are on their guard, fearful about what will happen and whether they will be blamed. In this case, the therapist should be as welcoming as possible and ensure that the atmosphere of the meeting is warm and positive. The following are a selection of possible opening introductions:

- Thank you for coming today. It can be difficult to make time to all be together. Anorexia nervosa is such a complex illness with a variable and sometimes protracted time course and a lot of uncertainties. One clear fact is that it helps if we work together as a team and share as much about the illness as possible. There are questions that I might be able to answer for you about anorexia nervosa in general. However, there are things that you know about your family experience that may help me structure how we work.
- In our experience carers often benefit from learning some of the skills and tips that nurses and therapists have found to be helpful when working with people with eating disorders.
- It is a natural reaction to be apprehensive, as if you have been summoned to a meeting with the headmistress. We are not here to apportion blame but to think about sharing information and working together to optimise care. All families have different stories. It is common for all therapists and families to make some mistakes when trying to help people with an eating disorder. We use supervision to reflect on, recognise and acknowledge mistakes or what with the benefit of hindsight we should ideally have done differently. This meeting is an opportunity for you as a family to have supervision, to reflect on what has gone well or not so well.
- Helping with anorexia nervosa is always a process of trial and error. Errors are as useful as successes because we can learn as much from what goes wrong as from what doesn't go wrong. Remember the audit adage – every mistake is a treasure. The added benefit of learning through mistakes with people with an eating disorder is that we know that they have a terror of making a mistake. Thus, if we can model how making mistakes can be a useful part of development, this is valuable.

It can be difficult to undertake and complete the whole assessment in the first meeting with the family. Family members are loyal to each other, wary of others and are eager for the individual with an eating disorder to engage with treatment. They do not want to rock the boat and they may be too aroused to see the bigger picture surrounding the problem. The main objective of the initial meeting is to engage with all the family.

The first phase of the meeting can be used to explore their understanding of the illness. Also, this meeting is a good opportunity to get greater detail about the family history and early developmental events. Here are some questions that can be used to structure and open the discussion onto their beliefs and expectations about the illness. We do not suggest that you fire off these questions in a series, but to use reflective listening to explore each domain in depth.

- What are the things that you see as symptoms of the anorexia nervosa?
- Which are the most worrisome and why?
- What are the things that have concerned you most about the anorexia nervosa both in the short and long term for your daughter and for yourself?
- Have you any ideas about what might be helpful or not?

The patient can then be asked to comment on what the parents have said and to give his or her own list of priorities, for example:

- Of all the things that your parents have mentioned, which are of most concern to you?
- How important do you think it is for you to deal with the concerns that your parents have raised?

During this phase you can feed into the discussion the known facts about anorexia nervosa and correct any misperceptions and ask the family if they would like more information. This feedback can be given as affirming reflection, for example:

- You are right to be concerned about the long-term consequences on the bones. Would you like more information on that?

You can help the family find information from books, videos or from the internet and from other sources. Emphasise that there are high levels of uncertainty in our current knowledge base. Parents can be mortified if they have read books that implicate them as causal in the disease process. In terms of understanding causal factors, the bottom line is that no one factor appears to have a large effect; rather, there appear to be numerous contributing factors that shift the balance of probabilities. This can be continued with a discussion about any family history of illness and care as these past experiences can shape the current situation.

Family assessment leading to a shared model of illness: case studies

The assessment with the family can help to build the picture of the patterns of care and nurturance than run through the wider family network. This can be important as the family may have their own idiosyncratic ideas about the eating disorder and how it would best be treated. In some cases these ideas can clash with the therapist's ideas, illustrated by the following two case studies.

Case study: Sally

Sally had a severe bulimic form of anorexia nervosa complicated by depression. Over time it emerged that Sally's mother had strong views about treatment and was eager to be involved.

Sally worked as a nurse. Her eating disorder began after two consecutive relationships ended unpleasantly. She had her first boyfriend at the age of 16. She accidentally fell pregnant and came to the difficult decision that she should have an abortion. Her relationship deteriorated after this and she broke it off. However, her ex-boyfriend continued to harass and follow her for several months. Her next boyfriend suddenly exploded one day and raped and trapped her for a period of time. She fell pregnant during this incident and had a further termination. Her eating disorder developed soon afterwards. After the assessment Sally and her therapist decided to try an antidepressant to supplement her psychotherapy as she had many features of depression and was highly aroused and not sleeping. Sally lived at home and so once the initial formulation was made, the therapist suggested that her mother be invited to the third session. It quickly emerged that Sally's mother did not approve of the anti-depressant that had been suggested in the prior session. She explained that she tried to avoid medication as much as possible. Part of the reasoning underpinning this was that Sally's mother had diabetes mellitus and was dependent on medication. She did not want Sally to be dependent on medication too. Sally's mother had a model of illness, which was that control and micro-management of the problem would be helpful and so she was very involved in Sally's eating.

This led to a discussion about how Sally related to her mother's diabetes. Sally as the oldest child had learned how to look after her mother when she became hypoglycaemic. She had learnt from an early age how to feed her mother sweet drinks, inject her with glucagon and call her father. This information helped the therapist understand the repeating patterns of interactions throughout Sally's life. Sally had a degree of role reversal in childhood during which she had to care for her mother, who was vulnerable. She therefore developed a strong caregiving schema. This is probably what attracted her into nursing. Her work as a nurse maintained this schema. In addition it coloured her choice of partner. She was attracted to men who had high levels of need. This served to maintain Sally's caregiving schema. Over time the men's needs became more and more demanding until they developed into gross abuse. Counterbalanced with this strong drive to care was a craving for perfect care. Sally had high expectations of others and would explode with rage when she was let down.

Sally's parents had become very over-involved and intrusive in relation to her eating disorder. This served only to make Sally more rebellious. During the session, Sally was able to say how she did not find this helpful and asked her mother if they could spend time together when they did not discuss her eating disorder. Following this session, Sally's mother stopped controlling and intruding upon Sally's eating and did not interfere with her medication. Sally and her mother started to spend time together on enjoyable activities such as shopping.

After this meeting, the therapist was able to work with Sally to see how this pattern of relationships in which she became drawn into giving or reciprocally wishing to receive perfect care worked its way into all aspects of her life. They discussed ways in which Sally could introduce more balance into her life and to create situations where she could be given 'good enough' care. She decided to enrol at the gym and book a session with a personal trainer every two weeks. Sally continued with individual therapy and she had a good response without the need for further involvement with the family.

Case study: Marion

In the case of Marion, the meeting with the family served to illustrate a different pattern of expectations about care, namely that needing care and affection was weak and disgusting.

Marion came to the clinic looking extremely fragile. Her hands were blue and mottled, her hair was unkempt and her clothes were ill assorted and brightly coloured. She had a dilapidated teddy bear tucked into her cardigan. Throughout the interview Marion would cry and blow her nose. She took control of the interview very assertively by asking what sort of treatment was available at the clinic. She had anorexia nervosa of the binge purge type associated with severe obsessive compulsive phenomena. She regularly stole from shops. She put herself through punishing exercise regimes, taking excessive amounts of exercise etc. Her electrolytes were severely disturbed with low sodium of 121. The doctor was concerned that it would not be possible to manage Marion as an outpatient. Marion refused to consider inpatient care. She wanted to have outpatient sessions three times per week.

In view of the severity of her illness, the therapist quickly called a meeting with the family. Both of her parents came. The family and Marion were told that Marion fulfilled all the criteria of a high-risk case and according to good practice guidelines, inpatient treatment was the recommended treatment of choice. Also, this would indicate that she was too unwell to work or continue with her studies. Marion refused to consider inpatient treatment and insisted on continuing with college. The option discussed with the family was the possible use of the Mental Health Act. However, as Marion was keen to work as an outpatient and her parents were willing to support her, a trial of outpatient treatment was started. When asked to state what her parents should do to help her, Marion asked them to help her by giving her emotional support. During the discussion Marion's father, David, pointed out that Marion's mother, Nancy, might have less sympathy with Marion's difficulties than he did because of her own experiences in childhood. Nancy had been brought up on a farm in Canada and at the age of 9 she developed tuberculosis (TB). She had been sent away from home to stay with family friends in Toronto where she received treatment. Nancy described how she had survived this period by not dwelling on her emotions but by putting on a brave face. This stoicism and intolerance for distress was something that she had maintained in adult life and in her interactions with her children. David explained that he had more empathy with Marion's illness and would be able to help. Thus Nancy held a model of illness in which the expectation was that you had to be stoical and endure whatever adversity came your way. Nancy had little tolerance of emotional weakness and vulnerability.

This information could explain why Marion had developed a strong care-eliciting schema as was apparent in her demeanour and interactions. It is possible that Nancy had interpreted Marion's distress and attachment behaviour as a sign of weakness. Nancy may have been repelled and disgusted at Marion's needs rather than being roused to protect and nurture. Marion may have experienced this as a further threat to her safety.

The anorexia nervosa developed when Marion started at boarding school away from home. This type of event might be expected to trigger Marion's care-eliciting schema. She was sent away from all of her home security. Marion recalled that her parents, acting on the advice of a family friend, got her admitted to a private clinic 100 miles from home when she first became ill. Thus, rather than her distress leading to a return to the safety of home, it led to a further perceived rejection and abandonment. This reaction possibly kindled the maintenance of her eating disorder.

In the session, both parents initially were very distressed. Nancy quickly became critical and hostile when discussing Marion's problems. The therapist tried to defuse the situation by developing a shared model of the illness. The therapist suggested that although stoicism was a useful reaction to a severe, treatable, infection, it might be less useful in a disorder of the emotions such as anorexia nervosa, where emotional coaching and mentoring was more helpful. The therapist shared the conceptualisation of anorexia nervosa as a stress-related illness, whereby processing rather than avoiding emotional reactions is needed in order to promote change. The rest of the session was spent planning how Marion would elicit help and support when she went home. Plans were made for Marion and her father to go out for walks together.

In the next individual session, Marion was able to reflect on how she craved for her mother to be tender towards her. The therapist and Marion were able to reflect on how Marion's care-eliciting schema played itself out both within the therapeutic session and in everyday life. The therapist discussed how Marion had a longing for fused idealised care from one person and brought the example of Marion's wish to have several sessions a week from the therapist. The therapist pointed out how Marion's overwhelming craving for care often backfired and led to people and friends withdrawing.

After a course of outpatient therapy and several sessions with the family, Marion chose to take up more intensive inpatient care as she recognised that change was difficult and that a magical transformation probably wouldn't occur if only she found the right person. Marion was then able to make a slow recovery from her illness. Marion would have experienced compulsory inpatient treatment early in the course of her illness as another rejection, whereas the process of engaging the family to be part of the solution helped her choose the help she needed.

These case illustrations indicate how the carers' models of anorexia nervosa can have a profound effect on the management of the eating disorder. There are often parallels between carers' relationships to the illness and the patterns of nurturance within the family.

Phase 2: Examining the consequences of the eating disorder on family interactions

The next phase involves an assessment of the interpersonal context related to living with a person with an eating disorder. How do severe food restriction, over-exercising, weight control measures, compulsions and perfectionist behaviours impinge on family life?

There are three important areas that can serve to either reinforce eating symptoms or OCD comorbidity or remove negative consequences disorders. First, *accommodating* to the symptoms and accepting them into family life, second, developing a reciprocal role by providing *reassurance* in relation to OCD symptoms, and third, *enabling* is when families cover up and protect the person with an eating disorder (or the family) from negative consequences. Families can accommodate to several of the eating disorder symptoms relating to food rules, safety behaviour and OCD symptoms. This can include calibrating or competing with other family members. We teach parents how to construct a functional analysis using some of the following questions:

- What happens before, during and after the behaviour?
- What other strategies have they used to intervene with the behaviour?
- Why did they change?
- What are their feelings about what they are doing now?
- Are they trying to conform to certain values or beliefs?

Examining how the family organises around the eating disorder

The following case example describes how the therapist can formulate care-giving difficulties and plan new interventions. In this family, the dominant mode of coping was for the mother to be a kangaroo and to be highly over-protective, even to the extent of being anxious about her husband's strategies. The mother had become depressed and exhausted in this role and the therapist focused on helping the mother to increase pleasant activities in the home.

Case study: Carol

Kate was the mother of a 17-year-old girl, Carol, with anorexia nervosa. The weight loss had started seven months earlier. Carol's weight had fallen from 60 to 44 kg. Kate and her husband Mark became concerned when Carol became panicky about eating on holiday. They went to their general practitioner, who referred them to child psychiatry where they had family therapy. Kate, the mother, requested to be seen for help for herself, as she did not think that she had been given enough help understanding the illness and how to manage it. She was concerned that not enough attention was being given to the physical aspects of Carol's illness, in that she had been given only a cursory physical examination. She found the family sessions difficult and felt that she was blamed for not being effective enough. She was a nurse and found it difficult to share her worries and concerns with her husband, who had no medical training. Mark shrugged off her worries, saying that she was too negative. Kate was very tearful in the interview. She herself had lost weight and was finding it difficult to sleep. She got no pleasure from her life.

The therapist explored how mealtimes were managed. Carol ate a breakfast of bran flakes, half a banana and a piece of toast alone in front of the television. The breakfast tray was set out by one of the parents, one of whom stayed at home slightly later to cover this time. This meal plan worked well. However, Kate felt somewhat embarrassed about letting Carol eat in front of the television. The therapist praised Kate for finding a successful strategy and indicated that using the television as a form of distraction was often a helpful method in anorexia nervosa. It is often difficult to make breakfast a family event when all members of the family have different schedules. Consequently, it is common for this meal to involve some sort of compromise. The therapist was able to help Kate resolve the conflict that she had between her values (in which it was regarded as not acceptable to watch the television while eating) and finding an effective strategy.

The evening meal was eaten together with Carol, her sister Susan and at least one parent. Susan and the supervising parent would try to engage in conversation, as Carol did not want the focus to be on her. Carol would be obviously distressed during the meal and would go up to her room and cry afterwards. Kate would often go up to Carol's room and try to comfort her. When she was asked to reflect on how this worked she said to the therapist, however, that this seemed to make Carol's distress last longer. She thought that if she stayed downstairs, Carol might become quiet quickly and would get on with her work. The therapist complimented Kate on her observation and suggested that she use this information in her management of Carol's problem. Rather than giving her attention to the anorexic side of Carol, which merely reinforces the anorexic distress (such as comforting the tears after eating), the therapist asked Kate to think of ways in which she could give attention and reinforcement to non-anorexic behaviours and to think of ways of scheduling these after a meal. Kate thought of things that she had enjoyed doing with Carol before the illness began. She knew that Carol would not opt to do anything herself that offered any pleasure. Since her anorexia had begun, she had chosen to cut herself off from people and to sit in her room working. She had even stopped practising her instrument. The therapist suggested that Kate gave Carol a forced choice of two options of behaviours, which did not relate to her anorexic side, such as going out for a walk or watching a TV programme together. It is wise not to leave any choice too open-ended as this produces a huge challenge for someone with anorexia nervosa who is so uncertain about her sense of self and finds decision-making difficult.

It is helpful if the therapist spends time reviewing reinforcers. Reinforcers do not have to be bought gifts, but rather other tokens of love and affection. The following are examples of activities which can act as reinforcers:

- listening to music
- watching a TV programme or DVD
- talking about mutually enjoyable topics, e.g. a magazine, news items
- joint games, crossword puzzle, jigsaw puzzle etc.

These should be linked to success in overcoming an anorexic behaviour or participating in non-anorexic behaviours. The carer and therapist may find it helpful to grade the attractiveness of each of these reinforcers to the person with anorexia nervosa on a linear 1–10 scale (how much pleasure would the person with anorexia nervosa find in it?). The following guidelines are useful to have in mind when considering reinforcers. They should be objects, behaviours, comments, activities that are:

- pleasurable for the person with anorexia nervosa
- inexpensive, if not free
- available to deliver immediately
- comfortable for the carer to deliver.

The therapist explored how Kate and her husband managed this supervision of the eating disorders behaviours. Kate and her husband had divided meal supervision between them. This meant that each of them had an evening off when they went out with a friend. Kate did not find this easy as she worried about what her husband expected of Carol. She thought, for example, that her husband was too strict about the issue of fat on meat. He expected Carol to eat it whereas Kate thought that it was not reasonable to expect anyone to have to eat meat fat. The therapist discussed how it was important that she and her husband spent as much time as they could, agreeing on matters of principle such as this. The therapist encouraged them to spend some time out together. Kate expressed concern about this, as she did not want Susan, Carol's sister, to have to be responsible for her. Nevertheless, she agreed with the therapist that she and her husband would sample the effect of taking small amounts of time out

> together, such as going out for a 15 minute walk, and gradually extending this period if all went well.

It can be helpful to practise positive communication skills and role-playing. Some examples are as follows:

- Have the carer describe the problematic scenario well so that you are able to get in role as accurately as possible.
- Try as much as possible to enter into the drama – it may help to stand up or move.
- The therapist as the person with anorexia nervosa makes the first move.
- Keep role-play brief so you can give feedback.
- Invite the carer to critique their performance first – start with what they liked and finish with what they would like to do better. It is helpful if they can judge themselves specifically against the criteria of positive communication.
- Give your feedback, sandwiching any constructive criticism between positive remarks.
- Repeat the role-play and feedback to shape their behaviour.
- Set a homework task to practise role-play.

In this case the therapist used modelling, shaping and role-playing to help Kate plan how she would increase the non-anorexic time she spent with Carol. Here is an extract from their conversation:

Therapist: How do you think you could ask Carol if she would spend some time with you?

Kate: I am worried about how you shut yourself away. It's not good for you to work all the time.

Therapist: Remember to be positive and yet express your own feelings.

Kate: It's not easy because I recognise that I am on a short fuse at the present time. OK, let me try . . . it may sound a bit artificial.

Therapist: Yes, I appreciate that.

Kate: I enjoy being with you. I get sad when you shut yourself away all night. I realise that the anorexic part of you drives you to be on the go, working all the time. I know I am tense and irritable at the moment. I would like you to spend half an hour an evening doing something pleasant with me. You could choose what we do. I had thought we could go out for a walk or watch a TV programme together. We could watch a section of one of these comedy videos we have.

Therapist: That's great! Do you think you will be able to ask her like that?

Kate: I'm not sure. However, now I think about it I can see how we may have both been winding ourselves up. It's worth a try.

Therapist: You are right that your concern and worry can lead to things spiralling into a trap of despair. It's not easy to climb out. I am impressed though with your observational skills. You have been able to see a pattern in all of this. That is the most important step. The next is trying to change things. Do you think you will be able to put it into practice?

Kate: I will try. I'm not sure what will happen.

Goal setting for the carers in close contact: working on interpersonal maintaining factors

Following the assessment, if it seems that interpersonal reactions to the illness are important perpetuating factors, then it may seem appropriate to work on this. Carers are often, however, not open to the idea that they might need to change. They merely want their daughter to change. It can, therefore, take a longer period with the carers alone before they are willing to change some of their own behaviours.

Often the issues that need changing seem to be minor but on further exploration they have many layers of difficulties. Thus, family members may be unwilling to change for fear of negative consequences for themselves or the individual with the eating disorder. Families may fear that conflict may threaten the love between family members. They are loath to cross the individual with an eating disorder for fear that she will stop loving them. Families may need support to share out the care, so that one family member is not singled out by the eating disorder and seen as a block to change, for example Mum is always the one who gives in first. A motivational interviewing approach can examine and hopefully resolve any ambivalence about change.

It is usual to frame any goals or attempts at behaviour change as experiments in the first instance. They can be introduced on a trial basis just for a short period, a week or so. Change is hard work and it is easier to continue for a short period in the first instance. The family can then report back to the therapist their reflections on the results of the experiment. In the reflection and review session, the therapist enquires about rebounds or adverse reactions, such as an increase in conflict, disruption, danger and risk. This work may need to be continued over time to gradually reduce enabling behaviours. Apart from this individualised support, families benefit greatly from meeting with other families in a workshop format.

Involving carers in strategies to overcome the eating disorder

In some cases, it is appropriate to engage carers in a more cooperative model of caring, in which carers are actively involved in delivering aspects of care. The groundwork for this in adult cases is often done on an individual basis. When working on the issue of readiness to change, for example, individuals often identify that it is important for them to change but feel lacking in confidence that they can change. When asked what might help improve their confidence, many suggest that a family member or friend may help. This is followed by a detailed discussion about how such help could be implemented, considering all the roadblocks and difficulties that might arise.

This preparatory work can then lead into a meeting with the key carer. A solution-focused rather than problem-focused approach is useful when discussing models of joint care. The aim is to set small but achievable goals for both the person with an eating disorder and the carers. The following questions can open up the discussion about how families can be engaged into providing help and care.

• What has discouraged you about trying to help in the past?
• What do you see that is encouraging now?
• Are there any green shoots where you see non-eating disorder behaviours?
• Are there things you have been able to do together which make you think you are pulling in the same direction now?

The emphasis is on change and the atmosphere is kept warm and positive. Sometimes the goal for the carer is not to be actively involved in eating but rather to increase their commitment to work jointly to improve the psychosocial deficits that are common in eating disorders. One way to address this, is to ask about those aspects of the relationship that are seen positively. This then can be deepened, by asking each of the family members about the others' strengths and positive attributes. The following questions can help this process:

• What were the things you most liked about or liked doing with X before the eating disorder?
• How could you help to increase the connections between X and world and others which have been stunted by the ED?

The linear 1–10 scales of readiness and confidence are useful tools to foster positive change talk. Steer the meeting away from interactions in which there is complaining, denigrating or criticising each other. Any negative atmosphere will impede change. Sidestep any negative comments by reframing them as features, which are to be expected with a chronic illness. Use externalising and attribute negative features to the illness:

• You must feel very frustrated with the eating disorder.
• This phase of development is tricky for both parties and steering through it is difficult.

Take it slowly. Do not get so carried away engaging the family that your patient feels excluded. Carers may be ambivalent about helping and it is useful to explore the mixed feelings they will have about this. Acknowledge any setbacks they may have had, but shift the focus back into what they have learnt so that they will be able to put it into practice next time. Some of the reasons why carers may be burnt out, and have less energy to invest in helping the patient to move on, include the following:

- They may have tried and failed in the past.
- Their attempts to help may have made things worse.
- They may have mixed feeling about change.

Carers benefit from developing skills that can help in the management of these problems. The therapist can instil a sense of optimism as here:

- Our research suggests that it is common for carers to get exhausted and dispirited, but we have found that they can be rejuvenated if they are given management skills, especially if they share doing this with others in the same boat. Are you interested in coming to a workshop?

Conclusion

There is no simple 'painting by numbers' approach in dealing with family members. The therapist has to have a scientific practitioner attitude in which mini-experiments are designed and trialled. There needs to be a continuing process of reflection and evaluation. There are some clear givens. The therapist must show respect and empathy to all members of the family and not adopt a superior powerful position. The therapist should at all cost avoid being drawn into interactions, which involve confrontation, criticism and contempt.

Chapter 10 describes the use of writing as a tool for developing reflective capacity and emotional processing. We begin by examining research into the therapeutic effectiveness of writing and then go on to look at some commonly occurring themes that manifest themselves in the narratives and which can then be deconstructed using cognitive behavioural analysis techniques.

References

Bardone-Cone, A. M., Wonderlich, S. A., Frost, R. O., Bulik, C. M., Mitchell, J. E., Uppala, S. et al. (2007). Perfectionism and eating disorders: Current status and future directions. *Clinical Psychology Review* 27: 384–405.

Blair, C., Freeman, C. & Cull, A. (1995). The families of anorexia nervosa and cystic fibrosis patients. *Psychological Medicine* 25: 985–993.

Dugas, M. J. & Ladouceur, R. (2000). Treatment of GAD: Targeting intolerance of uncertainty in two types of worry. *Behavior Modification* 24(5): 635–657.

Dugas, M. J., Gagnon, F., Ladouceur, R. & Freeston, M. H. (1998). Generalized anxiety disorder: A preliminary test of a conceptual model. *Behaviour Research and Therapy*, 36: 215–226.

Enten, R. S. & Golan, M. (2008). Parenting styles and weight-related symptoms and behaviors with recommendations for practice. *Nutrition Reviews* 66(2): 65–75.

Kyriacou, O., Treasure, J. & Schmidt, U. (2008). Expressed emotion in eating disorders assessed via self-report: An examination of factors associated with expressed emotion in carers of people with anorexia nervosa in comparison to control families. *International Journal of Eating Disorders* 41: 37–46.

Lopez, C., Tchanturia, K., Stahl, D., Booth, R., Holliday, J. & Treasure, J. (2008a). An examination of the concept of central coherence in women with anorexia nervosa. *International Journal of Eating Disorders* 41(2): 143–152.

Lopez, C., Tchanturia, K., Stahl, D. & Treasure, J. (2008b). Central coherence in eating disorders: A systematic review. *Psychological Medicine* 38(10): 1393–1404.

Lopez, C., Tchanturia, K., Stahl, D. & Treasure, J. (2008c). Central coherence in women with bulimia nervosa. *International Journal of Eating Disorders* 41(4): 340–347.

National Collaborating Centre for Mental Health (NCCMH) (2004) National Clinical Practice Guideline: Eating disorders: Core interventions in the treatment and management of anorexia nervosa, bulimia nervosa, and related eating disorders. National Institute for Health and Clinical Excellence. Available at www.guideline.gov/summary/summary.aspx?doc_id=5066 (accessed 30 April 2009).

Sassaroli, S., Romero Lauro, L. J., Maria, R. G., Mauri, M. C., Vinai, P. & Frost, R. (2008). Perfectionism in depression, obsessive-compulsive disorder and eating disorders. *Behaviour Research and Therapy*, 46: 757–765.

Schmidt, U. & Treasure, J. (2006). Anorexia nervosa: Valued and visible. A cognitive-interpersonal maintenance model and its implications for research and practice. *British Journal of Clinical Psychology* 45(3): 343–366.

Sepúlveda, A. R., Kyriacou, O. & Treasure, J. (2009). Development and validation of the Accommodation and Enabling Scale for Eating Disorders. *BMC Health Service Research* 9.

Soenens, B., Vansteenkiste, M., Vandereycken, W., Luyten, P., Sierens, E. & Goossens, L. (2008). Perceived parental psychological control and eating-disordered symptoms: Maladaptive perfectionism as a possible intervening variable. *Journal of Nervous and Mental Disease* 196: 144–152.

Southgate, L., Tchanturia, K., & Treasure, J. (2005). Building a model of the aetiology of eating disorders by translating experimental neuroscience into clinical practice. *Journal of Mental Health* 14: 553–566.

Treasure, J., Tchanturia, K. & Schmidt, U. (2005). Developing a model of the treatment for eating disorder: Using neuroscience research to examine the how rather than the what of change. *Counselling and Psychotherapy Research* 5(3): 187–190.

Treasure, J., Lopez, C. & Roberts, M. (2007a). Moving towards the use of endophenotypes in eating disorders in order to make progress in terms of aetiologically based diagnosis, and treatment focused on the pathophysiology. *Paediatric Health* 1: 171–181.

Treasure, J., Smith, G. & Crane, A. (2007b) *Skills-Based Learning for Caring for a Loved One with an Eating Disorder: The New Maudsley Method*. Hove: Routledge.

Treasure, J., Sepúlveda, A. R., Macdonald, P., Whitaker, W., Lopez, C., Zabala, M. et al. (2008). The assessment of the family of people with eating disorders. *European Eating Disorders Review* 16: 247–255.

Ward, A., Ramsay, R. & Treasure, J. (2000a). Attachment research in eating disorders. *British Journal of Medical Psychology* 73(1): 35–51.

Ward, A., Ramsay, R., Turnbull, S., Benedettini, M. & Treasure, J. (2000b). Attachment patterns in eating disorders: Past in the present. *International Journal of Eating Disorders* 28, 370–376.

Ward, A., Ramsay, R., Turnbull, S., Steele, M., Steele, H. & Treasure, J. (2001). Attachment in anorexia nervosa: A transgenerational perspective. *British Journal of Medical Psychology* 74(4): 497–505.

Whitney, J., Haigh, R., Weinman, J. & Treasure, J. (2007). Caring for people with eating disorders: Factors associated with psychological distress and negative caregiving appraisals in carers of people with eating disorders. *British Journal of Clinical Psychology* 46: 413–428.

Writing as a tool for developing reflective capacity and emotional processing

Janet Treasure and Jenna Whitney

Introduction

Therapeutic writing is an important component of our individual work with people with eating disorders (Schmidt et al., 2002; Treasure & Schmidt, 2008; Wade & Schmidt, 2009). We have used this approach with families in order to help us understand how eating disorders impact on family life and also as a reflective tool to examine processes of interaction. In this chapter we discuss how to use this writing as part of the therapeutic process. The parents' writings presented here were generated within a treatment trial of anorexia nervosa; however, many of the themes would equally arise or be applicable to other eating disorders as would some of the therapeutic considerations outlined. We deconstruct the content of the writing to analyse carers' attributions about the illness and their emotional reaction. The themes that arise inform the cognitive behavioural conceptualisation relating to the interpersonal element of anorexia nervosa. Later on, Chapter 12 expands on the process further by describing the use of written exercises in an intensive day-care context.

Research into the therapeutic effectiveness of writing

Writing about difficult experiences has been shown to have a beneficial effect on well-being. Writing appears to work by transforming emotions and images into words and into a coherent narrative. This helps an individual to integrate and reorganise their experiences. It allows a person to step away from the problem and see it from a different perspective. It is as if, once an experience gains meaning and a coherent structure, it becomes more manageable because there is some control over it (for a review of this approach, see Smyth & Pennebaker, 1999).

The use of writing as a means of processing emotions has been the focus of research by Pennebaker and colleagues. This group have compared the effectiveness of writing about stressful experiences (with the explicit instruction of writing about thoughts and feelings) with the effects of writing about neutral topics. They have found that writing about trauma increases long-term physical health, psychological well-being, immunological functioning, employment and academic functioning (for a review, see Smyth & Pennebaker, 1999). In the short term, during and immediately after writing, there can be an increase in measures of autonomic arousal and distress but this gradually settles. Emotional processing through writing in this way was superior to either cognitive restructuring and problem solving, or to pleasure and mastery oriented distraction, in terms of improving mood following a depressing life event (Hunt, 1998).

In a meta-analysis of studies using the Pennebaker paradigm, moderate effect sizes of 0.5 were found representing a 23 per cent improvement in subjects assigned to the experimental condition compared to control subjects (Smyth, 1998). Other findings from this meta-analysis were that the number and length of writing sessions were unrelated to the overall effect size. Studies with sessions spaced out over longer time periods showed a greater effect size. Overall, the author concluded that the effects of written reflection were clinically relevant and generalisable across age, gender, race/ethnicity, social class and a variety of other demographic variables. Some individuals benefit more from writing than others. Health benefits after writing seem to be greater for those who are more inhibited (Smyth, 1998) and have alexithymia (Páez et al., 1999). This is interesting for our work with people with eating disorders as they commonly exhibit these traits.

Using writing as a reflective tool in therapy

We use two writing tasks in the therapeutic setting for families. The first is to write a letter about 'What my daughter means to me'. The second writing task is 'What it is like to live with anorexia nervosa'. We set the task by asking that the writing be unrestrained, uncensored and express spontaneous and intuitive feelings or even irrational thoughts. We suggest that the person writing should 'start the task freely with a view towards destroying the letter afterwards if wanted'.

We use the writing task, 'What it is like to live with anorexia nervosa', to give us an insight into the emotional and practical reaction to anorexia nervosa within the family. Often these narratives illustrate some of the misconceptions about anorexia nervosa. These tasks also enable the therapist to develop a formulation about the processes that may be maintaining the anorexia nervosa. This information will then be used to shape the intervention in an endeavour to break these unhelpful traps.

The letter, 'What my daughter means to me', is a very different exercise. The aim of this is to strengthen the attachment bond between the family member and the person with anorexia nervosa. Parents often write this as a letter addressed directly to their daughter with anorexia ('What you mean to me'). In the parent, writing such a letter often puts them back in touch with and strengthens their love and compassion for their daughter. In the daughter, reading this letter or hearing it read aloud by her parent often serves to challenge and weaken her dependence on the pro-anorexia nervosa belief, which is 'anorexia nervosa makes me safe and secure', by introducing an alternative idea, namely that 'my relationships with close others can help make me safe and secure'.

In the day patient workshop for patients with severe anorexia nervosa and their families, we typically work with two families where we encourage family members to read their letter out to the group. We often find that the letters of love, 'What you mean to me', are an important means of improving communication within families, particularly when they are given to the person with anorexia nervosa. The therapist reflects on the letters with the group, asking the family members how emotionally engaged they had become while writing their letter, and whether they had found themselves interested or surprised at what had emerged in their written work.

Understanding the carers' perspective

We have not used the exact protocol developed by the Pennebaker group, as we asked carers to write on only one occasion about their experiences. The classical paradigm involves writing about an emotionally hot or confusing experience several times. However, Pennebaker (2004), in an excellent self-help book on therapeutic writing, has developed a range of alternative writing tasks that allow people to write about the same experience from different perspectives, including, for example, writing from different protagonists' points of view, alternating emotional with factual accounts, writing for different audiences, and taking bigger picture versus detail-focused perspectives.

In the carer context, the overall aim is to use writing as a tool to get a deeper and different perspective on caring for someone with anorexia nervosa, to find meaning in suffering, and to open new avenues for change. We use the written tasks as a springboard for discussion and reflection in the group. Many carers continue to use writing as a means to guide them through the process of change.

Text analysis

We analysed some of the parents' writing using the computerised text analysis program, the Linguistic Inquiry and Word Count (LIWC) developed by Pennebaker & Francis (1999). This programme analyses text according to emotional, cognitive, structural and linguistic processes used within the writing. LIWC conducts a word-by-word analysis and assigns words to over 70 categories. It calculates the percentage of words for each category. Results from 43 individual studies were compiled by Pennebaker & Francis (1999) to produce mean reference values for 'emotional writing' (when individuals are asked to write about deeply emotional topics) and 'control writing' (when asked to write about non-emotional topics). In our analysis we found that carers included a high proportion of emotional words, particularly negative emotions (Whitney et al., 2005). The proportion of fear and anxiety words were double that reported in emotional writing norms. There was a gender difference in the use of emotional words. Mothers used a higher proportion of emotion words, particularly negative emotions, with the greatest difference in the sadness and depressive domain.

This text analysis approach validates our previous research using questionnaire-based measures of depression and anxiety and highlights the distress that caring for someone with anorexia nervosa engenders.

A qualitative analysis of narratives describing living with anorexia nervosa

We have undertaken a qualitative examination of parents' writing (Whitney et al., 2005). Many themes related to Leventhal's model of illness perception emerge in the writings, i.e. themes relating to causation, cure, time course and consequences both on the patient and the family (Leventhal et al., 1992). Carers, especially the mothers, described the variety of emotions they experienced in response to the illness:

- It overwhelmed me: I often cried myself to sleep.

The description of the intensity of the symptoms, and how they interfere with sleep, concentration and many other activities, suggests that often carers have clinical levels of depression and anxiety. Others describe the cognitive strategies they use to cope practically, such as self-distraction or wishful thinking:

- I have to bury myself in work, and if I am very busy I can forget, the pain is eased, but it always comes back again.
- I keep reassuring them that B will come home and that she will be happy and well again.

Other family members such as siblings and children of the sufferer note how the illness contributes to greater friction within family relationships, more arguments, and an overall stressful atmosphere in the household.

Emotional processing within the narratives

Within the letters, carers express a wide variety of intense emotions. These emotions vary from overwhelming sadness and distress, to fear, anger and even hostility. Many carers also feel self-blaming emotions, such as guilt, coupled with a sense of failure and inadequacy. Perhaps unsurprisingly, it is mothers and other family members, rather than fathers, who talk about their emotional response to anorexia nervosa. Fathers often talk about the strategies they use to manage the illness. This pattern of response is seen in many other illnesses. There are several explanations for this. First, male caregivers may be less attentive to their emotions and, therefore, less likely to identify and report distress. Second, women may be socialised to use emotional coping strategies.

Deconstructing the themes for a cognitive behavioural analysis: 'What is it like to care for someone with anorexia nervosa?'

In this section, we have deconstructed some of the writings to illustrate themes within them, and the emotions, thoughts, beliefs and values that underpin them. These themes provide pointers towards the family atmosphere, the interpersonal maintaining factors, the coping capacities and the quality of life of different family members. Thus they are highly informative for the development of a cognitive behavioural conceptualisation and subsequent treatment plan, tailored to the specific circumstances of a given family.

Within the therapy context, for example, individual family meeting or carers' skills workshop, it can be useful for the therapist to reflect on the emerging themes in a motivational way. Using a more extreme reflection (overstating what has been said), for example, can help the person writing in a catastrophic extreme way to take a more moderate position. Alternatively, double-sided reflections which join together in one reflection discordant opinions can help accentuate and build up discrepancy. These fairly basic strategies can help the carer change some of their attitudes and behaviours.

The following excerpts illustrate some of the core themes. We have included a commentary on some of them and have used italics to highlight key parts of the themes in the carers' narratives.

Helplessness

- Totally disempowering. The nearest, as a woman, I will get to understanding how a man must feel if he is impotent . . . to watch your child waste away.

Comment: This is a misperception about parents' perceived lack of ability to have an effect on the outcome of their daughter's illness. A possible therapist reflection in response to this is to overstate the parents' helplessness and hopelessness which, it is hoped, would result in the family contradicting this reflection by coming up with some illustrations which contain a glimmer of hope. The therapist, for example, may say: '*You feel utterly helpless. You are not sure that anything you might do would improve this situation by even the smallest iota.*' The therapist illustrates and enacts practical strategies as to how they can impact on improving their daughter's ability to care for herself. Sometimes a form of black-and-white thinking colours parents' response:

- Unless my daughter is cured, I am doing nothing.

Comment: When reflecting back this polarised response, the therapist might spread out their arms full span to indicate the extreme divergence between the two statements.

Dependency

- To realise that love is not enough – talking, reasoning, cajoling, empathising, encouraging. *Sitting with her on your knees while she sobs and sobs, rocking her to and fro in your arms, gently, this frail, spiky skeleton, with the eyes of a 30 year old and the body of a child.*

Comment: This poignantly illustrates how anorexia nervosa elicits care with behaviours that involve a regression to the dependency of a child. However, the aim of work with the family is to help their daughter move from this degree of dependence. It is helpful to explore this in more detail, because it is possible that the parent's reaction displayed here may be unhelpfully over-protective (kangaroo). The therapist would spend time analysing this pattern of interaction.

- I never knew the mental pain; the misery and dark, dark fog of depression it entailed. The nightmares from which she would cry out; and if she didn't, *I would steal into her room to make sure she was still breathing, and hadn't finally cut herself. We tried not to leave her alone in the house.*

Comment: This statement, too, illustrates how parents are drawn into giving high levels of care and protection to their child, which is out of line with the child's developmental age, and often with the actual level of risk. Often this tendency to hold onto catastrophic beliefs about the dangers of the illness arises because the parents are not given enough information to make effective decisions about risk. One of the aspects of this treatment is to share with the parents the requisite knowledge and skills so that they can make such judgements realistically. There is a pronounced tendency for mothers to be drawn into being over-protective (part of the kangaroo response). The therapist works gently to analyse with the parents what underpins their fear and helps them to step back from this over-protective reflex. A problem-solving approach can help structure this sort of analysis.

False attributions of 'conscious intent'

- . . . is the most appalling thing? *It is appalling because she has chosen it.*
- *To find that your child doesn't want to grow up, stops the clock, and takes a road to a slow death.*

Comment: These statements ascribe a degree of intent behind the symptoms that is not supported by current evidence.[1] Clinicians have developed theories about unconscious mechanisms. The eminent anorexia researcher, Professor Arthur Crisp, for example, conceptualised anorexia nervosa to be caused by a fear of growing up, but there are no data to support this theory; nowadays, few, if any, clinicians would consider that the person with anorexia nervosa has made a conscious decision not to grow up.

The next quote is from a brother who again carries the misperception about the illness as if it has been a voluntary decision intentionally made:

- I managed to carry on ignoring any problem until the summer when we went away. Mum was clearly really worried and M and I were getting on pretty bad. But then we're brother and sister – we are supposed to argue once in a while. *I made a bargain with M that she was not going to lose any more weight – I've often been able to get round M in the past, and she agreed – case closed, I thought. I talked to her for ages about it, and I hoped that she would just get better.*

Comment: The assumption is that the intentional decision can be arrested by a similar conscious decision. Bribes or rewards, however, usually fail to work. Rather, it is necessary to provide emotional support and regular sessions of coaching or mentoring in order to help the person to see another way of coping other than anorexia nervosa.

False attributions of self-blame and guilt

- So how does the mother feel? *Failed, useless, bad, stupid, guilty, guilty, and guilty.*

Comment: There is no evidence that family factors cause eating disorders. There may be a small genetic risk but, of course, this is not something over which parents have any control and so guilt is inappropriate. These negative self-descriptions by a carer are not evidence based and serve only to make them depressed and may fuel a negative emotional atmosphere within the home. The therapist needs to help the family challenge these unhelpful beliefs and restructure their conceptualisations about the cause of the illness.

The therapist aims to work with the family to alleviate guilt. The therapist may reflect on this statement like this:

It is a natural human response to look for cause and effect. It makes us feel safe but this approach may not be helpful for anorexia nervosa.

What we want you to do is to focus now on what you can do to help your offspring connect with non-anorexic aspects of the world. I can give you a general idea of the kind of factors that psychologists and psychiatrists think contribute to why people develop anorexia nervosa. There are many different factors, such as genes, events and information processing styles that are thought to play a role in this. However, nothing is proven, it all remains uncertain. One thing is certain and that is blaming yourself and feeling guilty will not help your daughter to progress and get over her illness.

Inability to accept negative emotions in self

* And in the midst of all the pain, *you still get angry, so you feel even worse, a horrible person.*

Comment: Here we see that this mother shows how she is intolerant of having negative emotions: she labels herself as 'a horrible person'. The therapist would question statements such as these. It is a normal human reaction to be angry as part of the response to a loss. It is inappropriate to describe oneself as horrible because you have an emotional reaction such as this. This intolerance and shame about holding a negative emotion is rather similar to the type of the personality trait of 'avoidance' seen in people with anorexia nervosa themselves. We have found in our analysis of the written response to scenarios that carers commonly deny or neglect their own emotional response and this emotional neglect or invalidation is a trait that we aim to moderate within our work with families. We try to help parents model a judicious use of emotions in order to guide their daughter's decision-making and help her plan behaviour. Anger against the anorexia nervosa can be a useful motivator for parents to foster persistence to help their daughter. The therapist works to help family members use the intensity of their emotional reaction to drive adaptive behaviours, rather than trying to deny that they exist or bottling them up.

Threats to sense of self and self-esteem

This next excerpt is from a mother of a daughter with a persistent form of anorexia nervosa:

* At the beginning I can remember feeling so resentful because I had to tell strangers about every detail of our lives and I felt everything had been taken away. I had nothing left that was mine.

Comment: This mother felt violated by the process of a psychiatric assessment. It is possible that she is sensitive to the level of intimacy that such an assessment entails because she has some avoidant personality traits or insecure attachment style. In previous research we found that it was common for both mother and daughter to have insecure avoidant attachments (Ward et al., 2001). This loss of her privacy increased her levels of stigma and shame.

Enmeshment

- Mealtimes are sometimes stressful, *as T treats eating as a punishment; this means I am the one giving out the punishment all the time.*

Comment: There is some fusion of thoughts here with the mother taking on her daughter's perspective in that it joins her in the belief that she is punishing her by making her eat. This degree of empathy and enmeshment is unhelpful. Rather it is helpful to teach the family how to approach meals with a degree of clinical detachment, as a necessary medical procedure that has to be carried out. Using the analogy of chemotherapy for cancer, for example, can be helpful. The therapist might use a reflection with an overstatement to illustrate how this belief is unjustified such as:

> Your daughter is very anxious about eating and the anorexic part of her thinks eating is a punishment and you now firmly believe that you are torturing her on a daily basis.

Needs of other family members

- I feel under constant stress and as if walking on eggshells all the time. *I know X gets annoyed because I spend so much time talking with T.*

Comment: This clearly illustrates how the needs of other family members are neglected. This quickly leads to jealousy, resentment and guilt within the family environment. The statement 'as if walking on eggshells' suggests that the mother tries to protect and keep the peace. It may be that this mother is showing some kangaroo behaviours. Carers need to find a judicious balance between striving for change and accepting that the process may take time and a great deal of courage and energy on their daughter's part.

Siblings can feel particularly neglected.

> And now for the whiney, spoilt child bit. M and I have always competed for Mum's attention, and since she's been ill M has had 100 per cent of it. I dreaded ringing home for most of last year to hear about poor M for two hours and only really did so under duress. *I always used to ring Mum to get things off my chest and to make me feel better. But now whenever I ring Mum, we just talk about poor M and all her problems, and whenever I spoke to M it was even worse. A*

monologue about how terrible life was and how cold she was etc. Mum sends me emails quite regularly – but they're usually a page and a half about M! Is it unreasonable to think that's a bit off? I'm her son too! All this moaning reminds me of the parable of the prodigal son. ('You didn't kill the fatted calf for me and I've been a good boy all my life!!')

Comment: This letter illustrates very clearly how anorexia nervosa means that the needs of other family members are neglected and ignored. It is common for siblings to have mixed feelings or rather negative feelings of jealousy and envy like this, but it is rare for them to have the courage and ability to articulate them. Other family members get neglected by the illness and resent the fact that so much time is taken up with this issue. We have often found that it can be helpful for siblings to link up with other siblings and share these experiences. Probably one of the best ways to defuse jealousy is to be open about it and talk to others.

The therapist should praise this clear articulate expression of need and would bend over backwards to indicate that this ability to express feelings and needs clearly is a natural mature response rather than a childish reaction. Indeed, the therapist might want to indicate that the brother is modelling a healthy expression and acceptance of emotions, which is a great example for their sibling with anorexia nervosa. It is only if someone is able to make a clear expression of their emotional reaction and needs that other people can help think of solutions.

Differences in 'stages of change' between carer and sufferer

• *I feel very frustrated T will not or cannot accept help.*

Comment: This illustrates the difficulty that arises because patient and carer are at a different stage of change. It is common for carers to focus about wanting to see change in their daughter. It can be harder for them to think that they may need to change their own behaviours first. This recognition that ambivalence is a common part of the change process can provide helpful insight into the anorexia nervosa challenge and can lead to compromise and realistic goals.

Positive aspects of caregiving

• *On a positive note I am a more patient person now and less critical of others. I feel if T was to get better we would be stronger as a family and I would like to think we might be able to help others in the same way.*

Comment: These positive statements need to be treasured and used by the therapist to add an antidote to gloom. It is common for families to say after recovery that they have gained wisdom from the experience and have become closer as a result. The therapist might say:

> It is interesting that part of you recognises that despite these difficulties, you have been able to grow and develop your reflective capacities and this experience has taught you things you can pass on to others, can you tell me more about that?

Enhancing self-reflection in both carer and sufferer

The following excerpt is from a father:

*   My daughter's *illness has made me more aware of my son's feelings and needs and also to listen to him* as he makes a more positive contribution to family life.

Comment: The therapist listens out for and reinforces any positive comments such as this. Parents commonly voice that the skills needed to help their daughter through her illness enable them to communicate and listen to other family members.

The therapist can elicit positive comments by questions such as:

> We often find that despite the pain and difficulties some families find that they have been able to gain and learn from what has happened to them. Have you had any experience of this?

Focusing on the positive affirmations

*   If anything she is worse but, on the other hand, it depends on what is worse. Her weight is no better, but she has learned a lot and gained a lot of friendship and insight from other people. So not all is lost.

Comment: The therapist would use this opportunity to praise the mother for finding positive things in her daughter's life to comment on, for example with the following reflections:

*   It sounds as if you are noticing that your daughter is working hard to make her life bigger.
*   What other green shoots have you noticed that are signs that she has begun to connect with the world?

Sense of loss

This next excerpt from a mother's 'What is it like to live with anorexia nervosa' letter clearly describes all the losses endured by a parent when their daughter has a very chronic form of this illness:

- At the beginning it never occurred to me that S would not get better.

Comment: Many parents and, of course, many doctors do assume that an episode of anorexia nervosa will be a transient phase. It is not easy for clinicians to balance a realistic discussion of progress and likelihood of recovery and also to convey an atmosphere of hope. In this case, after duration of illness of 18 years the chances of the daughter making a full recovery are extremely low. However, if the family are given accurate information, they can be responsible for their reaction to the illness and make appropriate plans and decisions for the future with this in mind.

- I see groups of girls walking, running along and they may be giggling and happy; leading a so-called normal life; whatever that conjures up. *I wish S was one of them.*

Comment: There is an inevitable human tendency to grieve for the loss of a healthy child. The therapist could use this statement to increase the motivation to undertake 'non-anorexia nervosa' activities with their offspring,[2] for example:

- It is a challenge that carefree activities are so tough for your daughter. What do you think you could help her with so that she gets some opportunity to do this?

Wishful thinking such as this can be a maladaptive coping response. The therapist would aim to move the discussion on from dwelling on problems onto finding solutions, such as:

- Have there been any green shoots that might suggest that your daughter is reaching out to the world?

Stigma

- We go to the shops and people turn round. Sadly, they do not turn round for any other reason than the desire to have another look. *I get hurt, angry and embarrassed.*

Comment: Since anorexia nervosa is so obvious to others, the problem of stigma is particularly pronounced. Family members often feel humiliated, frustrated, angry and ashamed by the reactions of others. There is no correct way or rules for dealing with this, but an approach in which parents are open about the problem is probably most adaptive. It can be confusing because the reaction of the person with anorexia nervosa is often to withdraw from others and attempt to keep the illness a secret. This imposed avoidance may prevent the family from coping adaptively and they need to resist such strictures. The therapist coaches family members into using interventions such as the following:

- I need to let my friends know what is wrong with you otherwise they will worry as they can see that something is wrong but do not know what it is.
- I hear you say that you do not want other people to know about your illness. I need to get support and comfort from friends so that I can support you.
- I need to open up to family and friends about my feelings and reactions.

Inability to plan ahead

- *I can never look ahead with confidence.*

Comment: The inability to plan ahead is something that many people note with sadness. The therapist should work with the family to examine how they can plan but with contingencies built in for dealing with any crisis.

- At the weekends when she comes home, *it is difficult for our lives not to revolve round her.*

Comment: This illustrates the caregiving cycle swinging into action, with perhaps too much of an over-protective kangaroo response.

The need for causal understanding

- I want M to know that my unwavering love for her would always overrule every-thing. *I would love her to open up to me and express her feelings in explaining her problems* and indeed when they first started. *I really do need to know and I am prepared to listen to anything.*

Comment: This wish for intimacy and perfect understanding may be too high an expectation. People with anorexia nervosa are highly avoidant and are not able to conceptualise their problems easily. Furthermore, they are at a developmental stage at which intimacy with parents may be particularly difficult. On the other hand, the ability to communicate with others is an important stage of recovery. Consequently, the therapist might ask:

- What would you do to be able to set the scene so that your daughter would be able to feel safe and secure enough to be able to open up more to you?

This quote below, on the other hand, describes the difficulties and futility in utilising instrumental measures in the hope of a positive result, such as offering rewards to a sufferer:

- *We have tried several 'holidays of a lifetime'* as a mechanism to encourage O to eat. While the holidays will remain with us for a lifetime they did not provide a solution to her illness.

Comment: Providing the person with anorexia nervosa with the opportunity to reflect on, and understand her emotions and her own strengths and difficulties is a more useful skill and reward than material rewards.

Perfectionism

Parents sometimes share some of the same high standards and perfectionism of their daughter. This can lead them to make negative judgements about themselves and their abilities. The therapist, therefore, needs to moderate perfectionist standards both in the carers and in the patient. A good joke from Bob Palmer is to suggest that families with high perfectionism are missing the 'oh sod it' gene and they have to learn to make up for this.

The following father's quote illustrates how the perfectionism and obsessive compulsive temperament, which are risk factors of anorexia, both have positive and more problematic aspects. However, there is the danger that parents (and schools) can reinforce these traits so much that they becomes counterproductive and are taken to an extreme:

- O has been a most extraordinary child . . . *She has an extraordinary ability to plan and organise things and her work rate in all that she does has been beyond any experience that I have had in business.* She is multi-talented and yet excessively self-critical concentrating on the failures rather than the successes.

The carer's balancing act

The following father's quote clearly documents the difficult decisions that parents of people with anorexia nervosa have to face. The balance between being intrusive and over-protective and being neglectful is a hard one to negotiate.

Living with this is painful and debilitating. To watch someone you love have this happen to her is genuinely awful. On a practical level, you have to make almost impossible decisions and judgements day by day. Like do you believe her when she says she has eaten something? Do you insist on someone being with her when she eats her lunch or do you trust her? Trust her when you know that the anorexia will tell her to lie about this? Do you cajole her into meeting up with old friends? Is that mollycoddling and treating her like a child again? Is she right when she says leave that to her? Even though you know she means she'll never do anything about it. Do you ignore the blackmailing threats of the illness, when she insists on something that you know is unhealthy, obsessive and wrong? Or do you try and skirt round the problem? Negotiate? Or will that be colluding with the enemy? Do you insist on her keeping a medical appointment? Or do you say, 'No, she must take responsibility for herself as an adult'? Can you do that even though you know she must go and see that doctor or she may collapse because her bloods, or whatever, are out of balance?

(Father of anorexic woman)

Comment: This clearly illustrates the difficulties parents have in getting the optimal balance between being protective or controlling and fostering autonomy or neglect. There is obviously no easy answer. Rather there has to be an experimental 'try it and see' approach. Parents are often able to note signs and symptoms that indicate that their daughter's nutritional state is becoming perilous and it is helpful if they can feed back both to their daughter and to professionals about this. Ideally the therapist should negotiate this openness in communication at the start of treatment. If parents have severe worries about their daughter's health, the therapist might coach the parent to say something like:

• I have observed xyz, I think your life may be at risk, if this is the case it is out of our hands. As parents we are legally obliged not to be negligent about attending to your health.

Externalising the illness

The externalising approach to the illness, i.e. distinguishing the illness from their daughter and refusing to collude or communicate with the anorexia or dysfunctional behaviours, can help to reduce parents' perception that there is a battle between them and their daughter.

I used the word demon some time back. It conjures up medieval times, people being possessed. Sometimes it feels like that, talking to her, when the anorexia is strong. There is a haunted look in her eye that isn't D the daughter I know and love. It is as though she has been taken over. Then, some hours later, it has gone. We can talk again rationally. She actually laughs and smiles. D is back in control once more. There is indeed hope. That is what we live for – hope.

Comment: Again, it is helpful for the therapist to spend time discussing these glimmers of hope and exploring how and when they happen, with the aim of completing a functional analysis in order to facilitate setting up the environment so that these highlights occur more often and the consequences are such that non-anorexic behaviour gets strengthened.

Feelings in others evoked by emaciation

- I had no idea how to help Mum. *I kept my distance from M because it was so horrible to look at her.*

Comment: The emaciation of anorexia nervosa, if extreme, does induce feelings of horror and revulsion in others. It is almost like a piece of performance art: it produces a reaction. However, this automatic recoil and distancing of others serves only to reinforce the person's core beliefs that underpin the eating disorder, such as 'I am horrible, people do not want to be with me etc.'

Themes within the letters 'What my daughter means to me'

We have described above the themes arising from parents' writings about life with someone with anorexia nervosa. The letters on 'What my daughter means to me' are very different: these letters uniformly express positive emotions of gratitude and love. We find that these letters can form a bridge and start the process of an emotional reconnection between the person with anorexia nervosa and her parents. This can mean that the person with anorexia nervosa can start to appreciate the nurturance and love that her parents want to provide. We find that these letters can rekindle reparation in the relationship. This is important as one of the key positive aspects of anorexia nervosa is that it makes the person with the disorder feel safe and secure.

Conclusion

Therapeutic writing is a useful tool in working with families of eating disorder patients, because it can open up and give the therapist easy access to some of the misattributions, which can make adjustment to the illness difficult. These parental narratives also give helpful pointers to important emotional themes that facilitate the development of an individually tailored cognitive behavioural formulation adapted to the needs and circumstances of particular families. Furthermore, they are an excellent vehicle for emotional processing and can increase warmth, support and understanding within the family and begin to repair strained relationships.

Notes

1 In our clinical experience, the idea that there is conscious intent and that symptoms can be 'put on or stopped at will' is even stronger for bulimia nervosa than for anorexia nervosa. As a result, carers are often extremely critical of the person with bulimia. This may also have something to do with the fact that bingeing by

many people (parents, patients, general public) is seen as being 'gluttonous and self-indulgent' and purging as 'wasteful'.

2 This does perhaps – in this very chronic case – presuppose that there is an acceptance on the mother's part that her daughter is unlikely to change very much vis-á-vis her anorexia nervosa.

References

Hunt, M. G. (1998). The only way out is through: Emotional processing and recovery after a depressing life event. *Behaviour Research and Therapy*, 36(4): 361–384.

Leventhal, H., Leventhal, E. & Diefenbach, M. (1992). Illness cognition: Using common sense to understand treatment adherence and affect cognition interactions. *Cognitive Therapy and Research* 16(2): 143–163.

Páez, D., Velasco, C. & González, J. L. (1999). Expressive writing and the role of alexythimia as a dispositional deficit in self-disclosure and psychological health. *Journal of Personality and Social Psychology* 77(3): 630–641.

Pennebaker, J. W. (2004). Theories, therapies and taxpayers: On the complexities of the expressive writing paradigm. *Clinical Psychology: Science and Practice* 11: 138–142.

Pennebaker, J. W. & Francis, M. E. (1999). *Linguistic Inquiry and Word Count (LIWC)* (Computer software). Mahwah, NJ: Lawrence Erlbaum Associates Software and Alternative Media.

Schmidt, U., Bone, G., Hems, S., Lessem, J. & Treasure, J. (2002). Structured therapeutic writing tasks as an adjunct to treatment in eating disorders. *European Eating Disorders Review* 10: 1–17.

Smyth, J. M. (1998). Written emotional expression: Effect sizes, outcome types, and moderating variables. *Journal of Consulting and Clinical Psychology*, 66: 174–184.

Smyth, J. & Pennebaker, J. W. (1999). Sharing one's story: Translating emotional experiences into words as a coping tool. In C. R. Snyder (ed.) *Coping: The Psychology of What Works*. New York: Oxford University Press.

Treasure, J. & Schmidt, U. (2008). Motivational interviewing in the management of eating disorders. In H. Arkowitz, H. A. Westra, W. R. Miller & S. Rollnick (eds) *Motivational Interviewing in the Treatment of Psychological Problems*. New York: Guilford.

Wade, T. & Schmidt, U. (2009). Writing therapies for eating disorders treatment. In S. Paxton and P. Hay (eds) *Interventions for Body Image and Eating Disorders: Evidence and Practice*. Sydney: IP Communications.

Ward, A., Ramsay, R., Turnbull, S., Steele, M., Steele, H. & Treasure, J. (2001). Attachment in anorexia nervosa: A transgenerational perspective. *British Journal of Medical Psychology* 74(4): 497–505.

Whitney, J., Murray, J., Gavan, K., Todd, G., Whitaker, W. & Treasure, J. (2005). Experience of caring for someone with anorexia nervosa: Qualitative study. *British Journal of Psychiatry*, 187: 444–449.

Chapter 11

Family and carer workshops

Janet Treasure, Ana Rosa Sepúlveda, Wendy Whitaker,
Gill Todd and Carolina Lopez

Introduction

Family members and carers are eager to have as much information as possible in order to help their loved one get over their illness and, although highly motivated, they are all too often excluded from helping by adult services. This is either because the person with an eating disorder is not ready to change and so has not yet engaged in treatment or because health professionals are reluctant to include the families and carers of adults in treatment. As discussed in Chapter 4, an issue that causes confusion among professionals is that of confidentiality. A solution that we have developed to overcome some of these problems is to run workshops for people who care for someone with an eating disorder. We have included all types of carer (parents, partners and siblings), for all forms of eating disorder (anorexia nervosa, bulimia nervosa), at all stages of the illness and with all levels of severity.

The workshops are framed as an opportunity for participants to develop the skills to be 'expert' carers so that they can act as a mentor or coach to help the person with an eating disorder through her or his illness. We have a group of carers who co-facilitate the workshops with us and whom we have trained in the skills of motivational interviewing. We find that this is a way that the expert patient concept, which has been of use for chronic medical conditions, can be applied in the context of psychiatry to carers.

Aims of the workshops

As discussed above, the aim of these workshops is to give carers skills so that they can become more effective at helping their relative with an eating disorder. Essentially, we offer carers a course in the management of eating disorders, similar to that which we offer specialist health professionals. These skills improve their own coping strategies and reduce burn-out and stress. We teach carers how to avoid reacting with high expressed emotion to eating disorder symptoms. The process of training involves demonstrating how the principles of the trans-theoretical model of change and motivational interviewing can be applied in the context of carers themselves changing their relationship with the eating disorder. Finally, we teach carers how to implement these skills to help their loved one with an eating disorder change their behaviour.

The workshop format serves to defuse some of the guilt and stigma attached to having someone with an eating disorder in the family. Issues of unwanted intrusiveness, privacy and confidentiality do not arise. This format may be of great benefit in developing early interventions, as the individual with an eating disorder does not have to be present in order to obtain the requisite resources.

Format and protocol of the workshop

The format is two-hourly sessions, delivered on a weekly basis for six weeks. All carers are given a copy of the carers' book and toolkit and a slide presentation programme to accompany the practical sessions. The sessions follow the booklet, so the need for didactic teaching or psychoeducation is reduced. Consequently, most of the time is used for discussion and developing practical skills. This involves the use of coaching through scenarios, role-playing, live demonstrations etc. The format follows that recommended for adult learning, with plenty of time for reflection and observation. The use of writing is encouraged in between the sessions, to enhance self-reflection.

Session 1: Changing maladaptive interpersonal behaviours with the eating disorder

This session introduces the model of carer coping described in Chapter 5. First, we ask carers to think about whether they can make changes in the areas on the diagram of the model of carer coping in which they have direct control. These include:

- spending less contact time
- getting an optimal balance with other roles
- balancing the relationship
- caring for self.

First, we explain how to develop a balanced relationship avoiding the traps of extreme emotions or over-directiveness as described in Chapter 6. The animal metaphors are a playful way of introducing these unhelpful relationship patterns. A light-hearted discussion follows on from their observations and reflections of how these patterns emerge in their own day-to-day interactions. Carers often fall into extreme patterns of emotional responding, either having too intense an emotional reaction with anguish or anger (jellyfish), or denying that they have any emotions (ostrich) and withdrawing. In terms of directedness, carers can be overly protective (kangaroo), taking over all roles, or overly directive (rhinoceros), taking logic to an extreme and invalidating the eating disorder symptoms. Most carers recognise that their relationship pattern may often fall into one of these animal roles.

During the workshops, carers work in small groups discussing their default patterns of interaction. The aim is for carers to gently recognise and reflect on the possibility that they may play a role in maintaining the eating disorder symptoms. We teach about issues such as 'readiness to change' and how to increase motivation to change, by asking the carers to reflect on whether they might be willing and or able to work on changing *their* role in these patterns of interaction. The realisation not only that it is their daughter, son, relative or partner who might have to change, but also that they too share a role, is an interesting milestone in the process. In other settings, this can be a roadblock for some parents, especially if they feel they have to commit to family 'therapy' when they do not see the family as part of the problem. The process of commitment to change within the workshops is more gradual and also more clear, structured and contained.

Emotional intelligence

To be an effective mentor for their relative with an eating disorder, carers have to hone their emotional intelligence skills. This involves being able to be reflective about their own emotional reactions, using them as a guide in decision-making rather than becoming captured and swept up by the emotion. Thus, advice to remain calm and yet warm is a constant refrain within the workshops. This ability to reflect on their own emotions is a core skill that can usefully be transferred to their offspring. People with eating disorders find this difficult, preferring to avoid and dismiss emotions altogether.

We suggest, therefore, that a useful role for any carer is to serve as an emotional coach, modelling emotional intelligence. All too often, carers react to eating disorders by denying or invalidating their own emotional reaction. If they are suspicious that their loved one has skipped a meal or thrown it away, for example, they may challenge their loved one, who may, in turn, respond angrily, accusing the carers of not trusting her or him. Carers will often deny that this is the case, even although they do not trust her or him. Alternatively, they may deny being angry or irritated when provoked. This is all done in an effort to keep the peace. Dishonesty or avoidance of emotions, however, is harmful as it invalidates emotions. This inhibits the person with an eating disorder from developing and feeling confident about their own emotional intelligence. Peacemaking should not be at the cost of truth and honesty.

We end the session by small group discussions about the carers' coping model and whether they recognise that the demands of this model are relevant to them.

Session 2

This first phase of the workshops asks carers to analyse what it is about their own situation that contributes to high stress levels. The small group work focuses on their needs, and how to increase their coping skills. In many cases, this involves taking a step back with less of an intensive, full-on response. The workshops give carers both the opportunity and permission to think of themselves as individuals with their own needs. Professionals and other carers provide a safe context to consider taking time off from the caring role and to fit in activities that are rewarding and pleasurable. We emphasise that a distressed carer is a less effective carer. Furthermore, they need to model self-nurturing behaviours for their offspring.

This early phase allows for re-evaluation of their caring behaviour and whether they might want to change. This process of thinking about the importance of changing to a different pattern of interaction with the eating disorder and whether they can be confident that they can do so is a paradigm which also helps them to understand the process that their relative may undergo to change eating disorder behaviours.

At the beginning of every session, the facilitators elicit feedback from the previous session to enhance reflection and integrate meaningful information. We may, for example, ask participants to tell us one thing they learnt from the last session, or one new behaviour that they had to put in place after the last session.

The next session starts with a discussion of the array of possibilities about how they might set about changing their relationship with the eating disorder. We teach and practise the technique of externalising the illness. This serves to correct some of the common misattributions about the illness such as 'she is just doing it to annoy' or 'because she is stubborn and naughty etc.'. We then discuss possible ways in which the eating disorder might control the family, by discussing how some families accommodate their behaviour to allow or maintain OCD rituals, or become controlled by the eating disorder. We then discuss and validate the splits, hostility and anger that commonly arise. Finally we end with a description of the trans-theoretical model of change.

Carers are then split into small groups to reflect on their readiness to change, using the readiness ruler, a tool designed to elicit change talk. They are often surprised to become aware of their own mixed feelings. Often they recognise the disparity between their ratings of importance to change and confidence in their ability to instigate change. They might, for example, recognise that by accommodating their daughter's rigidity about what she will eat (e.g. only Waitrose's tinned celery), they may not be helping her fight the eating disorder. Nevertheless, they are terrified of rocking the boat and whether they will be able to cope with the backlash.

We close the session by having carers undertake small group work, in which they reflect on their readiness to change some of their behaviours in relationship to the eating disorder, considering the pros and cons of change. This involves thinking about the two constructs of importance and readiness to change.

Session 3

In this session the focus is on developing good communication skills including listening skills, the ability to understand non-verbal aspects of communication and developing the skill of making understanding statements in reflective listening. We use demonstrations and role-plays based on carers' own experiences, to facilitate this key aspect of the workshops. We also analyse transcripts of carer and eating disorder interactions, as it can be easier to read and plan this new language of listening and reflection before being competent at speaking it.

Carers practise using elements of positive communication, such as solution-focused questioning, within the safety of small groups. We teach reflective listening skills, using the principles enshrined in the acronym, OARS – open questioning, affirmation, reflection and summaries. Many carers find that this new pattern of interaction is extremely liberating, albeit not always easy to master. Carers use these techniques to explore their own mixed feelings about changing the way they interact with the eating disorder. Carers reflect on both their own and their offspring's readiness to change and what any discrepancy means for the relationship regarding how they manage anorexia nervosa.

This third workshop session ends with a discussion about how to match interventions with the stage of change. Again, we use the principles of adult learning, in that once a concept has been defined; carers examine how this fits with experiments in their own environment. Observations are reflected back to the group. A step to change their own behaviour is made on an experimental basis and they analyse and reflect on the implications. We introduce the concept of expressive writing (Chapter 10) as a means of deepening and tracking their progress. The narratives can help them step back, take an overview and see things from a different perspective.

Session 4

The aim of this session is to develop more advanced motivational interviewing skills. Thus, carers are introduced to the skills of tracking micro emotions and using complex reflections to deepen the meaning and increase the impact or value of their emotional reflection which, in turn, improves empathy. Another important skill is how to roll with resistance by sidestepping eating disorder talk and not entering into arguments. We teach carers how to move from the detail of the eating disorder into a bigger picture by framing the conversation within the context of their life course and core values.

Carers learn to use the skills embodied in the acronym DARN-C (eliciting the desire, ability, reasons, need and overall commitment to change). The final aim is for carers to expose any ambivalence their loved one might have about the eating disorder and increase the discrepancy between the current position and bigger ideals. By the end of this session, we hope that carers have started to commit themselves to some plan to change their own behaviours.

Session 5

In this session we move carers on from thinking about changing their own behaviours and interactions with the eating disorder to tackling how they can foster change in eating disorder behaviours themselves. The theory underpinning behaviour change is explained. Carers are taught to observe the conditions that increase or decrease the likelihood of an unwanted behaviour. They move from this to undertake a functional analysis; in other words, to examine the antecedents and consequences of the behaviour. The functional analysis of problematic eating disorder scenarios leads into discussion about problem solving. In small groups, carers apply the skills of motivational listening by using OARS and DARN-C, in order to encourage a commitment to setting goals towards some small behaviour change. Group work focuses on negotiating these changes in eating behaviours, increasing the importance and confidence that change can take place as well as making a plan for an 'experiment'. Coaching is used to set, implement and review goals.

Session 6

In the final session, we rehearse changing some of the other eating disorder behaviours such as obsessive compulsive behaviours, temper tantrums and self-harm. Obsessive compulsive symptoms have consistently been found to impact on the outcome of anorexia nervosa. Consequently, it is important that we help parents modify this key maintaining symptom.

We teach parents key elements of change in obsessive compulsive disorder. We explain how extremely difficult it is for people with OCD not to undertake their compulsions as any attempt to interrupt them results in high levels of anxiety. Following any change in behaviour, there needs to be enough time to habituate to the feared situation so that the levels of anxiety can tail off. Part of the problem with working with people with OCD and AN is that it seems to be very difficult to unlearn some of these reactions. People who have successfully gone through this process describe it as 'going through hell' needing 'blood, sweat and tears'. Carers may find it difficult to tolerate such distress and they will be tempted to cave in and interrupt the process. Carers, therefore, need to understand the rationale and the expected effects of treatment.

It is important that parents know that reacting to reassurance seeking is counterproductive. Often it can be helpful to have a formal written contract, which gets signed before the implementation of a plan to tackle OCD behaviour. A key point must be that the task is not changed at all. There will be pressure from the person with OCD, who will find loopholes to avoid doing the task in order to escape from the severe anxiety. Carers learn to attend to behaviours they want to increase and disattend to behaviours they want less of. Carers need to be able to accept some of the weird thoughts and not try to argue against them by saying that they are stupid, unreasonable or irrational etc. A gradual step-by-step approach with small goals is usually effective. Finally, this session also includes a basic review and quiz.

Conclusion and outcomes

We have completed a pilot series of workshops for carers of people with an eating disorder. The mental health (General Health Questionnaire (GHQ) screening) of the carers improved significantly after the intervention using the experience of caregiving inventory ($p > 0.001$). In addition, we found changes in the experience of caregiving, i.e. a significant decrease in the Negative Aspects of Care ($p < 0.003$) and on the Eating Symptom Scales ($p < 0.026$).

Research into this intervention is ongoing and includes a project to assess the impact and acceptability of these workshops in a small randomised controlled trial, in which we will compare post-intervention carers' outcomes (after participating in the group) with outcomes from carers on the waiting list. We are trying to examine the process of learning within the workshop. One of the behaviours that we measure is whether there is a change in the carers' response to a challenging statement in a standardised eating disorder scenario. In order to measure this, we give them typical written and verbal scenarios and ask them to consider how they would respond. Their answer is scored according to the principles of motivational interviewing. We are also measuring expressed emotion. There are many questions that remain unanswered. One is whether streaming the workshops with the five-minute speech sample to have carers with similar needs grouped together, works better than with a mixed format (e.g. carers of people in different stages of the illness, adolescents/adults, out/inpatient settings). At the time of writing, the answer to this question is unknown.

Carers' reactions to the workshops have been overwhelmingly positive. Carers feel more able to understand the emotional content of the eating disorder and feel less guilty about their attempts to help.

Chapter 12

An intensive three-day programme with families preparing for transition from inpatient to outpatient care

Wendy Whitaker, Janet Treasure and Gill Todd

Introduction

In this chapter we describe a three-day intervention involving patients and their families. This approach offers a more intensive intervention than the workshops described in Chapter 11 or the family work used as part of outpatient treatment. We have used it primarily for people with treatment resistant anorexia nervosa during inpatient care, as preparation for transfer into the community. The risk for relapse following inpatient care is high and careful planning and preparation is essential. This intervention could also be used for individuals at high risk who have failed to respond to outpatient care. Most of our experience relates to using it to supplement inpatient care. Elements of this programme, such as the skills training, are common to the other interventions we use for carers. The context, however, is more individualised and tailored to the two participating families. In this chapter, we outline the structure and timetable of the three days and give some details of the exercises that we use.

Structure and timing of the treatment

In the inpatient setting, we have two families who come to spend three days working together on the ward. Our experience suggests that the outcome of this intervention is better if it is held in the early part of the admission, although this may be confounded by parental motivation. Another advantage of holding the sessions earlier in the admission is that it allows time for any change in approach to be practised on home visits and reviewed with the team. Currently the patient is included in almost all the programme. There is flexibility in the final part of the third day during the psychoeducation section to allow the patient to leave if they wish. The feedback from carers is that they welcome the opportunity to have time on their own and to address this we have developed the collaborative skills workshops (described in Chapter 11). We recommend that, where possible, families attend all three days if they can.

We work with all carers – parents (including separated or divorced ones), partners, older siblings and children of sufferers. The therapist aims to match the families, if at all possible, with a similar family structure and a similar illness profile. Occasionally we have used this programme successfully with just one family and it can also be used in shorter family work sessions.

The content of the workshops has gradually evolved over time and has been shaped by feedback from carers and patients. It is common for carers to be very apprehensive about the intervention initially, as they are concerned about issues of privacy and exposure. It also involves a large time commitment. With hindsight, however, they value the opportunity to share and reflect with another family about the impact anorexia nervosa has, and to collaboratively generate solutions. It is as if they have the opportunity to see themselves as others might see them. This enables them to step back, see their family from a different perspective and reflect on their interactions with anorexia nervosa. They are often surprised when they see their own patterns of behaviour acted out in the other family. Families are often more able to be direct and challenging with each other in ways that they may not accept from professionals.

Carers are given the timetable at the start of the three-day programme. They value both the transparency of knowing what will happen and the opportunity to clarify the aims of the three days. This is explained with a statement such as:

> An eating disorder is a very complex illness. We are not completely sure what is the best form of treatment – however, we do know that if we work together as a tripartite team of patients, carers and professionals we stand a better chance of beating the stranglehold of the illness.

Carers experience and value being involved in such a manner, as this sometimes contrasts with some of their earlier experiences of individual sessions, where they have been passively involved as part of the treatment or formulation process.

DAY ONE

9.30 am	Introductions and welcome
	Explanation of day's programme
	Ground rules
	Anorexia Nervosa: A Survival Guide (Treasure, 1997) distributed to carers
10.00 am	Coffee and snacks all together
10.15 am	What do you need help with?
	What I can cope with and what I cannot cope with
	Work in pairs – feedback and discussion
	(Patients work separately from their families – mums, dads and siblings work together)

10.45 am	Family maps or family tree, resources and strengths
	Past timeline of events around the time the illness started
	Present your family to the group
12.00–12.15	Short break
12.15–1.00 pm	Lunch
1.15 pm	What I can cope with and what I cannot cope with feedback
	Discussion of stages of change
	Plot where the family is in readiness to change and where they think their daughter is
2.00 pm	Draw a future family timeline 'A year in the family's life' (future planning) – everyone
3.00 pm	Snacks
3.20 pm	Set homework: Write a letter about 'What it is like to be the father/mother/sister/brother/partner of a person with an ED'
	'What it is like to be a person with an ED in my family'
4.00–4.30 pm	Check out how people are before leaving and finish

DAY TWO

9.30 am	Introduce today's programme and answer questions from previous day
10.00 am	Coffee and snacks all together
10.20 am	Homework feedback: 'What it is like to be the father/mother/sister/brother/partner of a person with an ED'
	'What it is like to be a person with an ED in my family'
12 noon	Lunch
12.45 pm	Break
1.15 pm	Family sculpt
	What is your family like now?
	How would you like your family to be?
3.00 pm	Snacks
3.20 pm	Set homework: Write a letter to your daughter/son/partner/sister/brother about 'What you mean to me'.
	The person with an ED writes about 'What the eating disorder means to me'
4.00–4.30 pm	Check out how people are before leaving and finish

DAY THREE

9.30 am	Introduce today's programme and answer questions from previous day
10.00 am	Coffee and snacks all together
10.20 am	Homework feedback on the letters: 'What you mean to me'
	'What the eating disorder means to me'
12 noon	Lunch

12.45 pm	Break
1.15 pm	Reflective listening practice
2.30 pm	Review of 'What I need help with'
3.00 pm	Snacks
3.15 pm	Families' feedback: 'What went well'
	'What we would have liked to have done differently in the programme'
	Summing up: professionals offer verbal motivational feedback
	Final questions
	Future plans: 'What we will work on'
	'What we may need more help with'
4.30 pm	Check out how people are before leaving and thanks.

Day 1

Introductions and welcome

The two therapists running the meeting welcome the families in a warm and hospitable style, acknowledging the time and effort they have made to attend. Name badges are given to everybody at this stage. Throughout the workshop the therapist models and uses the skills of motivational interviewing. The therapist starts by reflecting on the positive and affirming the family.

- You obviously care so much for your daughter and her health to take the time and effort to help in this way.

The therapist introduces the timetable and plan for the three days, including how the meals will be organised. The therapist sets the scene by describing the aim of the work, which is to form a partnership between professionals, carers and people with an ED. The aim is to share knowledge, experience and ideas between all parties. Everyone has something to teach and share with the others. The sort of conversation that it might be helpful to have with family members goes like this:

- We need you to help us to help your daughter.
- You are the experts when it comes to your daughter.
- We need to join forces to stop the eating disorder taking control.
- The information you have about your daughter is invaluable to us when trying to help you work to prevent relapse after discharge.
- The main aim of these meetings is to share together the information and skills that we all possess. We have found that working in this way can improve the quality of life for family members, and also the outcome for the patient.

The therapist shares the ground rules about the days. These follow basic rules of good communication:

- We stress the importance of needing to observe confidentiality about the other family's information.
- We ask that only one person speak at a time and people will take turns to speak.
- We explain that this is because we believe that what everyone has to say is important.
- We also ask everyone to respect what the other person is saying, even if they disagree with it.

It is the therapist's job is to make sure that everybody gets a chance to speak. This is always carried out with respect:

> We may delay some people's contributions in order to include the participation of people who may be shy. During the meeting if people start speaking at once, I will remind you of our ground rules and you will soon get the hang of it.

At times it may be necessary to move a family along faster or in different directions with different people contributing. Again, the therapist does this in a respectful way.

> We want to hear what you think about these different issues, and we appreciate how candid you are being with us. Also, we are conscious of the time so we are going to move us along because we have a lot to cover. It is important to understand as many different parts of your family life from as many perspectives as possible.

Everyone writes their name on a sticky label. A useful ice-breaker and way of starting to get to know each other is to ask people to say something about their name, if it has a meaning, who chose it, is it a family name, if they like it and whether they have a nickname. This is often very helpful because it tends to relax people as someone often has an amusing story and is a way of introducing the notion that humour can be an important tool to tackle the eating disorder. It may also provide information about family patterns that need discussing at a later point, e.g. 'My grandma chose my name but my dad wanted to call me something else'. The therapists start this process by sharing something about their name.

In this first phase, the therapist tries to understand the family background including their handling of problems and difficulties in the past. Whenever possible, the therapists support a spirit of mastery and hope, doing everything in their power to allay guilt. Also, the therapist indicates that blaming, scapegoating and recrimination are not part of the ethos of the meeting:

> With the benefit of hindsight mistakes are easier to see. If we are to optimise our choices in life, we have to be flexible and some decisions will not be as good as others. That is how we learn and get experience. Mistakes, in the process of review, can be regarded as treasures as they offer the opportunity for reflection, understanding (what happened) processing and reparation. You may want to talk about those decisions or behaviours that may have been less than optimal or not so helpful. It is important, however, to bear in mind that this is not about blame. None of us can see the future and we try to make decisions in good faith. One of the temperamental traits that people with anorexia nervosa have is a terror about making mistakes. We think that such a tendency shrinks their life. We will try and acknowledge our mistakes, as we think that this models a flexible way of handling life rather than expecting a mistake-free experience.

At an early stage the therapist needs to include the concepts expressed in the following examples:

> All families are different and need different things. Therefore, during the first day we will gather information in a variety of ways. The different exercises we do give you the opportunity to look at things from various perspectives. It may also prompt you to think of things you hadn't thought of before. We have a philosophical belief that the perfect family does not exist. All families have problems and it is how they try to resolve these that is important.

> One of the reasons we developed this form of intervention was because we knew that levels of high expressed emotion in families where a member had a mental illness could be a problem. High expressed emotion is defined in terms of critical or hostile remarks and over-involvement. This can also produce depression and anxiety in carers and lead to carers pulling in different directions. One aim of this intervention was to reduce these where they were present.

Exercise 1: Working in pairs to clarify 'What do you need help with?'

Following this introductory phase the therapist asks the group to pair up with a member of the other family, if possible, putting mums and dads together, and patients in a separate group, and asking each group to generate a list of things that they need help with (families are encouraged to work with different people when the opportunity arises). This procedure is intended to encourage families to get to know one another and prepare an agenda of issues they want help with. This way of working enables people to hear fresh perspectives and helps question fixed family attitudes. The groups take their turn to feed back their ideas to the group as a whole.

Examples of issues carers of people with an ED need help with may include the following:

- how to cope with refusal to eat
- how to cope with lies
- how to manage vomiting, mood swings, isolation, relapse or self-harm
- how to communicate
- how to deal with arguments.

Examples of issues that people with an ED need help with may include the following:

- how to be respected by their families
- how to communicate
- how to be allowed to become independent
- how to have a relationship with their siblings.

The therapist uses reflective listening approaches to clarify any difficulties or solutions that may arise during this process. During the feedback sessions, the therapist aims to defuse criticism and generate warmth through accurate empathy. The therapist will try to incorporate as many of these issues into the three-day agenda as possible. We also explain that some issues raised may need to be topics for further individual or family sessions. Deciding which to leave for other forums is part of the therapist's skill. As confidence with this model develops, however, it is our experience that most issues can be sympathetically explored with the other family 'bearing witness'. Examples of issues that have been discussed with families are a father's attempted suicide, sexual abuse, a parent's affair and a mother's death when the person with the ED was a child.

It is important to explain that these issues may not all be addressed and resolved immediately, by saying that the rest of the programme provides more reflective and problem-solving opportunities.

Exercise 2: Family maps or family tree, resources and strengths

Sharing these between families is a quick way for the two families and the professionals to get to know each other. We emphasise that families only have to share as much as they feel comfortable with, especially if there is some resistance.

We ask each family to stay together to draw their family tree, to cover three generations (including significant others, such as ex-partners or close non-familial relationships), identifying names, ages, deaths (all losses including siblings), marriages, births, divorces, separations, significant events including illnesses and any other mental health issues. Each family will take a turn to explain their map. The following questions may be asked:

- Who do they consider to be in the family?
- What does the extended family know about the illness?
- How has the family coped with previous difficulties? (It is important here to affirm their resilience.)
- What do they consider to be their strengths and struggles?
- Who is there to give them support?
- How big is the social network they can draw on?
- How do the families manage change and loss?

We are often surprised by families' honesty in telling their stories. The families are often surprised by the similarities between them. We stress there are no 'ideal' families but how families tell and retell their stories can influence its members, e.g. 'You're just like Auntie Sue who was shy/the rebellious one'. Sometimes a mother will realise she's falling into similar patterns with her own daughter as the one she experienced with her own mother. Gently enquiring about difficulties that are hinted at can be approached thus:

> I may have got the wrong end of the stick . . . when you were talking about how your mother responded to your miscarriage, you felt she was ignoring your painful feelings . . . have I got this right?

The beginning and end of this statement can be a useful way of taking a step-down approach to encourage the expression of difficult emotions.

Rarely do families refuse to share their histories. On one occasion when this happened, however, rolling with resistance helped, by acknowledging the family's right to privacy but asking them to clarify the one piece of information the mother had already shared. This opened up the issue of a bereavement that the daughter then explained was a factor in the mainten-ance of her illness because she felt she needed to protect her father from her emotions.

Exercise 3: What I can cope with and what I cannot cope with

The next exercise for the work in pairs is for carers to describe what they can or cannot cope with, some examples of which are listed here:

- the sufferer's depression
- outbursts or temper tantrums
- the possibility of the sufferer's death
- the fact that eating is such a natural, normal behaviour that their loved one won't or can't do
- stigma – what the neighbours are thinking about them
- the change in their loved one, from the loving, caring person she was to this prickly individual that they can't talk to
- looking at her the way she is
- not knowing what to do
- lack of services in the community and how to engage or get information from community services.

Throughout the exercise we weave in our understanding of the illness and the maintaining factors that underpin it. We model reflective listening to tackle unhelpful communication, for example we ask people who may be critical to address the person they are criticising by their first name, rather than as 'you', and encourage them to explain the impact that the behaviour they don't like has on them by encouraging a parent to ask, for example,

- Julie, when you isolate yourself, I feel at a loss to know how to support you. Could you tell me how I can reach you at these times?

Exercise 4: Past timeline of events around the time the illness started

This can help put the triggers for the illness into perspective. It usually shows a combination of factors that led up to the illness, some of which are external to the family – helping shift the sense of blame. It also identifies 'stressors', e.g. exams or bereavements that may need further therapeutic work or the learning of more helpful coping strategies, e.g. anxiety management. Stepping back from the present details of the ED can be used to help build discrepancy by looking at the 'bigger picture' and thus enhance motivation.

Exercise 5: Future family timeline

The therapist then asks the family to look towards the future and to comment on what everyone in the family will be doing in six months, one year and five years' time. This is done by drawing a timeline on a whiteboard or a piece of drawing paper and marking down how the different family members see the future. The therapist suggests the family starts by thinking about forthcoming events. As with Exercise 4 this work is done in family groups but brought back to the large group for discussion. The aim of this exercise is, first, to try to increase motivation by thinking about future goals, creating dissonance between the situation now and in the future, and second, setting appropriately sized goals in order to improve the quality of life.

The therapist must be mindful of the stage of change of the different family members. This is not always easy as illustrated by the following example. When asked to think about the future, K (a person with anorexia nervosa) got angry, loud and distressed:

K: This is impossible – you are asking me to do too much being here with my family and eating with them is hard enough. Expecting me to think about the future that's impossible.

Therapist: It sounds as if you are really struggling at the moment. Thoughts of the future are too much. Can you tell me a bit more about that, please?

K then talked about the changes that she had started to make and her struggle with them. This enabled the other family members to see how resistance arose because K had been asked to do something that was not matched to her stage of change. The therapist's reaction illustrates how to reflect and roll with resistance. In the interchange that followed, K talked about the fact that although she had gained the weight, in her head she was still struggling. This practical example illustrated to the families present how important it is for carers to learn to stay with the sufferer's distress rather than move to the stage of change they would like to see the sufferer at. Any discrepancy between the readiness of the person with anorexia nervosa to change and the family's perception of it can cause intense frustration and distress.

After K had talked about the awfulness of her situation and how bad she was feeling – she excitedly said she did want to have some home leave in about four weeks. Thus, the therapist was then able to go back to the future timeline, set it for four weeks rather than for months or years and look at what steps she would need to take to achieve the goal of home leave.

The therapist acknowledged this mistake and gives the family an affirmation.

> I made a mistake when I asked you to work at thinking of the future in several years. What I have heard you and your family say is that they need to be more practical and think of the future in terms of weeks. That is great as it shows that people want to work hard thinking of strategies that they can use now. Let's develop plans and think about the steps we will need to implement them.

Homework writing tasks – for the evenings after Day 1 and Day 2

The first homework task is for the members of the family to write letters. This is an exercise that ensures everyone has the opportunity to reflect on and express their thoughts and feelings. Written exercises have been found to help people process their emotions and we give more of the background of this in Chapter 10. The development of a narrative enables family members to get an overview and a different perspective on their situation. We ask all family members (parents, siblings and person with the ED) to describe how the ED has affected them and the family. If younger siblings are present, we may ask them to draw a picture. The letter writing is a good way of facilitating a discussion about emotions. A characteristic of people with anorexia nervosa is that they avoid or suppress thinking about emotional issues. This trait can also run within their family making communication about emotions incredibly hard. Written exercises are a useful means of getting to grips with difficult feelings and they enable people to reflect on problems and difficulties in their own time and at their own pace.

It is very rare for family members not to do these tasks in their own time. Occasionally this does happen and the therapist will give time during the session for people to do this writing task. The therapist may say something like,

> We'll give you ten minutes to write your thoughts and ideas. Here are some pens and paper. The morning won't go as planned unless we can all share our ideas.

When a father commented, 'I feel like a naughty child', the therapist apologised saying, 'I must sound like a nursery school teacher. It is not intended like that. However, *we need you* to do this part of the programme.'

Throughout all of the three days, it is important for the therapists not to be too straightlaced; they should use humour and warmth to encourage and motivate people to collaborate effectively. The therapist needs to be sensitive with regards to non-completion of homework. One mother, for example, confided in the therapist that she couldn't read or write. The therapist organised for this mum to use a dictaphone and her letter was transcribed for her. The therapist suggested to her that she tell the group that she found it too difficult to read the letter out loud and to pass it to the person next to her to read. People frequently get so emotional when reading that they often hand it over to be read by someone else.

The letters are a vital part of this aspect of family work, because they facilitate emotional processing. They can help the family to cope with living with an ED. It is hard for some people to be able to analyse what makes things problematic and how to recognise their emotional reaction. It gives all family members, even the most shy and tongue-tied, the opportunity to voice all of the things that are unsaid, in a way that they can be heard. This produces a new form of communication between family members. If families find letter writing useful, we encourage them to use this form of communication at home, that is to swap letters and read them out as a starting point for a home meeting. This can be very powerful if families are not used to affirming (affirmations are an important aspect of motivational interviewing). If there is a tendency for the carers to be critical, then having time to think about a positive comment can really move the person with the illness through the cycle of change.

Feedback from the written task on living with an eating disorder

The 'What it is like to live with an ED' letters can highlight difficulties and pinpoint areas that may be a useful focus of work. We discuss how the therapist might deconstruct these letters and work on them to build on more adaptive reactions to the illness in Chapter 10. These letters often contain the thoughts and beliefs that underpin the negative emotions which are rated as 'high expressed emotion'. They may, for example, contain misperceptions about the illness such as mistaken ideas about the cause of the illness or unrealistic optimistic or pessimistic ideas about cure and change. Often these letters mirror the temperamental traits of the person writing them. Thus, there may be evidence of high trait anxiety with exaggerated fears about the illness. This may underpin the tendency to act in over-protective ways. Parents may have some of the traits of an avoidant personality and have difficulty tolerating emotions and regard emotions as if they are something shameful.

Writing about anorexia nervosa can highlight the negative aspects of anorexia nervosa and the problems it causes within the family. The therapist is able to use this to facilitate motivation to change and to decide what issues and problem areas need to be addressed within the intervention. This task can also serve to illustrate the models of the illness that individual family members have in terms of causes, consequences, cure and so on. In some cases, maladaptive attributions about the illness can underlie some of the interactions that can reinforce the illness. We encourage all parties, parents, siblings and the person with anorexia nervosa to share with each other, if possible, the letters they have written that describe life with anorexia nervosa in the family. After each person has read their letter, we ask them, for example:

- What was it like to write them and to read them out loud?
- How do you feel now?

We ask the person with AN what she feels or thinks on hearing the letter and whether there any questions she would like to ask. Other participants are also asked for their responses. Although difficult emotions are often expressed, patients say they prefer to know, rather than guess, what their carer feels about living with the illness.

These letters can be the starting point of a general discussion about unhelpful thoughts, reactions and interpretations to anorexia nervosa. One strategy is for the therapist to normalise the common problems that arise and explore whether they are relevant:

> We commonly find that one of the difficulties in managing anorexia nervosa is being able to strike the correct balance between how much the individual with anorexia nervosa is left to take responsibility of caring for themselves and how much a carer is drawn in to help protect them from adverse consequences for both the short and long term. Do you as a family think that you have got this balance right – or do some of you feel uncomfortable with what you do?

The above question explores whether a kangaroo response, compulsive caregiving, is present, whereas the following question explores whether a rhinoceros approach is typical (see Appendix 1).

> Sometimes we find that many families like to have things very clear. They like life and people to follow consistent rules. Thus, they may try to apply such rules to the anorexia nervosa part and enter into protracted logical discussion, debates and arguments. Does this happen in your family?

Themes in the letters can provide a useful opportunity for practical cognitive restructuring with the family. When a causal misattribution appears, for example, the therapist may ask other family members or the other family how much they share that belief, e.g. self-blame. Sometimes it can be helpful to get everyone to score the strength of their beliefs in the identified theme, on a linear scale 1–10, and then compare scores. Also, the therapist can feed back how strongly the consensus of expert professional opinion would rate that belief. If the therapist considers that one or more family members have become stuck into maladaptive patterns, e.g. over-protectiveness, she may ask other family members to comment. An alternative response is to ask that person what they would say if a friend was behaving like they are doing. Similarly, if the therapist identifies controlling behaviour, fuelled by perfectionist standards, this can be explored with the group, in an effort to encourage more realistic expectations. If the other family is able to model more helpful responses, for example stepping back and allowing the sufferer to take safe risks this can encourage the 'kangaroo' carer to act in a similar manner. If both families exhibit parallel behaviours, it can be helpful to ask them to step into each other's shoes and to comment on how anorexia is controlling them. It may be easier for them to be honest with the other sufferer rather than their own offspring and for it to be heard as a new voice.

Day 2

Emotional expression and processing

Emotions can get very fraught throughout the intervention. Some people express their hurt directly whereas others find it more difficult. The therapist needs to set the boundaries about emotion expression for the group. The family are told that it is all right to express their distress and the whole range of human emotions from tears to rage and laughter. The aim of the family work, however, is not to dwell on negative emotions, but to use them as markers to point out where things may be less than optimal. They can help get an understanding of what the family might need to do in order to make the situation more bearable. Loss is a major theme among family members and the expression of sorrow for the tragedy caused by such a severe illness is common.

Family sculpt

The family sculpt offers a non-verbal way of communicating within the family which can 'fit' with different communication styles from the letters. It gives the people with anorexia nervosa the opportunity to communicate their needs and feelings about the family. It is a task that is used to highlight the sense of discrepancy between current family relationships and preferred relationships for the future. The therapist builds upon this discrepancy to engender the motivation for change.

The aim of the task is for the patient, first, to describe their current relationship with the family, and second, to describe their preferred family relationship using the family sculpt as a tool. If there is time, other family members may also do this task. Siblings, for example, offer an opportunity to model family relationships that are not distorted by the illness. The instructions given to the person directing the sculpt (the person with anorexia nervosa) is that she is to choose someone to be her to enable her to be the 'director' to position 'actors' (the members of her own family, plus people from the other family present to stand in for absent significant other members of her family, e.g. grandparents). She is asked to position them in such a way that it resembles how she feels currently in relation to her family that represents the emotional closeness or distance she has to family members and that they have to each other. The 'actors' can be standing, sitting or moving and can be inside or outside the room. The person with anorexia nervosa is then asked why she put people where she did and each actor is asked to report on their feelings on being placed in such a situation. It is important that the therapist and family members do not analyse or comment on other people's positioning or feelings at this point. It is common for the person with anorexia nervosa to position the person who is standing in for her a long way away from the rest of the family, illustrating the profound sense of isolation and alienation typically experienced by people with anorexia nervosa. This sculpt often raises a number of interesting issues that may need to be followed up in later work, such as how separated parents constructively communicate.

This is followed by an exercise in which the task is repeated, but this time illustrating how the person directing the sculpt would *like* the family to be. Once again, there is feedback from each of the actors about what it feels like to be in that position. In general, there is a wish to change the family interactions so that there are closer, more balanced connections between the family members. Once one family have done their sculpts, it is then the turn of the other family.

On completion of all the sculpts, time is then set aside for reflection. How does everyone feel about the sculpt? Does anyone have questions for participants? If families have conflicts, can the other family suggest strategies for resolution? How can the family get from the first sculpt to the second, preferred position?

A common portrayal is for one family member to be down one end of the room, another at the opposite end with the person with anorexia nervosa in the middle. The most common desired image is for the family to form a circle so that there is equal access and closeness to everyone but with parents closer to each other and slightly away from their children. The family sculpt, like the letters, develops a new form of communication within the family. The therapist uses this as an opportunity to reflect on whether the anorexia nervosa may be serving a positive function within the family. Sometimes what is wanted is not possible, for example for a deceased parent to be back with the living parent or for separated parents to reunite. Acknowledging this need and the associated emotions of sadness and anger for these powerful feelings to be heard and tolerated by the parents is a crucial step in moving on from the eating disorder.

One of the most common themes to emerge is the need for a sense of safety to help control the fear of threats posed by the world. A lack of this sense prevents family change and limits the children's move towards independence. Anorexia nervosa can allow an individual to develop a pseudo-autonomous stance, as if they are independent of others. This has some positive factors for them as it is simple, with no expectations and serves to avoid coping with interpersonal issues that are difficult. The downside of such an approach is that it leads to loneliness and an anxious and impotent family. In order to help the person with anorexia nervosa move from the pseudo safety of the illness, the family need to strike a balance between providing support or stifling them by over-protection. Many sufferers come up to the therapists afterwards and say:

- Thank you, I've never been able to tell my parents how I felt and I have been able to do it today.

Often the parents are shocked and surprised by the messages that get conveyed during the family sculpt:

- My goodness, I had to come here and do this to learn how my daughter feels.

Day 3

Feedback from letters

The second letter, set as a homework task at the end of the second day, is addressed to the person with an eating disorder telling them what she or he means to the family member. This letter generates warmth, compassion and other positive emotions. Sufferers often report that they didn't fully realise their families' positive emotions towards them or the loss of connection that anorexia nervosa causes. This can provide the sufferer with support to challenge the illness.

It is usual for the letters to be shared among the group, with the people with eating disorder present. This brings out an intense emotional atmosphere and there are often many tears. Although the majority of people want to share their letters with the rest of the family, they do have a choice about whether to do so, along with where and how. In most cases, however, this occurs within the sessions and can be used to increase warmth.

The 'What you mean to me' letters also elicit a great deal of emotion. If and when parents share the letters about what their daughter or son means to them, with the sufferer, the therapist asks the daughter or son how they reacted to the content of the letter and if they were aware beforehand of any of the issues raised in the letter. The usual answer is that they are surprised at the contents and knew very little of it. We have had cases where daughters have cried for a day after discussing the letter because they have been touched by the poignancy of the feelings.

Other family members are often very ignorant about each other's feelings, as there may be a family pattern to suppress rather than express emotions. A father might say how much he loved a child, for example, and it often happens that the reply goes

- I had no idea, because you have never told me you loved me, I never knew you loved me, I didn't even think you cared about me.

Many of the letters describe the life story of the person with anorexia nervosa:

- When you were born you were the most precious thing that ever entered into my life, you were perfect, beautiful and it is intolerable that anorexia has caused a change.

Some go back as far as a description of a seed in their body, which has now become the person.

- I've had to watch you fade away, it's unbearable, I feel powerless.

These letters can be a very useful way of helping the sufferer to move on, especially if the relationship between the parents and the sufferer has been somewhat barren, with little warmth and not much emotional content. Interestingly there is usually a lot of warmth, a lot of caring and also a lot of suffering expressed within the letters. People can usually separate their feelings about the illness from those they feel towards their daughter and they may say:

- I'm not getting at you, love, it's just the illness I cannot stand.

These letters can form a bridge for a family member who had previously been rejected by the daughter. As a result, new relationships can be forged within split families. After family separations, the children often use black-and-white thinking and assume that it was the father's fault or the mother's fault, attributing all blame to that particular person in the breaking up of the family. These letters present both sides of the argument. It allows the person with anorexia nervosa the opportunity to understand that both parents love her dearly, whatever the difficulties in the parental relationship. If there is animosity between separated parents, stress the importance of parents working together to support the person with AN. They don't have to be friends, only agree on the way forward.

The sufferers' letter on 'What the eating disorder means to me' usually incorporates the pros and cons of the illness (part of the individual therapy). This enables a safer discussion about the difficulties of change when, for the sufferer, anorexia provides both positives as well as negatives. When one family hears the sufferer from the other family describe similar gains from what to the family is so destructive, it is harder to simply refute these ideas. Encouraging reflective listening helps families and sufferers understand each other.

Often difficulties in the relationship have arisen because of the illness. The letters allow the families to discuss thorny issues in a controlled way. It may need two or three future meetings to go over the letters. It may be impossible to share it all in one meeting as it can become very emotional and too much at one time.

Teaching communication skills

In this part of the three days, the therapists discuss with the family, models of health behaviour change and basic facts about anorexia nervosa. They are introduced to the interpersonal maintenance model and asked to reflect on how much time they spend being either an ostrich, kangaroo, rhinoceros or a jellyfish. They are then encouraged to make a functional analysis of patterns of interaction within the family. The main part of this session is spent on teaching skills, such as good communication and reflective listening. This is a playful way of thinking about planning more helpful interactions. We encourage individuals to grade both themselves and other family members on these tasks and to monitor change over time. Most of the time is used to practise these strategies. In feedback about this intervention, it is common for families to ask for more time to practise reflective listening.

Reflective listening practice

Reflective listening shows that you have been listening carefully and remembering what the other person has said. It is used to re-emphasise specific aspects of what the person has said by including and highlighting these themes. It also allows the therapist to change direction in a gentle and positive way to draw your period of listening to a close and move on to the next task (Rollnick et al., 2008: 75). There are several ways of reflecting, for example, paraphrasing, emphasising inferred emotions, reflecting both sides of ambivalence, thus on the one hand, you find it hard to finish your meal and on the other hand, you notice you are tired.

Families' feedback: 'What went well?' 'What we would have liked to have done differently in the programme?'

This section is done in pairs, giving participants the opportunity to give us feedback about both their personal experience of the three days and how we could build on the work we do with families.

Summing up: professionals offer verbal motivational feedback

During the wind-up session, the therapists summarise the issues that came up during the three days. They draw on what has been said in the letters and the sculpt to formulate the families' difficulties and strengths. The families are encouraged to summarise what they have gained from the three days and how they plan for the future. The feedback is given to the group as a whole. We welcome each family to comment on each other's feedback. The therapist indicates that the three days is merely the start of a process that can then be continued as part of the agenda for future individual family work.

The feedback is given using the approach of motivational interviewing, in order to promote a sense of partnership with the family. This involves being honest and straightforward, avoiding jargon and avoiding being authoritarian or didactic. It involves a listening process, with the family given time and opportunity to react and talk about the feedback. The therapist uses reflective listening to deepen understanding about their comments. The therapist is warm and emphasises family strengths and does not focus just on weaknesses.

The therapist summarises the issues that the family have identified as important for further development:

> I am impressed with the commitment you as a family have shown to start to communicate about some difficult issues. I wonder whether you would like to spend further time on some of the themes you have talked about over these three days. There are several issues that have emerged and these may have prompted you to think of more. There are, for example, practical issues about mealtimes and managing anger. Also, the relationship between X and her siblings are difficult at the moment. Is this right? Are there other areas that we have not mentioned? Have you any thoughts about which of the areas you want to continue work on?

The therapist tries to set the goals collaboratively. The families are also asked about the good and not so good aspects about the days. Often parents say something like

• We've spoken more in these three days than we have spoken in all our married life.

Closing

The therapist thanks the families for coming and working together over the three days. A follow-up appointment is made. The therapist indicates that they will be interested in further feedback and reflection on the process. It is helpful to schedule follow-up sessions to review progress even if there is no plan to work with the family on change. These follow-up sessions can mop up unresolved issues. If the family have made improvements it can be helpful to examine what strategies they have implemented which can add to their sense of mastery and self-esteem. This validation and support can be very helpful.

A useful structure for follow-up sessions

The families are asked for an agenda for the meeting and think about:

- What difficulties did you experience as a family before the first meeting?
- What has improved and how did you achieve this?
- Which difficulties do you still experience as a family?
- Which task could help with these difficulties?

It is important to identify and encourage strengths while acknowledging how hard it is to fight anorexia nervosa.

Research findings

We have completed a quantitative and qualitative piece of research into both the process and the outcome of this intervention. We described the caring experience from a qualitative analysis of the texts of these letters (Whitney et al., 2005). We found that misperceptions about the illness and high expressed emotion were often embedded within the text.

In an exploratory study, we found that the level of carers' distress and the difficulties in their caring role were improved by a similar amount of three months and three years after the three-day carers' workshop, as with the more traditional form of family intervention. Also, the individual outcome of the people with anorexia nervosa was similar in that the average body mass index (BMI) had improved from 13.3 to 18.0 kg/m^2 at the end of treatment and settled at 16.5 kg/m^2 at the time of the follow-up at three years.

We have followed up this intervention by asking carers and people with eating disorders themselves about the helpful and less helpful aspects of the intervention. Some of this feedback has been synthesised into our treatment included in this book. The qualitative feedback suggested that there were differences between the treatment approaches with families preferring the structure and clarity of the intensive three-day approach as well as recognising the benefits of working with another family.

References

Rollnick, S., Miller W. R. & Butler, C. C. (2008). *Motivational Interviewing in Health Care: Helping Patients Change Behavior*. New York: Guilford.

Treasure, J. (1997). *Anorexia Nervosa: A Survival Guide for Sufferers and those Caring for Someone with an Eating Disorder*. Hove: Psychology Press.

Whitney, J., Murray, J., Gavan, K., Todd, G., Whitaker, W. & Treasure, J. (2005). Experience of caring for someone with anorexia nervosa: Qualitative study. *British Journal of Psychiatry*, 187: 444–449.

Chapter 13

Coaching methods of supportive skills-based training for carers

Pam Macdonald and Miriam Grover

Introduction

In Chapter 11 we discussed the rationale behind offering family workshops to carers. We discussed how these workshops offer family members and partners the opportunity to become 'expert carers' in their own right. Faced with inadequate knowledge as well as uncertainty over their own responses to the eating disorder, carers frequently experience a sense of helplessness. Feedback to date has shown that equipping them with the skills and training akin to those used by professionals can instil a great sense of mastery and empowerment over their loved one's illness (Treasure et al., 2007). In this chapter we will describe and discuss alternative methods of delivering skills training to an even wider audience. The rationale behind this is to address issues of high demand, scarce resources and geographical and time constraints.

The availability of specialist eating disorders treatments for patients across the UK remains patchy, demonstrating clusters of services in some areas (usually major cities such as London) and a paucity of services in some other areas. Gaining access to effective treatments for the patient is often a challenge. Services are often under-resourced with little time and personnel to offer any substantial form of intervention for carers. This, therefore, negates the possibility of delivering skills-based workshops within many clinical environments. Additionally, even if carers have the opportunity to attend workshops on a regular basis, they may lack the time due to work or other family commitments. Some carers may not feel that their needs are best met within a group format or feel that their learning needs are best met in other ways. An element of 'competition' can be generated in a group such this (as is often seen within patient groups) and this may also discourage some carers from taking part. Alternatively, some people may simply be too distressed to feel able to fully participate in a group-based intervention. Consequently, there remains a need for a range of interventions for carers of people with AN that allows for choice based around issues such as individual learning preferences and time commitments and is not restricted by concerns such as service resources and geographic location.

This chapter looks at ways in which skills training for carers can be administered as a distance learning or support medium via DVDs and the internet. Just as in the workshops, the aim of these programmes is not only to provide psychoeducational information and skills training to carers, but also to provide interpersonal support. Delivering effective interpersonal support is obviously more challenging when working with carers at a distance. Nevertheless, we hope that by offering a series of telephone coaching sessions or regular guidance and support via email, this can provide an acceptable substitute for the face-to-face contact that would be available in the workshop sessions.

Method 1: DVDs, manual and telephone coaching

The didactic and skills-based content of the workshops have been transferred onto a series of five DVDs. These consist of three theoretical DVDs (Collaborative Caring 1, 2 and 3) and two practical skills DVDS (Problematic Behaviour and Supported Eating). By using role-play scenarios, these DVDs illustrate those communication, assessment and motivational skills required to overcome abnormal eating behaviour. A book, written with a carer and a former sufferer, accompanies the DVDs and provides both theoretical and practical rationales for the training (Treasure et al., 2007).

In a pilot study (Sepúlveda et al., 2008), results showed that participants expressed high levels of satisfaction with most aspects of the DVD training, reporting some lessening of psychological distress and depression after the intervention. The study concluded that the DVDs appeared to be an acceptable and easily disseminated method of delivering skills-based training for carers.

As mentioned above, while the DVDs are designed to replace the practical aspects of the workshops, telephone coaching using motivational interviewing techniques is offered in a bid to replace the interpersonal element of the workshops. In these sessions carers are encouraged to identify manageable target behaviours using the strategies and techniques illustrated in the materials. Below we look at how the coaching process enhances the psychoeducational materials by attempting to boost carer self-reflection and action planning.

The coaching process: introductory session

During the pilot study (Sepúlveda et al., 2008), it was noted that the carers did not always know what to expect from the coaching process, or the philosophy behind motivational work. Consequently, we now send carers written information about what to expect, prior to starting the coaching sessions. This material details the principles behind motivational work along with a short description of the rationale for the programme:

Research shows that carers of people with eating disorders provide high levels of emotional and practical support to their loved one and that this role can often lead carers themselves to have high levels of distress which, in turn, can often lead to unhelpful emotions and behaviours and/or carers colluding with the symptoms.

Some of the key motivational principles are explained along with the fundamental aim of the process, i.e. to experiment with the ways the carer responds to the symptoms by using the techniques and strategies in the materials, in the hope that this will have a positive effect on the sufferer.

The coach will then follow this information up with a short introductory telephone call that reiterates some of the main points in the written guidelines providing clarification, if necessary. The introductory call is also an opportunity for the coach and carer to introduce themselves to each other and for the coach to gather some initial information in preparation for the first coaching session. The coach asks the carer to tell them a bit about their personal circumstances with respect to the eating disorder, how long their loved one has been ill, whether he or she is currently in therapy, an inpatient etc. Practical considerations are also discussed, such as the length of the DVDs and time required to absorb the information and put some of the techniques into practice.

An action sheet is then sent to the carer that lists behaviours they would like to target for next time period (their own and/or the sufferer's), action planning involved, potential obstacles, coping mechanisms they will use or experiment with, obstacles and possible strategies for addressing difficulties. Carers are instructed that this action sheet is merely a guide to encourage their own self-reflection and is entirely optional whether or not they complete it.

Building rapport

Building rapport is more difficult to establish with telephone coaching than it would be with face-to-face contact, as there are no visual cues to guide the coach. Despite the lack of non-verbal cues, such as facial expression or body language, it is, nevertheless, still possible to build rapport in a reasonably short period of time. The introductory session provides an excellent opportunity to set the foundations for a constructive working relationship by noting, for example, the carer's tempo, tone and general demeanour so that this can be matched and mirrored during the actual sessions in order to establish and build a positive connection with the carer. The advantages for the carer are that he or she knows exactly what to expect and whom he or she will be working with, indicated here by the following quote:

> It was really good that . . . because I knew what was going to happen and I knew who I was going to be talking to and everything.
>
> (Carer, in response to helpfulness of introductory session)

After the introductory session, three coaching sessions of about 40 minutes' duration are offered at two to three weekly intervals.

Coaching session 1

The aim of the first session is to work with the carer's self-reflection on their current behavioural and emotional responses to the illness. Open questions designed to elicit this information are used with the carer. The coach uses motivational techniques (discussed in Chapter 7) when working with the carer. Unique caring styles are discussed as well as their responses to the eating disorder and whether or not this is working for them. By frequently affirming the carer's strengths as well as reflecting back on what the coach is hearing, the coach attempts to strike up a communicative 'dance' approach (elicit, guide, elicit) in order to motivate and encourage the carer to come up with potentially different ways in which he or she can experiment with and implement some of the techniques and strategies in the intervention materials.

The coach, for example, may draw the carer's attention to the possibility that carer responses can sometimes play a role in maintaining or aggravating the illness. The carer is then asked for their feelings on this. The carer is encouraged to use this information to reflect on their own responses in guiding their goal setting and action planning. The session follows a semi-structured format but generally the main objective of the session is for the carer to think about the animal analogies that best represent their behaviour, along with any useful strategies for behaviour change utilising the techniques and tools in the materials. Towards the end of the session, carers are asked what goals they can think of that they can experiment with for next session. Carers are encouraged to set specific, achievable and realistic goals that can be attempted in a timely manner, i.e. ones that are not likely to set them up for possible failure but those that can also challenge the behaviours in an appropriate manner. Examples of questions for the first session include:

- Thinking about the animal model, which animal would you choose for yourself?
- Can you give me an example of your Kangaroo/rhinoceros/ostrich/jellyfish behaviour?
- How important do you think it is that you change?
- What do you need to change in your behaviour?

The following transcript exemplifies a typical excerpt from the first session where the coach and the carer engage in *change talk*. We have illustrated the process elements that are being used:

Coach: What were your thoughts on the animal analogies? [*Open question*]

Carer: Well, I can see very much, where I fit in. I'm overly protective and possibly need to change my approach to be more like the dolphin and less like the kangaroo?

Coach: The kangaroo. What examples of your kangaroo behaviour can you think of? [*Simple reflection + open question*]

Carer: Well, always sort of fretting, always making her feel that she can't make decisions off her own back any more, about all sorts of things, not just about food but particularly about food. I have to be the one who decides what she's going to eat. If, on the rare occasion, we do go out and she's faced with a menu, she can't make a choice off her own back. She has to ask me. I have to decide for her and I think what I've got to do is try and stop doing that and instead say to her, 'Well, you've got to decide for yourself' . . .

Coach: Leaving the food talk to the side for a moment, can you think of any ways you can allow her to make decisions outwith the eating? . . . You said you tend to make decisions in all areas of her life. [*Shifting focus + closed question + complex reflection*]

Carer: Well, because she's not really doing very much, it's quite hard to see how I can, but I suppose really it's just a way of encouraging her to try and get more involved in things outside of home and the illness and try and make arrangements to actually go out and see people and do things . . . I mean the exercising thing is a big problem for us because she goes mad with it and that's all she really wants to do, so I need to try and encourage her to do other things.

Coach: How important do you think it is for you to stop the kangaroo behaviours? [*Open question*]

Carer: Well, I can see that if I want her to change her attitude, then I probably need to change mine.

Coaching session 2

The second session begins with the coach asking for a brief outline of how things have been going since the previous session. Goals are discussed and whether or not they were achieved. If they were not achieved, the coach will then ask what has been going well. In most cases, there are some green shoots. If the carer finds it difficult to name any, then the coach will help out by reiterating the positives from the previous session. The motivational spirit is maintained at all times.

Meanwhile, the aim of the second session is to establish that the carer understands the concept of change in relation to whatever particular stage of change their son or daughter is in. They are then encouraged to tailor communication to personal circumstances using the tools illustrated in Collaborative Caring 2, e.g. OARS, DARN-C questions (see Chapter 11). If the carer has difficulty coming up with their own ideas to promote change in their loved one, the coach may ask permission to offer a list of strategies in whichever stage of change applies to their specific situation (pre-contemplation and contemplation strategies etc.) or reflect on strategies that other carers may have experimented with. Examples of questions and reflections from a typical second session include the following:

- What strategies or action plans can you make to help encourage your daughter to (further) contemplate change thoughts?
- Were you able to use open questions? If so, can you give me an example?
- Sounds like you're saying that you feel your unassertive behaviour is interfering with your ability to try out some of the techniques.
- It sounds like you've gone out of your way again and again to try and make things work for your son. What are the green shoots that make you feel a little bit confident?

In the following two excerpts we can see the coach using open questions and reflections in, first, addressing problematic communication, and second, encouraging change talk:

Addressing problematic communication

Carer: M wants to pack up her job and do a diploma in art, which I don't see as a problem but she's never done art, you know, and I'm thinking, 'Well, I don't see how you're going to get on an art course if you've not got a portfolio or anything like that'. We're very different in that respect. Whereas I like to have all the facts and would never just pack my job in before weighing up all the pros and cons, she's the opposite and with this latest idea of hers, she said, 'Well, you are never ever enthusiastic about anything I do' and she go really nasty.

Coach: It sounds like you find some of M's impulsive behaviour quite challenging. Can you tell me more about that? [*Complex reflection + closed question*]

Carer: Well, I wouldn't do anything rash and I have to say I'm torn because if that's what she wants to do and it's going to be good for her then yes, she ought to do it, but on the other hand, the organised part of me says how's she actually going to do it, how's she going to fund it, if she gives up her job where's the money coming from? You have to think of the practicalities but I can't say that because she then accuses me of being negative . . .

Coach: I'm really impressed by your skills of self-reflection and problem solving, A. On the one hand, you want what will make her happy, yet on the other hand, you worry about the practicalities. Can I make a wacky suggestion? [*Affirmation + developing discrepancy/complex reflection + closed question*]

Carer: Yeah go ahead . . .

Coach: What would happen if you said, 'Fair enough that sounds like a fantastic idea' . . . how do you think she would respond? [*Open question*]

Carer: She'd probably turn around and then . . . She'd probably be OK probably . . . It's maybe my fault . . . I have real difficulty with her rash decisions – it could be worth a try though.

Encouraging change talk

Carer: So if I go back to work after her exams, I'm just concerned that she's got the whole of the summer on her own in the house. She has already said, 'I know I'm not good on my own, I want to be as busy as possible and see as many people as possible' but when she wakes up and she's feeling low and sub- dued, the last thing she's sort of thinking about is motivating herself to get out. It's sort of me saying, 'Well, go on . . . you're going to go out, let's go for a walk . . .'

Coach: That's fantastic that you are coming up with all these ideas. It also sounds rather exhausting for you! [*Affirmation + complex reflection*]

Carer: Yeah it can be . . .

Coach: The statement, 'I know I'm not good on my own, I want to be as busy as possible' sounds interesting. What open question could you use to pass a certain amount of responsibility and control for her well-being back to her again? [*Complex reflection + open question*]

Carer: Well, I suppose I could have asked her what sort of ways did she have that she could keep herself busy . . .

Coach: That sounds like a fantastic open question [*Affirmation*]

Carer: . . . and start planning for that really – I think we need to start thinking about some action planning.

Coaching session 3

The third session again starts with a brief summary of the situation, posi- tives, difficulties encountered and how these were dealt with. The main aims of this session is, first of all, to clarify basic psychological rules and strategies that can be used in thinking about behaviour change using the ABC (antecedent-behaviour-consequence) functional model of analysis and to recap on understanding of previous DVDs. Carers sometimes find the ABC model difficult to implement in the home, so with the help of the role-play scenarios from the DVD, the coach and carer may use this session to discuss the triggers that lead to problematic behaviours. These may be 'high-risk' environmental factors, such as people, places and other occasions that spark off a certain behaviour. Triggers can also be internal, the sufferer's thoughts and feelings that can precede, for example, a binge. It can be beneficial to explore the antecedents because in doing so, it can help carers and sufferers realise that the problem behaviour is influ- enced by reasonably predictable external and internal factors. The con- sequences of colluding with or attending to a problematic behaviour may also be discussed. Examples from the third session could include the following:

- What do you think your daughter is *thinking* about right before a binge?
- What do you think she is usually *feeling* right before a binge?
- Can you think of any ideas as to how you can nudge your daughter forwards in any of these areas?
- If you were advising a friend, what would you tell her?
- What consequences are *you* avoiding?
- How do you feel about making those changes?

In another extract, we look at setting boundaries for unacceptable behaviour and how the coach works with the carer through the use of reflective listening and open questions, to encourage her to come up with her own solutions and plan of action to address the unacceptable or maladaptive behaviour:

Setting boundaries for unacceptable behaviour

Carer: I don't see how to get over this hurdle of her pacing up and down when I visit her in hospital.

Coach: So sounds like you're extremely concerned about this particular behaviour. [*Complex reflection*]

Carer: Certainly that one ... I mean I guess she could have a heart attack at any moment but it's not just that – she's in a dangerous place ... which is why she's supposed to be on bed rest.

Coach: That must be really frightening and distressing for you. ... so what are your choices here, P? [long pause] You sound to me frightened that she's doing all this pacing, because there's the risk to her heart. [*Empathy (MI Adherent) + open question +complex reflection*]

Carer: ... and also it's the travesty of the relationship we've had up until now. It's like that 'naughty toddler' and the way to deal with a naughty toddler is to draw the boundaries and yesterday I was allowing it to continue and I felt I shouldn't have done ... we were doing a crossword which we both enjoy and it was a case of colluding with em ... she was pacing up and down and I asked her not to and she just ignored me and I felt, you know, I'm colluding in it.

Coach: I'm impressed that you are reflecting on those interactions in terms of the ABC framework. [*Affirmation + complex reflection*]

Carer: Mmm.

Coach: It's really tough on you – this behaviour is really unacceptable to you. [*Complex reflection*]

Carer: It's unacceptable also for her own good! I'm not putting up with it any more

... I think that's what I've decided ... I'm not putting up with it any more ... I suppose I can go and just leave.

Coach: You're doing a lot of reflecting upon the interactions with your daughter by using the ABC framework, which is really impressive. You sound as if you're planning to change some of the consequences as an experiment ... to examine if it will help change the behaviour you find unacceptable. [*Complex reflection + affirmation + complex reflection*]

Carer: Exactly yeah ... I've decided I'm not putting up with it ... so that's my choice. I'm going to write to her and say that I find it unacceptable. I will come to visit but if you do that then I will leave immediately. I think that's what I'll do. That feels right ...

Coach: Can I make a suggestion? [*Asking for permission – closed question*]

Carer: Yeah go ahead ...

Coach: It's a really good idea to give some warning about how your behaviour will change and what you will and will not accept – a letter can help make it clear. [*Affirmative complex reflection*]

Carer: That's a great idea – thanks, that's what I'm gonna do.

Feedback

Such observations at this point, however, are merely based on anecdotal observation. Later we hope to address this issue as more data are collected. In the mean time, we will conclude by offering a few quotes from carers, thus far, on their experience of a DVD intervention with coaching:

> I felt really alone again after the process had finished ... the one thing that carers don't have ... we don't have the support we need because for a lot of the time we are the people who are, you know, day-to-day, week in, week out ... we are the people who are trying to help the young person and the support in the community's just not there really ... so I kind of put the phone down kicking and screaming on the last phone call I had. So that's a positive, you know, that's a positive comment.
>
> (Mother)

> It's been nice to talk to somebody other than the wife, otherwise you are too close to it. We are both too close to it with different approaches.
>
> (Father)

> It's been really encouraging to have somebody from the outside who's not involved in this at all ... just really, really refreshing.
>
> (Mother)

> It's been very helpful ... because I just got a few pointers and also it's been at a calm time so it's at a time to be calm and considerate and so often it's just so

much easier not to think about it unless it's the middle of the night . . . and that's when it's desperate isn't it?

(Mother)

It was good to kind of talk about what I had seen in the DVDs and applying it to E . . . and it gave me a lot of encouragement to continue trying. So that kind of gave me something to aim for. If I didn't have the telephone coaching to set those objectives then I would not have tried to implement as much of the stuff that I'd learned in the DVDs.

(Sister)

Method 2: Internet-based intervention with telephone or email support

An alternative method of delivering skills-based training for carers using a 'distance learning' style model is through the medium of an interactive internet-based programme (Overcoming Anorexia Online) supplemented with workbooks containing much of its contents (Schmidt et al., 2007) and supported by a clinician either by weekly phone calls or emails to the carer, depending on their personal preference.

The internet programme 'Overcoming Anorexia Online' (Schmidt et al., 2007) was developed in parallel with but separately to the workshops and DVDs. There is some overlap in contents with the workshops and DVDs, and also significant differences. It is underpinned by the philosophy, concepts and aims of chronic disease management (Lorig and Holman, 2003) and adopts the stance of a systemic cognitive behavioural model and techniques (Dummett, 2006).

Central to the internet intervention is a formulation-based approach, teaching carers to apply the use of simple user-friendly formulations to their own situation. This involves separate but interlinked formulations for key family members, designed to help carers understand and act on the difficulties of their family member with anorexia nervosa and their own problematic responses and difficulties in relation to this. This is illustrated through the use of real-life scenarios describing problematic situations, for example, a difficult mealtime interaction between parents and an anorexic daughter, and showing the different vicious cycles of each family member and their interactions and how this serves to keep anorexia going. Different ways of breaking out of vicious cycles are illustrated, for example, by challenging extreme or unhelpful thoughts, reinterpreting physiological responses more accurately, acknowledging and responding to one's own emotions differently or by adopting different strategies for dealing with difficulties.

'Overcoming Anorexia Online' (OAO) is accessible via a website, 24 hours a day, and carers have a variety of resources to access (e.g. accompanying workbooks and recordings of relaxation tapes). The intervention delivers nine multimedia sessions presented using a variety of online media, such as online self-assessment, audio clips and video presentations and role-plays as well as written information. The contents of the sessions and workbooks is summarised in Table 13.1.

Carers often identify a need for support from others who know of and have experienced the particular difficulties and situations that they face as carers. In recognition of these needs, the OAO intervention contains online forums where carers can post messages on message boards asking for advice, guidance and support and to chat with other carers. Such message boards are now common on the internet for a variety of groups of people and are extensively used.

An offline pilot study of OAO has been conducted examining the efficacy and acceptability of the Overcoming Anorexia Online interactive workbooks together with limited (up to 20 minutes) weekly support by phone or email from a clinician. After the intervention, carers experienced many positive changes, including significant reductions in levels of anxiety and depression, expressed emotion and negative experiences of caregiving in addition to improvements in positive experiences of caregiving (Grover et al., in preparation).

At the time of writing, the OAO intervention is being used for the first time in a pilot randomised controlled trial (RCT) comparing the efficacy and acceptability of the programme with informal support provided by 'beat' (the UK's largest charity devoted to supporting people with eating disorders and their carers). It is too early in the research programme to discuss the efficacy and acceptability of this intervention. The multimedia delivery of an online intervention, however, is richer than that of a workbook intervention and therefore may be more engaging for carers, potentially making the information easier to absorb and process. The online delivery also means that OAO can provide some of the benefits of a group-based format (i.e. contact with other carers) without carers actually having to be present at the same place at the same time.

The workbooks are an important component of the internet-based intervention. While the use of a workbook in today's ever more technologically advanced society might seem a rather low-tech choice of delivery method, one of the benefits of this is that the workbooks are themselves highly portable and also very discreet and easy to use. Carers who completed the pilot project commented on this. Some used the workbooks on the bus on the way to work, while others kept them at work to use during their breaks. Carers often created their own binding and referencing systems so that they were able to access the most personally relevant subjects easily. Carers were also able to take the workbooks away with them while on holiday, thereby enabling them to use them as resources if they encountered difficulties while away.

Table 13.1 Contents of Overcoming Anorexia Online

Module 1 and Workbook 1	This gives key information regarding symptoms and diagnosis and discusses myths and misconceptions. It introduces the five-areas approach to conceptualising and understanding problems and the process of CBT. It also introduces Anxiety Control Training (ACT), a form of relaxation technique.
Module and Workbook 2	This focuses on helping carers to understand ambivalence and the difficulties of change using the 'Stages of Change' model (Prochaska and DiClemente, 1984). It focuses on developing the skills needed to communicate effectively with a person who is ambivalent about change and how to avoid unhelpful communication.
Module and Workbook 3	This addresses how anorexia affects families and uses the five-areas approach to identify and understand how unhelpful behaviours and avoidance can result from difficult situations. Carers are encouraged to use the five-areas approach to understand unhelpful behaviours and/or avoidance within the family and break these vicious cycles.
Module and Workbook 4	This concerns how to talk about meal support with the sufferer and make a collaborative plan to address this need. It suggest tools and techniques for giving meal support to facilitate recovery.
Module and Workbook 5	This is about risk and prognosis, including understanding and talking about medical risk with the sufferer and how to prepare for an appointment with health professionals. It identifies situations in which medical risk may increase and how to deal with these.
Module and Workbook 6	This tackles understanding the function of difficult behaviours such as bingeing, purging or self-harm. Carers are encouraged to challenge their own negative beliefs about these behaviours so that they can assist the sufferer to understand and manage them.
Module and Workbook 7	This deals with relapse prevention by helping carers to identify the risk of relapse, helping the sufferer to maintain improvement without 'policing' them, avoiding entering the vicious cycle of reassurance, dealing with setbacks and looking for NHS support.
Module and Workbook 8	This describes the roles of different professionals and different types of treatment for AN, how to access them and their evidence base. It also gives details of additional sources of help such as organisations, books and web-based resources.
Additional Workbook – Carers' Own Needs	This attends to carers' own needs, helping them to identify their own needs, challenge negative beliefs about meeting their own needs and assists them to develop a plan to meet their own needs.

Clinician support

As previously mentioned, OAO is designed to be used with a low level of clinical support. The aim of this is to help carers make the best use of the programme, and to tailor this to their needs, by helping them decide which modules to work on and in which sequence, as is appropriate to their particular personal circumstances. Thus the support is very flexible, and clinicians take their cue entirely from the needs of the carer. This is akin to what happens in Specialist Supportive Clinical Management of anorexia nervosa (McIntosh et al., 2005). Carers are asked whether they would like to receive support via email or the telephone and are encouraged to make their decision based on such factors as their preferences, availability and level of privacy they would have to receive support. The decision to choose one form of support is not set in stone and carers can alter their support medium according to changes in their situation or needs. In the workbook pilot study, about 50 per cent of carers chose email and 50 per cent phone support.

During the first support session, the clinician discusses the format of these and their role in helping the carer with getting the best out of the programme, by helping them choose and guiding them through the most appropriate modules and workbooks. It is emphasised that there is no right or wrong way of using the support and that they can use this as much or as little as they want. Carers are provided with ideas and options for how they might want to use the contact: they may wish to focus on a particular area of difficulty that they are experiencing in their caring role that they were previously aware of or have become aware of during the course of completing the programme. Alternatively, they may wish to use the support to review different situations within their caring role that have occurred during the course of the week and to discuss their understanding of the situation and their responses and discuss the outcome of this and whether these situations could have been addressed differently. Carers may decide that they would like to use the support to reflect on their own emotional coping and to gain support from a qualified, knowledgeable professional who is sympathetic to their difficulties and needs to bolster their efforts. Lastly, carers may wish for a combination of the above methods of support according to their varying needs.

It is important that whatever medium that carers choose to use for their support, that the clinician maintains regular and consistent contact with each carer. In the pilot study, the carers and the clinician agreed regular times for telephone calls to enable the carer to ensure that they had the time and privacy to take the call. This also provided momentum and consistency to the support sessions. While one of the benefits of email to the carers is the ability to gain support without being tied to a particular time or day, it remains important for clinicians to regularly contact the carer by email each week if they have not heard from the carer. By doing this, carers are reassured that they have not been 'forgotten about' and that even if they do not have the time, want or need to contact the clinician, that the clinician remains concerned for them. This view was reinforced by one of the carers who took part in the pilot project, who expressed gratitude that although she often did not have the time to (or need to) email the clinician, she felt cared about and supported by receiving a brief email from the clinician expressing support and inviting a reply.

Building rapport

We have already discussed above how building rapport with a carer is more difficult during telephone interactions where there are no visual cues to contextualise comments and the clinician and the carer need to remain aware of this and mindful of the need to be very clear and unambiguous in their communication with one another. It is important to frequently check understanding to avoid miscommunication and it is important that clinician and carer have an open agreement from the first session that any concerns about what might have been said or any misunderstandings are identified at the time of occurrence and are addressed then.

These issues are even more important in relation to email support where there are even fewer contextual cues than during telephone interactions. In this form of communication, it is essential that information exchange is as clear as possible. The insertion of emoticons may help to clarify or emphasise affective contents. One might initially think that due to this limitation, email support would be the least desirable form of giving support. However, despite these potential problems, there are also unique benefits to giving and receiving support through email. For those carers with busy and irregular lifestyles, for example, email contact is not limited by the same timetable as verbal contact. It is perfectly acceptable to email someone at 2 am (as long as you are not expecting an immediate response!). But perhaps the most important advantage is therapeutic, rather than practical, as communication in writing allows carers to significantly reflect on their situation, by thinking about what issues to raise and how to raise them, how to describe what they have already tried and why this might have worked well or not so well, how they felt about what happened, what questions to ask and what solutions to aim for. This integration of the cognitive and emotional aspects of the issues raised into a more coherent narrative addressed to an empathic, non-judgemental and knowledgeable other (the clinician) are at the heart of what produces change in people using therapeutic writing (see Pennebaker, 2004). Moreover, carers can review their emails before sending them to be sure that they have included all issues they would like to discuss and can keep a record of emails for future reference. These can be used to apply the principles and ideas given by the clinician to a number of different situations.

The medium chosen to receive support does however affect how information is shared between the carer and the clinician. During telephone support the clinician is able to adopt a more clearly CBT-style method of communication. An example of this is the use of the 'Socratic dialogue', where the clinician uses a style of questioning to assist carers to resolve their own difficulties by developing a full understanding of the nature of the problem and how this might be resolved. This can be realistically achieved only through direct conversation because this Socratic questioning is very difficult to conduct meaningfully via email. However (as mentioned above) email allows both carer and clinician to consider and reflect upon the situation at more length and allows the clinician time to consider not only the particular situations addressed within the email but also the bigger picture and to incorporate this within a measured response. Email support may at times be rather more directive than telephone support, although the carer still can be encouraged to develop a greater understanding about the problem and to think of methods of resolution. Receiving a personalised email response giving thoughts and ideas about their difficulties can be very important to carers, and a resource for future use.

Below are some extracts of issues raised and the support given via email from the pilot project using the interactive workbooks.

Developing the confidence to care effectively

MOTHER OF ADULT AN SUFFERER

> I'm a bit late with the latest workbook, partly intentionally because [she] saw the dietician recently, and has been trying to make changes in her rigid eating habits, with mixed success. I thought Book 4 was particularly appropriate to the stage we're at. At first I thought the book not very much related to our situation, with her being an adult and very independent, but as I went on, I realised the essence of the messages and felt them to be very, very valuable . . .
>
> I'm not at all confident about being able to support [her] because she knows a great deal about calorific value, and the AN voice is so strong. I'm scared of damaging our relationship because I'm scared it will be detrimental to [her] health. However, yesterday, we met with [the doctor]: she made it clear how concerned she is and how seriously ill [my daughter] is. I'm scared, but I feel more confident to recognise the AN voice that poor [daughter] is unable to hear it and challenge it.
>
> Our family is pretty chaotic at times; I've had a row with my husband this week, about something completely different, but these things happen. We've

made it up now, but it scares me because we haven't got time to waste on this petty stuff. Overall, we all get on fairly well and care about each other, but for [my daughter], who's been used to living abroad for several years, to come home and return to her childhood bedroom and existence is very hard. She can't forget she's been the explorer of the family.

CLINICIAN

I am so pleased that you found Workbook 4 helpful. I also agree with you that at first it can seem as if the materials are less relevant because of [your daughter's] age, but as you say the essential message is the same and the ideas can be used, perhaps with some adjustment for the person's age and the relationship.

I'm sorry to hear that [your daughter] is struggling and is becoming more ill. I am pleased that her treatment has started. It is so good that you are able to understand how trapped she is in the illness right now. [Your daughter] is very lucky to have you there and for you to be able to spot AN influencing her when she can't see it. There will be a time when she will understand how much you have tried to support her.

I understand how easy it can be to have a row with your husband right now. You are all under a lot of stress and it has to come out one way or another. It's human nature to argue about stuff that feels 'petty'. Don't give yourself a hard time about it – you made up and ultimately being able to resolve these things is the important thing.

Poor [daughter] – I do appreciate how hard it must feel for her to have once been the adventurer and to now come back home. She is still that person underneath the AN and needs to get through it to let that side of her out again.

I also feel for you. You are so worried about her. Can I suggest you jump to Workbook 8 – the one about carers looking after themselves? I think this would be especially important for you as you are under so much stress and are feeling low and panicky. Perhaps you and your husband could look at that together? You could talk it through and make suggestions to each other about how to manage at such a hard time.

COMMENT

The clinician reinforces the carer's reflection and understanding that the materials may need some thought and adaptation to 'translate' them from a generic approach and to make them personally relevant to the carer's own situation. The clinician also reflects that despite the carer's fear of the effect of giving support, the carer does have an understanding of the illness and its effect on her daughter and that that in itself is a great skill and a step forward in helping her daughter. This is to help counter the carer's lack of confidence and to help the carer to recognise the changes that she has already made and put into effect. The clinician also wants to convey that people's understanding and perception of events can change over time according to the person's viewpoint and that while her daughter may not seem particularly happy to receive this support now, her perception at a later date may well change. The clinician reflects on the difficulties of the current home situation from all people's viewpoints (to reinforce the systemic CBT model) by empathising with both the carer and the daughter for the difficulties they are all having and also by inviting the carer to involve her husband in expressing the difficulties that both parents are having to help enhance their understanding of the other's difficulties and discuss how they can work together to support each other.

Dealing with dilemmas in caring

FATHER OF AN ADULT MALE, DIABETIC AN SUFFERER

We're concerned that he may be cutting back on his insulin again and becoming ketotic. The problem seemed to start on Christmas Eve when a friend haphazardly, and quite accidentally, mentioned something about the shape of [his] face. Poor chap looked as though he'd been hit in the stomach, and since then he's taken himself off his [antidepressants] and we've seen a number of symptoms of ketosis, namely: tiredness – falling asleep in the chair in the evening; confusion – playing [a board game] and he was repeatedly unable to move his counter to the correct square; increased thirst – drinking large quantities of water, including during the night, and obviously resulting in increased urination frequency; bingeing – eating large quantities at meals and extra food in between meals and most worrying a smell of ketones on his breath.

... [He] gets irritated whenever reminded about 'doing his insulin' after meals, and refuses to let us know anything about his weight or blood sugar levels. He doesn't look much different in appearance from the last few months, but considering how much he eats, we're surprised that he isn't filling out more.

His [previous] serious attack, the one which left him in Intensive Care for a couple of weeks, was almost exactly a year ago ...

I'm wondering whether to email his diabetic consultant in these circumstances, he is a very helpful and senior chap, but I'm unsure whether he would feel it appropriate to approach him directly. I have emailed and spoken to him in the past about [my son] but as he is such a senior guy, I'm a little nervous about contacting him again directly. However if [my son] is becoming ketotic again, it's obviously important that someone knows before he gets badly ill.

Any comment or advice would be most welcome.

CLINICIAN

I've given your questions a lot of thought and I think that although [he] may be unhappy about you doing this, I am inclined to think that due to the high levels of risk associated with his diabetes, that it would be advisable to explain your observations and concerns to both his Diabetic Consultant and the Eating Disorder Unit. It may also be an idea to be clear to [your son] beforehand that you are going to do this and the reasons for it being your concerns that he runs a risk of serious harm as you have all seen in the past. That way, you can give vital information to people without feeling that you are going behind his back.

It would then be an idea to approach both clinics and tell them of your concerns and what you have observed, as well as your concerns that he may not feel inclined to share all of this with them himself. Perhaps, also let them know that you have told him that you will be approaching them, so that they are aware that he knows. It is then in their hands to address this further with him. You may or may not get much feedback from them but you will know that you have made them aware.

I appreciate the position you are in because it means taking a course of action that may make [him] feel rather angry with you, but as a parent and a carer, it is important that you help him ensure his safety.

COMMENT

This extract shows a carer's request for guidance in a difficult situation. The carer clearly empathises with his son's unfortunate experience and how this must have affected him emotionally, yet this does not overshadow his concern about how his son has responded to this in terms of his behaviour. The carer has fears regarding his son's health that are based on familiar and recognisable signs and symptoms that have been experienced before when his son became very seriously ill. His dilemma on the one hand is that he is gravely concerned and wants to help protect his son's health in a situation that he believes (according the evidence of his observation) has triggered eating disordered behaviours (withholding of insulin) and on the other hand the carer is unsure whether his son or the health professionals involved will welcome his input. While this particular situation is perhaps pertinent to a small group of sufferers and their carers, the experience of a dilemma such as this is very common for carers in trying to establish what is the most appropriate course of action. The response of the clinician allows the carer to feel that his concerns have been taken seriously and acknowledges that dilemmas such as this do occur for carers. The clinician confirms that the carer's inclination to want to discuss this with his wider care team is the responsible thing to do and in effect gives the carer 'permission' or perhaps the confidence to follow through with this course of action.

Establishing a united approach

MOTHER OF AN ADULT FEMALE AN SUFFERER

> Another big problem is balancing the way other members of the family react to my daughter, particularly my husband. He will make a remark that I can see upsets [her]. I want to make everything better and jump in and try and smooth things over and he says I make the situation worse and that [she] was over it. My husband then feels that I take [her] side and he feels left out.

CLINICIAN

> We often advise parents to sit down together and develop a joint strategy on how to deal with situations so that you don't feel split into being the 'good guy' and 'bad guy'. This could take a while because you may need to talk through your respective feelings about how you and each other deal with situations and reach a consensus on how you want yourselves and each other to deal with them in the future.

COMMENT

Again it is a common experience for carers of people with AN to find that they disagree on how to communicate with that person or the situations that arise, with one carer finding themselves in the role of pacifier and others feeling 'pushed out' or excluded. The clinician guides the carer to discuss this with their husband and for each of them to try to understand the other person's feelings about these situations and point of view by understanding what they are thinking in particular situations and how this influences their behaviour. This is in keeping with the Systemic CBT approach. The aim is to resolve such difficulties by helping them to understand how each other's behaviour can often either help resolve a difficulty or reinforce it with the eventual aim of deciding how best to approach certain situations collaboratively.

In summary, despite the limits that telephone and email support can place on communication, there are merits and benefits to these methods as well. Despite reservations that carers and clinicians may initially have, a strong rapport and working relationship can be established with a carer using these media if the potential issues are acknowledged from the start and there is agreement on how to address them. It is also important to remember that for some people, speaking openly to a stranger on a relatively anonymous basis is easier to do than speaking to someone familiar to the person, particularly when talking about issues where there may be stigma attached, hence the popularity of online forums and treatments such as computerised self-help where people have treatment with a 'friendly' computer program and are able to be honest regarding the severity of a problem without fearing judgement or stigma (Duffy and Waterton, 1984).

Carers who took part in the pilot study examining the efficacy and acceptability of the workbook-based intervention with limited clinician support completed feedback questionnaires and/or in-depth qualitative interviews regarding their experience of using the workbook intervention with clinical support. Carers invariably reported that they found the intervention very helpful and that they wished they could have had access to an intervention like this when the person that they cared for first became ill.

Feedback

Extracts from carers' feedback are given below.

Regarding the clinician support

> I think the idea that I was asked whether I wanted to take the support by email or phone call – I think that was really good. Because, you know, it's a choice of what people want to choose. Whether they want to speak to you by email or by phone, and I think it was a really nice personal touch.
>
> (Mother of a young female sufferer)

Telephone support

> I would say that that was you know, one of the main benefits really . . . I just felt that was very, very useful.
>
> > (Mother of a young female sufferer)

> I think it's really good that you can have someone to chat to who seems to know about the situation. Because not . . . obviously not everybody does and they might show their sympathy and . . . feel like they want to offer you their support but it's not the same if you don't really know the illness. I mean, it's a difficult . . . it's a difficult illness I think for people to get their head around.
>
> > (Mother of a young female sufferer)

Regarding email support

> with email, I find, you've got time to think about what message you want to get over more clearly. I mean, when you're talking on the telephone, you can forget . . . some of the things you want to say. If you're emailing, then you've got the opportunity to think a bit longer and get things right.
>
> > (Father of an adult male sufferer)

> email is better for me because I can actually keep the email and go back to it . . . it's actually much better for me to have it in black and white because I can talk on the phone and then I think: 'Oh no, what was it she said? I'm sure that was really useful.' So email's better.
>
> > (Mother of an adult female sufferer)

Regarding the workbooks

> It broadened my knowledge of eating disorders . . . the best thing in it for me was . . . giving me training in communications, which I found excellent and to get the back-up references to be able to go and look things up on the internet.
>
> > (Father of an adult male sufferer)

> I found it very positive. Very positive experience using them and it certainly made me think and . . . assess the situation that I'm in and actually look at things differently.
>
> > (Mother of an adult female sufferer)

> Well, I think it's very useful . . . you feel like you're taking part and being involved and you feel like you're maybe you're contributing to your daughter or relative's recovery because you're doing something positive.
>
> > (Mother of an adult female sufferer)

I was really quite impressed with it actually . . . I wish I'd had it in the beginning because I think it's very, very well presented and I think it's very clear and I think it's very well structured. And I think if you had this right at the beginning when [they] were first diagnosed with anorexia, it would be really helpful and really useful.

(Mother of an adult female sufferer)

The workbooks were really comprehensive. That they touch on every area that . . . major area that you are likely to need to know something about – dealing with somebody with an eating disorder. That they give you sort of knowledge and the confidence and the feeling of support that would actually help you as a carer to help you to look after yourself . . . and will in turn have an effect on the person suffering. So in the long run will be a very important part of their recovery.

(Mother of an adult female sufferer)

Regarding the Anxiety Control Training (ACT)

I found the relaxation [CD] really helpful . . . it's something that I've never really done. I mean it's a good stress management, anxiety management . . . I don't think I've always really thought enough about taking that time out to do that. And I didn't think it would have a huge impact . . . and it just had such a calming effect . . . I was actually quite surprised.

(Mother of an adult female sufferer)

Conclusion

Research into the efficacy and acceptability of the DVD and coaching intervention and the OAO web-based intervention are still ongoing. At the time of writing, both quantitative and qualitative data are still being collected and analysed. It may be that these interventions will be cost-effective vehicles for reaching out to large groups of carers who might otherwise struggle to find interventions to support them as carers. While each of the interventions described appears to have its own merits and deficits, it remains to be seen whether any short-term 'distance-learning' style intervention for carers is adequate to address such a large-scale problem of helping carers, some of whom may have longer-term needs.

Should these interventions demonstrate efficacy in clinical trials, then this will open the door to further questions regarding the different approaches, some of which have already been anticipated. As each intervention contains several different component parts, it may be interesting and necessary to identify whether the efficacy of the intervention lies in particular component parts and whether all parts are necessary.

Again, at the time of writing, several different carer interventions are available. We have little or no data on what motivates a carer to choose a particular intervention over another. It is possible that the particular method of support, clinical approach or style of delivery may influence a carer's choice.

Additionally, no trials have been completed to date, where the different interventions described have been compared against each other. Consequently, we are unsure whether these interventions are equivalent in their efficacy and so, further investigation would be needed to establish whether health-care services should apply a 'horses for courses' approach of having access to a variety of interventions from which carers could chose according to their needs and preferences.

All the interventions described within this chapter are delivered with support from people with in-depth knowledge and experience of working with people with eating disorders and their families. Whether these interventions can be delivered with support from non-specialist sources (for example in primary care or community mental health facilities) also remains to be seen.

Advancements in technology may also assist the delivery of such interventions, for example, support and coaching could potentially be delivered through real-time online contact via webcam. The use of this type of technology would mean that carers could benefit from support with visual as well as verbal contact that could involve several carers at a single time and even involve the sufferer as well. Interventions conducted on this basis would retain the benefits of being used as distance learning style interventions, while benefiting from virtual face-to-face contact.

To conclude, such interventions, while having been made available to carers of people with other mental disorders for some time, are still relatively new in the field of eating disorders. Clinicians and researchers developing and testing these interventions are undoubtedly going to encounter many more questions in their quest to discover what intervention works for whom and why.

References

Duffy, J. C. & Waterton, J. J. (1984). Underreporting of alcohol consumption in sample surveys: The effect of computer interviewing in field work. *British Journal of Addiction* 79: 303–308.

Dummett, N. (2006). Processes for systemic cognitive-behavioural therapy with children, young people and families. *Behavioural and Cognitive Psychotherapy* 34(2): 179–189.

Grover, M., Williams, C., Eisler, I., Fairbairn, P., McCloskey, C., Smith, G. et al. (in preparation). An off-line pilot of a web-based cognitive-behavioural intervention for carers of people with anorexia nervosa.

Lorig, K. R. & Holman, H. R. (2003). Self-management education: History, definition, outcomes, and mechanisms. *Annals of Behavioral Medicine* 26(1): 1–7.

McIntosh, V. W., Jordan, J., Carter, F. A., Luty, S. E., McKenzie, J. M., Bulik, C. M.

et al. (2005). Three psychotherapies for anorexia nervosa: A randomised, controlled trial. *American Journal of Psychiatry* 162(4): 741–747.

Pennebaker, J. W. (2004). Theories, therapies and taxpayers: On the complexities of the expressive writing paradigm. *Clinical Psychology: Science and Practice* 11(2): 138–142.

Prochaska, J. & DiClemente, C. (1984). *The Transtheoretical Approach: Crossing the Traditional Boundaries of Therapy*. Homewood, IL: Dow Jones Irwen.

Schmidt, U., Williams, C., Eisler, I., Fairbairn, P., McCloskey, C., Smith, G. et al. (2007) *Overcoming Anorexia: Effective Caring*. Series of nine unpublished workbooks.

Sepúlveda, A. R., Lopez, C., Macdonald, P. & Treasure, J. (2008). Feasibility and acceptability of DVD and telephone coaching-based skills training for carers of people with an eating disorder. *International Journal of Eating Disorders* 41(4): 318–325.

Treasure, J., Smith, G. & Crane, A. (2007). *Skills-based Learning for Caring for a Loved One with an Eating Disorder: The New Maudsley Method*. London: Routledge.

Part IV

Special cases

Chapters 14 and 15 offer insights into two distinctive areas. Chapter 14 explores problems that can arise when people with an eating disorder become parents themselves. It looks at the long-term consequences, offers tips on how to prevent eating disorders in their own children and if traits and/or symptoms do appear, how then can they be minimised. Genetic and pregnancy-related factors are examined as well as personality traits that shape parenting styles.

Chapter 15 looks at the role fathers may play in increasing the risk that an eating disorder will develop, along with evidence that points to the protective role that fathers can have, both in reducing risk as well as supporting recovery. The chapter looks at the father's role in maintaining factors for an eating disorder. It ends by considering treatment implications in areas such as communication, as resources for self-esteem and resilience and highlights the importance of promoting a collaborative teamwork approach to the recovery process.

Chapter 14

Reproductive function and parenting in people with an eating disorder history

Janet Treasure, Nadia Micali and Fabrice Monneyron

Introduction

In this chapter we discuss the particular problems that can arise when people with an eating disorder (ED) history become parents. Several questions are commonly voiced:

- What are the long-term consequences of an eating disorder history on pregnancy and motherhood?
- What can be done to prevent an eating disorder developing in children of mothers with an ED?
- How can an eating disorder in the offspring be managed if one of the parents also has an eating disorder?

What are the long-term consequences of an eating disorder history on pregnancy and motherhood?

Most of the evidence about the long-term consequences of eating disorders on reproductive health comes from clinical case series. A major problem with the interpretation of these findings is that the case mix between studies varies greatly. Often there is not a well-matched comparison population and many studies are underpowered. In this brief summary of the literature we prioritise the most robust research findings from epidemiologically valid sources such as the Avon Longitudinal Study of Parents and Children (ALSPAC).

Maternity rates

The fertility and maternity rate of women with anorexia nervosa are reduced (Brinch et al., 1988; Hjern et al., 2006) whereas this does not appear to be the case for bulimia nervosa.

Eating disorder symptoms in pregnancy

In general eating disorder symptoms decrease in women with ED during pregnancy. They do not, however, disappear completely and some women with a past ED history can have a resurgence of symptoms in pregnancy (Micali et al., 2007b). It is not unknown for binge eating to develop during pregnancy (Bulik et al., 2007).

Symptoms of anxiety and depression during and after pregnancy

Women with AN and BN have high levels of anxiety and depression throughout pregnancy and in the post-partum period. In part, this is associated with ED symptoms also (Micali et al., 2009b).

Perinatal outcomes

Women with anorexia nervosa are more likely to have lower birth-weight babies; in part this is related to low maternal BMI before pregnancy and in part due to smoking. A maternal history of eating disorders particularly is associated with miscarriages (Micali et al., 2007a). High rates of premature birth have also been reported (Brinch et al., 1988; Bulik et al., 1999). Studies on Scandinavian case registers have similar findings (Sollid et al., 2004; Ekéus et al., 2006).

Feeding problems

Women with current or past eating disorders have been shown in several studies to report problems with feeding in their infants and children (Stein et al., 1994; Agras et al., 1999). We found that the most common feeding problems reported in the first year of life included: (a) slow feeding, (b) the infant eating only small quantities of food at each feed, (c) being dissatisfied or hungry after feeding and (d) not having established a feeding routine (Micali et al., 2009a).

A higher proportion of infants born to women with a past history of BN had accelerated growth between birth and 9 months and were overweight at 9 months (Micali et al., 2009a). Stein and colleagues have reported on a case series of women with eating disorders and found feeding difficulties persisting throughout development up to mid-childhood (Stein et al., 1994; Stein & Fairburn, 1996; Stein et al., 1996, 2001, 2006).

What can be done to prevent an eating disorder developing in children of mothers with an ED?

The children of mothers with an eating disorder are at increased risk (approximately 5 per cent more than children of 'healthy' mothers) of developing an eating disorder themselves. In part, this is because of genetic effects. Also their development may be shaped by the familial environment created by having a parent with an eating disorder (Bulik et al., 2005). Some putative risk factors are summarised in Figure 14.1, which illustrates how these mechanisms lead to later psychiatric outcomes.

The putative risk factors including mechanisms and vulnerabilities responsible for the transgenerational transmission of eating disorders include the following:

- genetic factors
- pregnancy-related factors (maternal anxiety, baby small for date, etc.)
- relapse of maternal ED with an increased salience of food, weight and shape
- parental personality traits and lifetime comorbidity with anxiety and OCD shaping the style of parenting and the parental marital relationship.

Genetic factors

Twin studies suggest that over 50 per cent of the risk of developing an eating disorder comes from genetic factors. In part, the genetic risk is a broad vulnerability overlapping with that of anxiety, depression and addictions. This is an area of active research and new technologies are producing rapid changes in the field. The genes that have been implicated include those related to appetite, anxiety, inhibition and compulsivity.

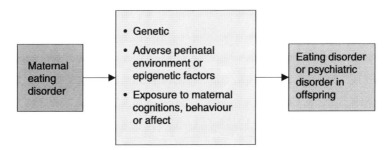

Figure 14.1 Putative mechanism of risk for the intergenerational transmission.

Pregnancy-related factors (maternal anxiety, baby small for date, etc.)

The intrauterine and early perinatal environment can shape development through a fetal programming effect. In part, this is mediated by epigenetic effects, a process by which the environment moderates which genes are available for later transcription. Stress and nutritional factors can impact on neurodevelopment through changes in neurotransmitter function (Mokler et al., 2007) and both are of relevance in mothers of people with eating disorder.

Nutritional factors

Under-nutrition in early life can have profound effects on metabolic programming throughout life. This theory was developed by Barker and colleagues (Barker, 1998; Hales & Barker, 2001). Extreme natural experiments such as the Chinese and Dutch famines have provided evidence in support of this theory. Poor fetal nutrition impacts on brain development and the risk of neuropsychiatric disease is also increased (Altschuler, 2005; Kyle & Pichard, 2006; Penner & Brown, 2007).

Stress related factors

Animal studies have found that intra-uterine stress produces an impact on the stress response over development (Meaney et al., 1996; Durand et al., 1998; Gorman et al., 2002; Wadhwa et al., 2002). The early hormonal environment is thought to play a role in mediating this effect (Sarkar et al., 2007, 2008). O'Connor et al. (2002) were the first to show the effect of maternal anxiety and depression in pregnancy on emotional and behavioural problems in the offspring in childhood (O'Connor et al., 2002). More recent research has shown that stress during pregnancy also affects cognitive development and fearfulness during early childhood (Bergman et al., 2007).

Relapse of maternal ED with an increased salience of food, weight and shape

A relapse of the eating disorder problems may affect the family environment increasing the importance given to weight, shape and food and can have several effects:

- Maternal extreme attitudes to eating, body shape and weight may have direct effects on the child (e.g. fear of fatness may lead to under-feeding or over-concern about food and shape issues may lead to meal conflict and criticism).

- The maternal disturbed eating behaviour may make the mother a poor role model.
- The maternal preoccupation with food, shape and weight may impair her overall concentration, reducing the mother's working memory and can reduce her sensitivity to the child's needs.
- The maternal eating disorder may impinge on the quality of the parental relationship.

Research from several longitudinal studies supports these links. Children with feeding problems often have mothers with eating problems themselves (Pike & Rodin, 1991; Stein et al., 1995; Whelan & Cooper, 2000). The influence of maternal eating disorder symptoms on childhood risk factors has been reported in prospective studies: maternal body dissatisfaction, bulimic symptoms, dieting and higher BMI all predict childhood eating problems (Stice et al., 1999). The effect is more pronounced in girls (Agras et al., 1999; Jacobi et al., 2001). Parental over-control, over-eating and pressure to be thin (especially from fathers) is related to the child developing a preoccupation with thinness (Agras et al., 2007). Being teased about weight, shape or dietary issues and a strong internalisation of the thin ideal can also have a profound impact, particularly on the development of bulimic disorders (Jackson et al., 2002).

Parental personality traits and lifetime comorbidity with anxiety and OCD shaping the style of parenting and the parental marital relationship

Obsessive compulsive traits such as rigidity, attention to detail and perfectionism and anxiety are associated with eating disorders and commonly remain as part of the personality after recovery. A mother with an eating disorder will have vulnerability traits, for example OCD personality with perfectionism, attention to detail, and rigidity, all of which can predispose to over-controlling and somewhat authoritarian parenting, and/or high anxiety, associated with concerns about being a mother. These personality styles can have a profound impact on all relationships including the parenting role.

Perfectionism can impact on parenting. The transmission of maladaptive perfectionism across generations is mediated by parental psychological controlling behaviour, especially through fathers (Soenens et al., 2005, 2008). This is of particular relevance for bulimia nervosa (Soenens et al., 2008). Perfectionism in the parents means that they make extreme efforts to care for, teach and spend time with their children. Sometimes these beliefs can be underpinned with maladaptive assumptions with extreme black-and-white or catastrophic thinking styles.

- Unless I thoroughly check my children's homework every night, I am a failure.

- If I let my child stay overnight with a friend he may develop poor sleeping habits or not be able to get on with his homework the next day.

Parental controlling behaviours such as excessive regulation during parent–child interactions are linked with shyness and anxiety in the child with medium to large effect size (Chorpita & Barlow, 1998). If parents fail to provide the opportunity for their child to engage in self-mastery behaviours, they are not able to develop a sense of self-control or mastery. The development of autonomy is stunted and they become dependent and have low self-esteem (Chorpita & Barlow, 1998; Barlow, 2000). The parenting style of mothers with a past eating disorder tends to veer towards the over-control end of the spectrum, with difficulty tolerating the 'mess' of mealtimes or exploration during play (Stein et al., 1994). Parental criticism can lead to an increase in wariness in their offspring who will develop negative views about themselves and others.

Anxiety in parents can promote or maintain anxiety, for example when their child is faced with a novel situation they can reinforce the child's anxieties by focusing and giving excess attention to the beliefs related to threat and physiological arousal. Later, play and social activities can pose threats and anxiety and parents can model avoidance and over-protection. Stein et al. (1994), for example, found that the mothers with a past eating disorder had a tendency to be over-involved, intrude into their child's play by showing them the 'correct' way to play. Another form of over-protection is preventing time away from the parental home (Shoebridge & Gowers, 2000).

Excessive parental responsiveness and over-solicitousness in situations that elicit anxiety serve only to reinforce anxiety. The immediate consequence of a reduction in anxiety, in response to this form of parenting behaviour, may reinforce parents to carry on with this behaviour. This sensitises children to these situations and prevents exposure and habituation so that significant life transitions, such as starting school or university, living away from home, or staying with a friend, present more difficulties for the child or young adult. Children who are more inhibited in a social context may be slower to habituate to novel situations and this elicits from the parent's protective behaviour, which interferes with the child's learning how to cope with new environments.

Some mothers with an eating disorder tend to stifle their own emotional reactions and may have modelled unhelpful emotional regulation. This may mean that they can be intolerant if their child shows excessive fear. They may, therefore, encourage the child to be stoical and to ignore and cover up their fears, perhaps by using avoidance invalidating the emotional response, e.g. 'You are not frightened of that are you?'

The opposite, however, has also been reported in the literature. Role reversal and the child taking on the caring role can also happen when parents with an eating disorder might feel overwhelmed by parenting demands (Woodside & Shekter-Wolfson, 1990; Franzen & Gerlinghoff, 1997). Parents with an eating disorder might also recruit their children's help to manage the eating disorder.

Bryant-Waugh and colleagues have examined the issues that mothers with an eating disorder who have young infants highlight as areas of difficulty (Bryant-Waugh et al., 2007a). Some of the themes that emerged in their qualitative study include: 'Passing on traits', 'Food preparation and provision', 'Interactions around food and mealtimes', 'Mother's intake', 'Self care', 'Self identity and parental expectations', 'Impact on general parent–Child relationship' and 'Need for control'. They developed a group intervention to address these issues which women found helpful (Bryant-Waugh et al., 2007b). Below we describe in detail the strategies they used.

What can be done to prevent transmission?

In terms of primary prevention it is possible to moderate risk areas:

- optimising nutrition in pregnancy
- developing a network of supportive relationships to buffer the mother's stress and anxiety levels during pregnancy
- managing maternal concerns about food, shape and weight issues
- moderating maternal extreme personality traits (so that they do not have an adverse impact on relationships and roles as a wife and mother)
- problem solving.

Optimising nutrition in pregnancy

A healthy weight at conception is an important first step. Techniques of assisted conception can sidestep the need to be at a 'healthy weight'. Sometimes women who have chronically restrained their eating let themselves go during pregnancy and gain an excess amount of weight during this time; they then stringently diet again when the baby is born. Bingeing and vomiting during pregnancy may cause large swings in glucose. These extreme metabolic swings may adversely impact on fetal development through fetal programming.

Managing maternal concerns about food, shape and weight issues

As food is so salient to mothers with a past history of an eating disorder, this can be a key area of difficulty. There may be fears that infants will not be able to know what the correct amount to eat is, or may be unable to master the skills needed to feed themselves. The tendency to be over-controlling and perfectionist can intrude into this process. During infancy, simple practical measures can help develop this process, like spreading a plastic sheet on the floor along with two bowls and spoons allows both infant and mother to take part in feeding.

Later there are several strategies that a mother with an eating disorder history may need to put in place to stop the salience of food and shape intruding on the family environment. These include:

- Not focusing on the calorie content or being excessively judgemental about 'good' or 'bad' foods.
- Eating meals with the family with portion sizes equivalent to most other family members.
- Not voicing explicit instrumental rigid rules about eating, for example avoiding statements such as 'I am not going to eat lunch now because I am going out for a meal later in the evening'.
- Not voicing critical comments about shape, weight and eating in others.

Managing maternal extreme personality traits

It is often helpful to review with the mother an optimal balance between her heightened need to be in control and the need to allow her child freedom, in order to foster the development of self-esteem and autonomy.

There are simple strategies that can help with an over-controlling tendency which include reflecting on the logic of extreme over-protection. Questions such as 'What is the worst that could happen?' and/or 'What are you trying to avert?' can help mothers to develop a realistic appraisal of the threat. A series of small steps can be built to plan for 'safe' risks. These aim to foster the child's autonomy and the development of their self-esteem and yet have some layers of protection built in. It can be helpful if this planning occurs with the father in order to ensure that this less controlling approach can be implemented consistently.

Balancing the level of control and the tendency to be perfectionist requires skills in three areas:

- How to be assertive and set age-appropriate rules.
- How to coach the child in sticking to the rules.
- How to respond when the child breaks a rule.

First, there is the need to set realistic age-appropriate rules. In order to set reasonable rules, both parents need time for respectful discussion with each other, enlisting the help from families or friends, if and when necessary. Second, a somewhat hands-off approach to implementation is required, with positive attention to encouraging steps towards the overall desired behaviour, while coaching the child through any difficult roadblocks. Third, if rules are broken, the parent may need to manage their emotional reaction to temper any intense feelings of anger, threat or disappointment that arise in them.

Such intense negative reactions can instil in their child a fear of making mistakes or getting things wrong. Frequent parental criticism that constantly attempts to shape and mould may increase a child's wariness and general anxiety. Nurtured in an environment with this form of hostility, children can develop a negative perception of themselves.

A contrasting style of parenting is one in which parents are able to grant a degree of autonomy to their children, with help available when necessary, to learn how to solve problems and cope with the world. At times, this will mean not responding by imposing consequences on a behaviour the parents do not condone. Thus, children have to accept that their parents have expressed concern or disapproval for the behaviour and have let them choose to explore it and undertake an experiment to discover the consequences for themselves. This strategy can help children internalise control and develop their own reasons for adopting a chosen behaviour or not. The adage 'every mistake is a treasure' is a helpful motto to remember!

Table 14.1 contrasts various parental behaviours.

Problem solving

As there is a tendency for people with eating disorders to show avoidance, an important parenting skill is to teach children how to approach situations and potential problems positively and assertively. The first step is to be clear about the problem, that is what, how and why it is a problem. It is helpful if there is

Table 14.1 Parental behaviours which can buffer against or foster the development of an eating disorder

Control	High	• Parent dismissing the child's individuality by not listening, ignoring, interrupting or criticising the child's ideas and behaviours and 'taking over' and doing things for them.
	Low	• Parent promoting autonomy by encouraging the individuality of other family members and affirming their ideas and behaviours.
		• Parent demonstrating this trait by listening and showing interest and respect for the other person's point of view.
		• Parent being prepared to make time and effort to understand and clarify what the child is thinking and how the child wants to approach particular situations.
Warmth	High	• Using non-verbal signs of listening.
		• Maintaining eye contact using a pleasant tone.
		• Attuning with the other's state.
	Low	• Using non-verbal signs of impatience or uninterest.
		• Looking away, being distracted.
Doubt	High	• Repeatedly questioning the ability of the other to complete a task, e.g. 'Are you sure you would be able to do that?'

(Continued Overleaf)

Table 14.1 Continued.

	Low	• Fostering self-efficacy, coaching, mentoring, role-playing to practise difficult scenarios. • Discussing times in the past when a similar thing has been done. • Reflecting on and encouraging examples of vicarious learning such as how peers tackle similar problems. • Teaching skills such as problem solving to generate strategies. • Expressing the belief that their offspring can solve a problem or achieve a result. • Helping offspring set achievable goals. • Fostering independence and autonomy. • Modelling independent thinking. • Encouraging other members of the family to think. • Reflecting ideas that are offered to encourage their development by questions such as 'Tell me more about that?' • Reflecting on the successful events in the past and how or reflecting on friends or other family members have tackled problems.
Avoidance	*High*	• Avoiding the topic being discussed. • Showing impatience and lack of interest. • Looking away. • Withdrawing from the conversation, redirecting a conversation, e.g. 'I am tired of this.' 'How should I know?'
	Low	• Being open to broach and act on difficulties or mistakes in an honest and direct manner. • Letting others express difficult emotions and dissenting opinions. • Taking the lead in novel or somewhat uncertain situations.

some clarity about what solution is wanted. The second step is for parents to teach their child how to generate a variety of solutions (these can be both playful and serious). The penultimate step is to model a process of reflection, whereby each solution and consequence is discussed. The final stage is to model how to make plans, set goals, and to review and assess the situation. This skill is of particular benefit because the temperament of people at risk is one of rigidity, fear of making mistakes etc. Problem-solving strategies coach the person in how to be flexible.

Prevention is best achieved if there is openness and honesty among all parties. This is not always easy, given the stigma that surrounds eating disorders, and many women (and their husbands) choose to forget their own eating disorder. However, we think that by becoming more aware of the possible pitfalls, it is possible to avert the development of an eating disorder in the offspring.

Case study: Joy's mother

The following extract is from a mother with an eating disorder describing her daughter:

> I have a 9-year-old daughter who, for some time now, has been showing subtle but recognisable traits of anorexic behaviour. Joy, my daughter, came into this world with an *acute* fear of food and is very reluctant to try new food, consequently eating a limited diet. [This suggests that part of the temperament of this individual is a fear of novelty with behavioural constriction. The relationship of this individual to food parallels their relationship with people and the world.] What has become apparent in recent months is her unconscious need to use food to deal with her emotions. If Joy has an anxiety she will, on occasion, refuse to eat or discard food deceitfully. Obviously, given my long history of anorexia, I am able to recognise the signs and address the problem with her.
>
> Not surprisingly, Joy is a high achiever and a perfectionist. She puts tremendous pressure on herself at school, despite our repeated reassurances that we do not have any expectations of her academically. She is an extremely anxious child and very sensitive to others' needs. Joy is also quite obsessive, as are my younger two children, and all have shown traits of OCD from a very young age, a condition I have been acutely afflicted by and now manage with reasonable success. I hasten to add I have done my utmost to shield my children from my illnesses and to set a good example. I do believe these traits are inherent.
>
> Fortunately, Joy does not have the mindset whereby she is obsessing about her body shape and weight, although she does have an interest in the nutritional element of food which, although not obsessive, could exacerbate should anorexia take hold.
>
> Her self-esteem is very low and I have occasionally found notes declaring how much she hates herself. My husband and I have given all our children enormous love and tried to instil a good foundation of self-esteem. I am coming to the conclusion that Joy is an absolute clone of me and that alarms me greatly!!!! Joy has not suffered any trauma in her life but it would seem her personality traits could be instrumental in triggering the potential for anorexia.

This mother clearly highlights the temperamental traits that can lead to the development of an eating disorder. These traits need to be sensitively handled. Here we outline strategies that women with a previous history of eating disorders have used in order to protect their child having a similar problem. We include the difficulties that some mothers have had mastering these skills in their own life.

1   Let your child be the person he or she is. Don't lay your expectations on your child. Give your child the space to develop his or her own potential.

2   Don't isolate yourself or your family. Surround yourself with people, both friends and relatives. Allow yourself to ask for help and support when you need it – and forgive them if they don't always do things exactly as you would yourself.

3   Keep your own worries about food and body image to yourself. Don't openly judge other people or your own appearance – and try to make the best of your good points. Kids seem very quick to pick up on parents' judgements on just about everything. Difficult to do in practice, but the more you learn to love and respect your own body/self, the more your child will do the same.

4   Don't be afraid to let your child see you make mistakes and get things wrong – and most importantly to see that it isn't the end of the world. Learning how to make do or make the best of a bad job is much more important than trying to do it right first time.

5   Give your child control in as many areas of his or her life as possible where this is developmentally appropriate, i.e. food, education, relationships, hobbies etc.

6   Have a quiet chat with your child's teacher, informing her of your son or daughter's inherent traits, i.e. perfectionism, obsessive tendencies, high achiever, over-anxious and sensitive traits, so that these can be handled cautiously to avoid anorexia being triggered by the demands of the education system.

7   Gently draw your child's attention to his or her eating behaviour, should it become apparent that your child is using food to deal with his or her anxieties. Any loss of appetite is a signal of ill health, physical or emotional. Compulsive snacking or over-eating can also be an atypical signal of distress. Enquire tentatively whether there is any worry or upset behind the change in behaviour related to food. Find a calm, quiet time to bring up the subjects of emotions and what they might signal, e.g. sadness (need to grieve what is lost and make reparative connections), anger (frustration about not achieving a goal – what help may be needed in attaining that goal), anxiety (what might be needed to make them feel safer). Suggest that eating and relationship to food may mask or numb emotions. Inform your child that it is important to be able to understand emotional responses and make judgements as when and how to use them to guide wise decision-making. There are dangers associated with avoiding emotions as a coping mechanism.

8   Educate your child on the importance of eating food from all the food groups in order to sustain good health and apply the adage 'everything in moderation'.

9   Talk openly and honestly about the mother's experience of anorexia,

giving emphasis to the dangers to one's physical, mental and emotional health.

How can an eating disorder in the offspring be managed if one of the parents also has an eating disorder?

Awareness and early detection

While a multicentre study from Europe suggests that the outcome of treatment is poorer if there is a family history of an eating disorder (Steinhausen et al., 2008), preliminary findings from our research indicate that children of parents with an eating disorder are, on the whole, more likely than other eating disorder sufferers to access treatment early on. This may offset some of the raised risks of poor long-term outcome as early treatment optimises outcome.

The parental factors that may get in the way of successful treatment of the offspring are discussed below. Extreme guilt is the common reaction of parents with an eating disorder when they notice that their child too has developed an eating disorder. They may question what they have done to cause this to happen. Furthermore, to make matters worse, once their child's eating disorder symptoms become marked, this may rekindle their own eating disorder attitudes. The high levels of maternal guilt and self-recrimination may also act as trigger for an exaggerated maternal stress response which can lead to a self-perpetuating cycle of anorexic behaviours in which ultimately both the mother and her offspring become trapped.

Issues and problems

The issues and difficulties that arise when the child of a parent with an eating disorder also develops eating problems can include:

- under- or over-sensitivity to eating problems
- competition and calibration of eating behaviours
- unhelpful expectations about treatment
- unhelpful expectations about consequences and prognosis
- accommodation of the family around eating disorder behaviours.

Specific problems relating to treatment include the following:

- unwillingness to accept treatment goals
- uncertainty over competence to deliver and support treatment
- perfectionist goals regarding recovery
- parental guilt and/or irritable moods.

All of these issues also occur in families without an eating disorder history and so general management strategies are of value, such as eliciting a detailed assessment of family functioning (Treasure et al., 2008) and sharing information and skills with the parents. The therapist needs to be kind and sensitive to the high level of guilt and shame that will be present.

Issues for the therapist

There are several issues that are of relevance for the therapist and that need to managed carefully. These include the following:

- There is a lack of openness and loyalty about the family's secret. If the parent's eating disorder is a secret, do you try to 'out' it or not?
- Do not assume that the family have all of the necessary skills and knowledge. There may be more barriers of misinformation, unhelpful attributions and ambivalence to be overcome.
- It is helpful to widen the discussion of risk factors to a broad range of personality traits in order to depersonalise the issue of blame and stigma.
- The tendency for non-eating disordered siblings to be excluded may be increased.

Avoidance of eating disorder history

Eating disorder talk is so painful for some mothers that they avoid thinking about their own issues. They may deny that they either have or did have an eating problem themselves. This confuses other family members because although they can observe the overt signs of poor nutrition or an unusual reaction to food, it is a secret that cannot be mentioned.

When mothers are unable to be open about their own eating disorders, whether this is due to guilt or shame, it can make treatment difficult. Children with an eating disorder become angry and resentful and want to 'out' their mother. Children are very sensitive to any hypocrisy or what they see as injustice. People with an eating disorder become angry and resentful if the people helping to feed them are themselves on a diet or skip meals.

In some treatment settings, it may be helpful for the mother to be more explicit about her own difficulties. However, it may be inappropriate to discuss the mother's eating disorder in family sessions as it becomes very confusing. In such a scenario, it may be better if the mother has some individual sessions where she can reflect on her own issues relating to eating food and shape, thus modelling appropriate behaviours, as much as possible.

There can be barriers that impede the mother coming for help; was she 'really' anorexic? Was her illness severe enough? Was she a fraud? Was she wasting the therapist's time?

Treatment issues with two generations of eating disorders

The mother's sensitivity to food, weight and shape issues may make it extremely difficult to set up a joint approach with their partner about meal planning and rules related to eating. Such a mother may perceive, for example, that her partner is being unfair if he makes general approximations, such as substituting a treacle pudding for a fruit flan. The mother's attention to detail over such issues may blind her to the bigger picture of helping her child attain better nutritional health. It is important, therefore, that parents in these circumstances spend more time together reviewing their management plans of the child's ED. Ideally, the non-ED partner should take the main role in setting the rules about eating, shape and weight. This is often not possible, however, as most mothers are the primary caregivers and spend more time supervising meals. In this case, careful planning with agreed contingencies is needed. It is helpful to involve the father in care as much as possible. We encourage fathers, for instance, to come to the carers' skills workshops. We have found that fathers respond well to the taught information, probably because they have less emotional over-reaction. This makes it somewhat easier for them to implement the skills.

Here are some comments made by a mother with a past eating disorder on the treatment process for her daughter:

> When your daughter develops an eating disorder you, as a parent and sufferer, feel overwhelming guilt. You must be responsible and as a previous sufferer you are familiar with GUILT, self-blame.
>
> It is much, *much worse* watching your daughter sink into anorexia than having the disease yourself – there you had control, or thought you had. With your daughter, however, you can only watch her sickness, suffering, withdrawal and gradual disappearance. She is beyond the stage when cuddling and a kiss will make it better. These she rejects.
>
> I thought that to help Jane overcome anorexia, all I had to do was be her constant support, companion and carer. She got worse. I thought by giving Jane all my love and attention she would beat this illness. She couldn't.
>
> What was helpful:
>
> One-to-one counselling (Jane only – reasonably helpful to Jane – she stabilised her weight).
>
> Family therapy: mainly held with Jane, Dad, myself and occasionally elder sister once every 2–3 weeks. These sessions definitely intensified *my* guilt, especially when sessions were discussed at home. It certainly made me even consider leaving home as I felt I must be a bad influence, the cause or the reason Jane was not recovering.
>
> One-to-one for me. This was a breakthrough for me! It really helped to be able to voice my feelings. It was very helpful – crucial even – to write my life journal; to realise how I react to given situations; to realise why I can't express

anger and hurt and bottle emotions up; to understand that actually, it is fine to tell other people when you don't feel happy with their behaviour. How can they know to treat you differently if they are unaware that you are upset?

This in turn got me thinking that maybe Jane felt the same. I tried this out on Jane and it worked. This armed me with new tactics that REALLY worked – for both of us. What this involved was looking for signs of distress in Jane and patiently easing out her worries. Definite progress in Jane.

15–18 months. Carers' workshops:

Wow! I could have my life back and gosh I was a kangaroo. I needed to give Jane back control over her life – to make her own mistakes and triumphs. How else could she learn and regain her self-esteem?

I took a back seat and allowed Jane to become self-sufficient. There were slight hiccups as husband became a kangaroo – especially when I was away for five days. He is still a bit kangaroo'ish but a bit better. He is definitely inclined to jump into primary carer/kangaroo role when I go out!!

Conclusion

In this chapter we have reviewed the long-term consequences that a maternal history of an eating disorder has upon reproductive function and the offspring. There is an impact on fertility, pregnancy outcomes, maternal psychological health and feeding. In addition parental extreme obsessive compulsive and anxiety traits can impact on parenting and the marital relationship. We have described some of the strategies that can be used to prevent an eating disorder developing in their children. Finally, we have summarised some of the therapeutic issues and dilemmas that can arise in this situation.

Summary of prevention tips

- Ensuring adequate nutrition in pregnancy for women who have or have had an eating disorder
- Developing a network of supportive relationships to buffer stress and anxiety levels during pregnancy and once the baby is born
- Managing maternal concerns about food, shape and weight issues
- Exploring and aiming to change maternal extreme personality traits so that they do not have an adverse impact on relationships and roles as a wife and mother
- Helping women to foster independence and self-worth in their child
- Helping women to be open to their child.

References

Agras, W. S., Hammer, L. D. & McNicholas, F. (1999). A prospective study of the influence of eating-disordered mothers on their children. *International Journal of Eating Disorders* 25: 253–262.

Agras, W. S., Bryson, S., Hammer, L. D. & Kraemer, H. C. (2007). Childhood risk factors for thin body preoccupation and social pressure to be thin. *Journal of the American Academy of Child and Adolescent Psychiatry* 46: 171–178.

Altschuler, E. L. (2005). Schizophrenia and the Chinese famine of 1959–1961. *Journal of the American Medical Association* 294: 2968–2969.

Barker, D. J. (1998). In utero programming of chronic disease. *Clinical Science* 95: 115–128.

Barlow, D. H. (2000). Unraveling the mysteries of anxiety and its disorders from the perspective of emotion theory. *American Psychologist* 55: 1247–1263.

Bergman, K., Sarkar, P., O'Connor, T. G., Modi, N. & Glover, V. (2007). Maternal stress during pregnancy predicts cognitive ability and fearfulness in infancy. *Journal of the American Academy of Child and Adolescent Psychiatry* 46: 1454–1463.

Brinch, M., Isager, T. & Tolstrup, K. (1988). Anorexia nervosa and motherhood: Reproduction pattern and mothering behavior of 50 women. *Acta Psychiatrica Scandinavica* 77: 611–617.

Bryant-Waugh, R., Turner, H., East, P. & Gamble, C. (2007a). Developing a parenting skills-and-support intervention for mothers with eating disorders and pre-school children. Part 1: Qualitative investigation of issues to include. *European Eating Disorders Review* 15: 350–356.

Bryant-Waugh, R., Turner, H., Jones, C. & Gamble, C. (2007b). Developing a parenting skills-and-support intervention for mothers with eating disorders and pre-school children. Part 2: Piloting a group intervention. *European Eating Disorders Review* 15: 439–448.

Bulik, C. M., Sullivan, P. F., Fear, J. L., Pickering, A., Dawn, A. & McCullin, M. (1999). Fertility and reproduction in women with anorexia nervosa: A controlled study. *Journal of Clinical Psychiatry* 60(2): 130–135.

Bulik, C. M., Reba, L., Siega-Riz, A. & Reichborn-Kjennerud, T. (2005). Anorexia nervosa: Definition, epidemiology, and cycle of risk. *International Journal of Eating Disorders* 37: S2–S9.

Bulik, C. M., Von, H. A., Hamer, R., Knoph, B. C., Torgersen, L., Magnus, P. et al. (2007). Patterns of remission, continuation and incidence of broadly defined eating disorders during early pregnancy in the Norwegian Mother and Child Cohort Study (MoBa). *Psychological Medicine* 37: 1109–1118.

Chorpita, B. F. & Barlow, D. H. (1998) The development of anxiety: The role of control in the early environment. *Psychological Bulletin* 124: 3–21.

Durand, M., Sarrieau, A., Aguerre, S., Mormede, P. & Chaouloff, F. (1998). Differential effects of neonatal handling on anxiety, corticosterone response to stress, and hippocampal glucocorticoid and serotonin (5-HT)2A receptors in Lewis rats. *Psychoneuroendocrinology* 23: 323–335.

Ekéus, C., Lindberg, L., Lindblad, F. & Hjern, A. (2006). Birth outcomes and pregnancy complications in women with a history of anorexia nervosa. *BJOG* 113: 925–929.

Franzen, U. & Gerlinghoff, M. (1997). Parenting by patients with eating disorders: Experiences with a mother–child group. *Eating Disorders* 5(1): 5–14.

Gorman, J. M., Mathew, S. & Coplan, J. (2002). Neurobiology of early life stress: Nonhuman primate models. *Seminars in Clinical Neuropsychiatry* 7: 96–103.

Hales, C. N. & Barker, D. J. (2001). The thrifty phenotype hypothesis. *British Medical Bulletin* 60: 5–20.

Hjern, A., Lindberg, L. & Lindblad, F. (2006). Outcome and prognostic factors for adolescent female inpatients with anorexia nervosa: 9- to 14-year follow-up. *British Journal of Psychiatry* 189: 428–432.

Jackson, T. D., Grilo, C. M. & Masheb, R. M. (2002). Teasing history and eating disorder features: An age- and body mass index-matched comparison of bulimia nervosa and binge-eating disorder. *Comprehensive Psychiatry* 43: 108–113.

Jacobi, C., Agras, W. S. & Hammer, L. D. (2001). Predicting children's reported eating disturbances at 8 years of age. *Journal of the American Academy of Child and Adolescent Psychiatry* 40: 364–372.

Kyle, U. G. & Pichard, C. (2006). The Dutch Famine of 1944–1945: A pathophysiological model of long-term consequences of wasting disease. *Current Opinion in Clinical Nutrition and Metabolic Care* 9: 388–394.

Meaney, M. J., Diorio, J., Francis, D., Widdowson, J., LaPlante, P., Caldji, C. et al. (1996). Early environmental regulation of forebrain glucocorticoid receptor gene expression: Implications for adrenocortical responses to stress. *Developmental Neuroscience* 18: 49–72.

Micali, N., Simonoff, E. & Treasure, J. (2007a). Risk of major adverse perinatal outcomes in women with eating disorders. *British Journal of Psychiatry* 190: 255–259.

Micali, N., Treasure, J. & Simonoff, E. (2007b). Eating disorders symptoms in pregnancy: A longitudinal study of women with recent and past eating disorders and obesity. *Journal of Psychosomatic Research* 63: 297–303.

Micali, N., Simonoff, E. & Treasure, J. (2009a). Infant feeding and weight in the first year of life in babies of women with eating disorders. *Journal of Pediatrics* 154(1): 55–60.

Micali, N., Simonoff, E. & Treasure, J. (2009b). Depression and anxiety in pregnancy and the postpartum in women with ED: Results from a longitudinal prospective cohort. Submitted manuscript.

Mokler, D. J., Torres, O. I., Galler, J. R. & Morgane, P. J. (2007). Stress-induced changes in extracellular dopamine and serotonin in the medial prefrontal cortex and dorsal hippocampus of prenatally malnourished rats. *Brain Research* 1148: 226–233.

O'Connor, T. G., Heron, J., Golding, J., Beveridge, M. & Glover, V. (2002). Maternal antenatal anxiety and children's behavioural/emotional problems at 4 years: Report from the Avon Longitudinal Study of Parents and Children. *British Journal of Psychiatry* 180: 502–508.

Penner, J. D. & Brown, A. S. (2007). Prenatal infectious and nutritional factors and risk of adult schizophrenia. *Expert Review of Neurotherapeutics* 7: 797–805.

Pike, K. M. & Rodin, J. (1991). Mothers, daughters, and disordered eating. *Journal of Abnormal Psychology* 100: 198–204.

Sarkar, P., Bergman, K., Fisk, N. M., O'Connor, T. G. & Glover, V. (2007). Amniotic fluid testosterone: Relationship with cortisol and gestational age. *Clinical Endocrinology* 67: 743–747.

Sarkar, P., Bergman, K., O'Connor, T. G. & Glover, V. (2008). Maternal antenatal anxiety and amniotic fluid cortisol and testosterone: Possible implications for fetal programming. *Journal of Neuroendocrinology* 20(4): 489–496.

Shoebridge, P. & Gowers, S. G. (2000). Parental high concern and adolescent-onset anorexia nervosa: A case-control study to investigate direction of causality. *British Journal of Psychiatry* 176: 132–137.

Soenens, B., Elliot, A. J., Goossens, L., Vansteenkiste, M., Luyten, P. & Duriez, B. (2005). The intergenerational transmission of perfectionism: Parents' psychological control as an intervening variable. *Journal of Family Psychology* 19: 358–366.

Soenens, B., Vansteenkiste, M., Vandereycken, W., Luyten, P., Sierens, E. & Goossens, L. (2008). Perceived parental psychological control and eating-disordered symptoms: Maladaptive perfectionism as a possible intervening variable. *Journal of Nervous and Mental Disease* 196: 144–152.

Sollid, C. P., Wisborg, K., Hjort, J. & Secher, N. J. (2004). Eating disorder that was diagnosed before pregnancy and pregnancy outcome. *American Journal of Obstetrics and Gynecology* 190: 206–210.

Stein, A. & Fairburn, C. G. (1996). Eating habits and attitudes in the postpartum period. *Psychosomatic Medicine* 58: 321–325.

Stein, A., Woolley, H., Cooper, S. D. & Fairburn, C. G. (1994). An observational study of mothers with eating disorders and their infants. *Journal of Child Psychology and Psychiatry* 35: 733–748.

Stein, A., Stein, J., Walters, E. A. & Fairburn, C. G. (1995). Eating habits and attitudes among mothers of children with feeding disorders. *British Medical Journal* 310: 228.

Stein, A., Murray, L., Cooper, P. & Fairburn, C. G. (1996). Infant growth in the context of maternal eating disorders and maternal depression: A comparative study. *Psychological Medicine* 26: 569–574.

Stein, A., Woolley, H., Murray, L., Cooper, P., Cooper, S., Noble, F. et al. (2001). Influence of psychiatric disorder on the controlling behaviour of mothers with 1-year-old infants: A study of women with maternal eating disorder, postnatal depression and a healthy comparison group. *British Journal of Psychiatry* 179: 157–162.

Stein, A., Woolley, H., Cooper, S., Winterbottom, J., Fairburn, C. G. & Cortina-Borja, M. (2006). Eating habits and attitudes among 10-year-old children of mothers with eating disorders: longitudinal study. *British Journal of Psychiatry* 189: 324–329.

Steinhausen, H. C., Grigoroiu-Serbanescu, M., Boyadjieva, S., Neumarker, K. J. & Winkler, M. C. (2008). Course and predictors of rehospitalization in adolescent anorexia nervosa in a multisite study. *International Journal of Eating Disorders* 41: 29–36.

Stice, E., Agras, W. S. & Hammer, L. D. (1999). Risk factors for the emergence of childhood eating disturbances: A five-year prospective study. *International Journal of Eating Disorders* 25: 375–387.

Treasure, J., Sepúlveda, A. R., Macdonald, P., Whitaker, W., Lopez, C., Zabala, M. et al. (2008). The assessment of the family of people with eating disorders. *European Eating Disorders Review* 16: 247–255.

Wadhwa, P. D., Glynn, L., Hobel, C. J., Garite, T. J., Porto, M., Chicz-DeMet, A. et al. (2002). Behavioral perinatology: Biobehavioral processes in human fetal development. *Regulatory Peptides* 108: 149–157.

Whelan, E. & Cooper, P. J. (2000). The association between childhood feeding problems and maternal eating disorder: A community study. *Psychological Medicine* 30:
69–77.

Woodside, D. B. & Shekter-Wolfson, L. F. (1990). Parenting by patients with
anorexia nervosa and bulimia nervosa. *International Journal of Eating Disorders*
9(3): 303–309.

Chapter 15

The influence and importance of parents in care and treatment of an eating disorder

Olivia Kyriacou, Janet Treasure and Simone Raenker

Introduction

The parental influence on eating behaviours and the parent–child (particularly mother–daughter) relationship has been intensely explored in clinical research in the context of eating disorders (Barber & Thomas, 1986; Arevalo & Escursell, 1997; Fassino et al., 2002, 2003; Woodside et al., 2002), but the role of fathers themselves has been somewhat neglected. We redress this balance in this chapter as there is some evidence suggesting that fathers can be particularly important. First, we examine the father's role with regards to risk and protective factors, and second, we look at evidence suggesting that fathers can also have a protective role in buffering risk, as well as contributing to recovery.

A common misperception present in the literature is that 'anorexia is a mother–daughter thing'. Blaming of mothers – as well as fathers – is unhelpful as it reduces confidence in their ability to help, paralysing them with fear over whether their actions are making the situation worse.

In this chapter, we summarise the literature that highlights the role that mothers and fathers can have in both the development and maintenance of eating disorders, priority being given to evidence that has the most validity, that is systematic reviews or prospective studies, if they are available. We then discuss the roles that parents tend to adopt in reaction to the eating disorder. Their responses can contribute to the inadvertent perpetuation of the disorder. Finally, we discuss how to engage parents, especially fathers, in treatment.

Importance of parents in the realm of eating disorders: reviewing the evidence

Among the many factors that increase the risk of developing eating disorders, the impact of mothers and fathers is noteworthy. This relates to the style of parenting, shared eating disorder vulnerability traits (endophenotypes) and also more specifically the salience of food, weight and eating.

Style of parenting

Paternal affection, communication, and amount of contact have a close response relationship with eating disorder risk (Johnson et al., 2002). Thus, the more distant and unavailable the father during childhood, the more likely it is that their daughter later developed an eating disorder. This link between lack of paternal care and eating disorder risk is also found in retrospective reports on parenting from clinical studies (Wonderlich et al., 1996; Rojo-Moreno et al., 2006). Weaker paternal boundaries with intrusive behaviours have also been found (Rorty et al., 2000; Agras et al., 2007).

Shared eating disorder vulnerability traits

Soenens et al. (2005, 2008) examined the association between paternal psychological control and eating disorder symptoms in a case-controlled study. The authors concluded that maladaptive perfectionism, a key vulnerability factor for eating disorders, is a significant intervening factor between parental (especially fathers) psychological control and eating disorder symptoms. Thus, controlling behaviour of fathers seems to have an impact on eating disorder symptoms.

Transmission of the salience of food, weight and eating

Two modes of transgenerational transmission of maladaptive eating and weight attitudes and behaviours have been identified in the area of eating disorders:

- communication of the importance of thinness and/or weight management and critical comments on appearance and eating, including teasing
- modelling or emulating problematic behaviours.

It is likely that both occur within families.

Fathers who highly value thinness can transmit this ideal to their daughters. Thus, there is a gradually increasing body of literature that suggests that fathers can have a profound impact on the development of the thinness ideal in their daughters (Agras et al., 2007). Paternal teasing significantly predicted higher levels of body dissatisfaction, social comparison, internalisation of the thin-ideal, restrictive and bulimic eating behaviours, depression and lower self-esteem (Keery et al., 2005). Paternal teasing was associated with sibling teasing, particularly by male siblings.

Problematic eating behaviours in the fathers can increase the risk of the child developing an ED. Early development of binge eating disorder (BED), for example, was associated with significantly higher rates of *paternal obesity* and *binge eating*, but not with maternal obesity or binge eating (Marcus et al., 1995).

Parental role in factors that maintain an eating disorder

Parental characteristics and treatment response

Engel and Stienen (1988) ranked the father–daughter relationship as third out of the ten most important prognostic factors for eating disorders, and several more recent studies support this observation. Individuals with bulimia nervosa whose fathers were obese responded less well to treatment than the individuals with a normal weight parent (Fairburn et al., 1995). Castro and colleagues found that parental rejection had a profound influence on the impact of treatment in the early phase. Higher perceived rejection and control or over-protection from both parents were associated with a poorer overall outcome (Castro et al., 2000). Lower paternal care was associated with a poor outcome for treatment of anorexia nervosa (Bulik et al., 2000) and high levels of paternal expressed emotion (EE) was found to be associated with dropout from treatment (Szmukler et al., 1985).

Emotional impact of an eating disorder on parents

Fathers usually do not get as emotionally engaged as mothers when their daughter has an eating disorder (Whitney et al., 2005). They show less of an over-protective reaction and their levels of anxiety and depression are also significantly lower than those reported by mothers (Kyriacou et al., 2008).

Fathers' interview accounts, however, tell a different story, especially those of fathers caring for daughters with AN. They suggest that fathers are equally affected and distraught but appear to cope better by managing to compartmentalise, continue their role as providers and achieve some adaptive emotional detachment from the illness (Kyriacou, 2008).

An illustration of some of the important themes relating to parents' caregiving experience

The following qualitative themes emerged from analyses of interviews and focus group discussions of women with either AN or BN, their fathers, as well as carers (fathers and mothers) of women with AN (Kyriacou, 2008). Excerpts from participants are provided as illustration of themes.

Awareness of eating difficulties as an illness

Fathers find it particularly difficult to conceptualise eating difficulties as an illness. Daughters with anorexia nervosa reported perceptions of fathers as rigidly seeking logical explanations and invalidating their experience by over-focusing on the symptoms of the illness rather than underlying unmet needs.

> I don't know whether that's a male thing but I think it was much more difficult for him to accept, and I don't know if he fully got it . . . I mean with any other illness, you would never have to sit down and explain it's real or prove how bad it is or justify it as an illness. And you can't rationalise it and he wanted me to rationalise it because he couldn't understand it, but I could not equally under-stand it.
>
> (Patient 3 with AN)

> One can understand if you've got a medical problem . . . it's sort of outside my training, knowledge, maybe I deal more with facts, numbers, you know.
>
> (Father of patient with BN)

Eating disorders using the divide and rule principle

Polarised responses and attitudes between parents as to their required roles in providing care can cause caregiving difficulties. Consequently, an important aspect of teaching skills to carers needs to focus on improving communi-cation between parents, while emphasising a mutually supportive and collaborative approach to care. Fathers often step back in order to provide a counterbalance to maternal over-involvement. This might not be always help-ful as it could produce an inconsistent parenting approach.

Empowering carers to openly discuss their views, share responsibilities and negotiate their tasks may help reduce friction and role strain within the family. A more balanced approach to caregiving can be beneficial for both parents, enabling one parent to take respite and recharge, while the other takes responsibility and vice versa.

> I say she over-controls it, and she'll say I'm emotionally sterile [laughs].
>
> (Father 6 of patient with AN)

> I try to encourage her just to be calm in front of [daughter's name] and not show her anxiety so much. But I think it does come across to [daughter's name], so what I try and do therefore, is, even more so, is try to keep very calm and more distant and try to avoid talking about it.
>
> (Father 3 of patient with AN)

I have to say for myself that I was partly over-protective and over-loving towards my daughter to kind of compensate for the lack of closeness with her father. So then the father comes into it, and also if he's not as close still I try and compensate for it, so you cannot look at the father's relationship with the child without looking at the mother's relationship with the child because they are totally meshed. I don't think you can look at one separately from the other.

(Mother 3)

Fathering as a healing tool

Daughters identified helpful paternal caregiving behaviours, characterised by calm encouragement, a welcome contrast often to maternal anxiety and over-protection. This balanced emotional response and the ability to cope with feeding and treatment instructions was particularly noted.

In comparison to mothers, fathers were able to step back from the 'hot emotions' and were able to keep their eye on benefits in the long run, rather than gratify their daughters in the present moment. Fathers were able to appreciate that resisting emotional over-involvement was essential in enabling them not to be overwhelmed by the illness. Fathers showed their care, in different but no less important ways, such as maintaining financial responsi-bilities and supporting their wives and alleviating maternal stress. Mothers welcomed support and input from their husbands. It is clear, therefore, that treatment needs to include fathers.

If my dad had been a part of it, it would probably have not gone on for as long because I would have maybe wanted to please him as opposed to antagonise her.

(Patient 5 with AN)

I can kind of get away with telling him stuff he won't, say, try to change my way of thinking 'cause he really doesn't understand at all so, it kind of baffles him, so he's like, alright, ok, rather than yeah, I understand but change this like a woman would say . . . my mom would sort of shout at me and be stressed with me. It's actually easier with my dad to be honest . . . I find that she is more judging of me, dad doesn't sort of seem to judge me.

(Patient 4 with BN)

her father, like for a lot of girls, is very important to her, and I realise how important this relationship is, I was wondering if you can talk about why that is so, if you can break it down? Is it also that there's something physical, the comfort, the father being bigger, giving that hug, making the daughter feel safe and protected . . . there seems to be something very special about those hugs.

(Mother 7)

I think often dads can be better at the meals, you know, especially as food has more meaning for women, the shopping and the rejection of it, so you get more irritated if you can't feed your child, and it's much better to be calmer and more detached and sometimes men are very good at doing that.

(Mother 10)

In contrast to AN, BN daughters were more likely to avoid involving their fathers in their treatment, expressing self-blame and shame for their illness, and considering it a private problem they had to resolve.

Treatment implications: promoting collaborative caring and teamwork

Collaboration between carers is a key factor in the recovery process. The aim of the clinician is to help the parents develop a collaborative approach. Thus, mothers can be helped and supported, rather than being expected to take on most of the caregiving task. In some cases, the opposite scenario occurs in that fathers may play a more dominant role as caregivers. The essential point is that both parents need to be involved in a collaborative, consistent and mutually supportive and affirming manner. Involving fathers may be a good way to help the family work together and to help bring a balance. Fathers are usually willing to help but uncertain as to what to do and welcome a structured, problem-solving approach. In our experience, they respond well to being given the opportunity to learn new skills through written material and structured methods of information sharing and skills training.

In my experience, and this is obviously not a definitive one in any way, men tend to read desperately about it because it's the easier way of dealing with the problem than actually necessarily talking about it (other men in the audience nod or speak in agreement), and men are absolutely obsessive about learning all they can about it.

(Father 4)

The following excerpt is some feedback from one father whose wife and daughter had both had an eating disorder.

Father: I didn't think there was anything to understand and so reading the book [Treasure et al., 2007] has really opened my eyes and I have to say has completely changed my view on things. I began to understand what some of the causes of the illness could be and what were the sort of reasons for S acting like she was and also there was some insight into the kind of things that could be done outside the hospital environment to help. I realised that those were things that we, and particularly I, could get involved with and do something and maybe think there was more hope to achieve something. Also to understand S a lot better because for a long time I have to say, I thought S was selfish at first whereas now I understand that's not the case. I find it very difficult to deal with selfish people, even my own daughter.

Clinician: Right, so did that stop you getting involved?

Father: Oh yes. My wife says she knows all about it because she's had it but quite honestly from my point of view her behaviours and symptoms are very different from S's. She was never selfish, never inward-looking and so on. My experience with her didn't help at all with S.

Conclusion

The findings presented in this chapter suggest a rich and multifaceted contribution of mothers *and* fathers in the area of eating disorders, underscoring the significance of the father–daughter relationship and highlighting the under-utilised resources that fathers can bring to both prevention and treatment of these disorders.

Families should be conceptualised as a resource in treatment and as an ally against the illness. *Psychoeducation* regarding the nature and causes of the illness is helpful along with *cognitive restructuring training*, that is addressing possible misperceptions of the illness. Also, fathers may not be aware that their role impacts on the well-being of their spouses, offspring (affected or unaffected) and the whole family unit, and so fathers may need to be actively encouraged to be more involved. The research evidence is consistent in finding that fathers *can* and *do* play a crucial role both in the psychosocial development of their daughters and their transition from illness to health and adult life.

Fathers are crucial in aiding psychosocial transitions, such as adolescence and leaving home for university, through maintaining consistent and supportive relationships with their children. Similarly, it is possible that fathers are key sources of support for specific aspects enabling transition to normal life and reintegration following treatment for an ED, such as returning to school or employment. Additional empirical work (ideally longitudinal) is needed to elucidate fathers' contribution to recovery and reintegration in eating disorders, by assessing paternal characteristics and involvement at onset of treatment, throughout the course of the illness, and also into recovery.

In clinical contexts, individual sufferers and their families may stand to benefit tremendously from increased paternal involvement, while the father–daughter relationship will, for many, be a primary focus in treatment. Empirically, longitudinal and genetic studies have important questions to answer, regarding the specific impact of paternal characteristics in the neurodevelopment and environmental pathways to eating disorders and their treatment. The efficacy of preventative interventions may also improve by harvesting the potential for fathers to act as protective and support factors, as their consistent involvement throughout a daughter's life, may buffer against the development of eating disorders and contribute to improved psychosocial functioning.

In summary involving fathers is helpful in the following ways:

- reducing the tendency for maternal over-protection
- reducing criticism, unrealistic expectations, and perceived conditional regard
- developing positive communication
- fostering secure paternal attachments.

Acknowledgement

This work was supported by a grant from the NIHR Biomedical Research Centre for Mental Health, South London and Maudsley NHS Foundation Trust and Institute of Psychiatry, King's College London. Furthermore, we would like to thank Nina Jackson and REID, who funded the PhD of Olivia Kyriacou.

References

Agras, W. S., Bryson, S., Hammer, L. D. & Kraemer, H. C. (2007). Childhood risk factors for thin body preoccupation and social pressure to be thin. *Journal of the American Academy of Child and Adolescent Psychiatry* 46: 171–178.

Arevalo, R. V. & Escursell, R. M. R. (1997). The role of family in eating disorders. *Psicologia Conductual* 5: 391–407.

Barber, B. K. & Thomas, D. L. (1986). Dimension of fathers and mothers supportive behavior: The case of physical affection. *Journal of Marriage and the Family* 48: 783–794.

Bulik, C. M., Sullivan, P. F., Wade, T. D. & Kendler, K. S. (2000). Twin studies of eating disorders: A review. *International Journal of Eating Disorders* 27: 1–20.

Castro, J., Toro, J. & Cruz, M. (2000). Quality of rearing practices as predictor of short-term outcome in adolescent anorexia nervosa. *Psychological Medicine* 30: 61–67.

Engel, K. & Stienen, M. (1988). Father types of anorexia nervosa patients: The bonding, the brutal, the weak, and the absent father. An empirical study based on a comparison with fathers of a representative normal group. *Psychotherapy and Psychosomatics* 49: 145–152.

Fairburn, C. G., Norman, P. A., Welch, S. L., O'Connor, M. E., Doll, H. A. & Peveler, R. C. (1995). A prospective study of outcome in bulimia nervosa and the long-term effects of three psychological treatments. *Archives of General Psychiatry* 52: 304–312.

Fassino, S., Svrakic, D., Abbate-Daga, G., Leombruni, P., Amianto, F., Stanic, S. et al. (2002). Anorectic family dynamics: Temperament and character data. *Comprehensive Psychiatry* 43: 114–120.

Fassino, S., Amianto, F., Daga, G. A., Leombruni, P., Garzaro, L., Levi, M. et al. (2003). Bulimic family dynamics: Role of parents' personality. A controlled study with the temperament and character inventory. *Comprehensive Psychiatry* 44: 70–77.

Johnson, J. G., Cohen, P., Kasen, S. & Brook, J. S. (2002). Childhood adversities associated with risk for eating disorders or weight problems during adolescence or early adulthood. *American Journal of Psychiatry* 159: 394–400.

Keery, H., Boutelle, K., van den, B. P. & Thompson, J. K. (2005). The impact of appearance-related teasing by family members. *Journal of Adolescent Health* 37: 120–127.

Kyriacou, O. (2008). Risk and maintenance factors in eating disorders: The role of the father. PhD thesis, University of London

Kyriacou, O., Treasure, J. & Schmidt, U. (2008). Expressed emotion in eating disorders assessed via self-report: An examination of factors associated with expressed emotion in carers of people with anorexia nervosa in comparison to control families. *International Journal of Eating Disorders* 41: 37–46.

Marcus, M. D., Moulton, M. M. & Greeno, C. G. (1995). Binge eating onset in obese patients with binge eating disorder. *Addictive Behaviors* 20: 747–755.

Rojo-Moreno, L., Livianos-Aldana, L., Conesa-Burguet, L. & Cava, G. (2006). Dysfunctional rearing in community and clinic based populations with eating problems: Prevalence and mediating role of psychiatric morbidity. *European Eating Disorders Review* 14: 32–42.

Rorty, M., Yager, J., Rossotto, E. & Buckwalter, G. (2000). Parental intrusiveness in adolescence recalled by women with a history of bulimia nervosa and comparison women. *International Journal of Eating Disorders* 28: 202–208.

Soenens, B., Elliot, A. J., Goossens, L., Vansteenkiste, M., Luyten, P. & Duriez, B. (2005). The intergenerational transmission of perfectionism: Parents' psychological control as an intervening variable. *Journal of Family Psychology* 19: 358–366.

Soenens, B., Vansteenkiste, M., Vandereycken, W., Luyten, P., Sierens, E. & Goossens, L. (2008). Perceived parental psychological control and eating-disordered symptoms: Maladaptive perfectionism as a possible intervening variable. *Journal of Nervous and Mental Disease* 196: 144–152.

Szmukler, G. I., Eisler, I., Russell, G. F. M. & Dare, C. (1985). Anorexia-nervosa, parental expressed emotion and dropping out of treatment. *British Journal of Psychiatry* 147: 265–271.

Treasure, J., Smith, G. & Crane, A. (2007). *Skills-based Learning for Caring for a Loved One with an Eating Disorder: The New Maudsley Method.* London: Routledge.

Whitney, J., Murray, J., Gavan, K., Todd, G., Whitaker, W. & Treasure, J. (2005). Experience of caring for someone with anorexia nervosa: qualitative study. *British Journal of Psychiatry* 187: 444–449.

Wonderlich, S., Klein, M. H. & Council, J. R. (1996). Relationship of social perceptions and self-concept in bulimia nervosa. *Journal of Consulting and Clinical Psychology* 64: 1231–1237.

Woodside, D. B., Bulik, C. M., Halmi, K. A., Fichter, M. M., Kaplan, A., Berrettini, W. H. et al. (2002). Personality, perfectionism, and attitudes toward eating in parents of individuals with eating disorders. *International Journal of Eating Disorders* 31: 290–299.

Part V

Conclusion and appendices

Throughout this book, we have provided numerous opportunities for the reader to listen to the carer's voice. We hope that this has provided considerable insight into the lived-in experience of caring for a loved one with an eating disorder. The book now draws to a close with two other all-important perspectives of what 'collaborative caring' means to them, i.e. that of the sufferer and also of two clinicians who have had immeasurable experience of working and building on our collaborative caring programmes during the last several years. We also hear from an individual who has crossed the bridge from a carer herself, to that of researcher and motivational interviewing coach for other carers.

Chapter 16 presents a case study from the perspective of both the carers and the sufferer herself. It explains the rationale behind the therapist's guidance as well as providing the sufferer's perspective on the process. Although data analysis is ongoing, the chapter also provides some recent qualitative insight into the effects on the sufferer of their carers participating in collaborative caring projects. Chapter 17 concludes with quotes from three individuals who work with the carer's model and the principles of motivational interviewing in their work with carers of people with eating disorders.

This book includes three appendices as an adjunct to the material and guidance provided in the main body.

Appendix 1, 'Toolkit for Carers', is a series of worksheets designed to help carers recognise their own unique caring styles. It offers a full description of the animal models which are referred to throughout the book along with questions aimed at boosting the carer's self-reflection. The toolkit also cites several resources for support.

Appendices 2 and 3 are two assessment instruments that may be useful to professionals and/or carers.

Appendix 2, Eating Disorders Symptom Impact Scale (EDSIS), was designed to examine the specific problems experienced by carers of people with eating disorders. It has twenty-four items and four subscales, Impact of Starvation, Guilt, Social Isolation and Dysregulated Behaviours, with high internal consistency (0.91) (Sepúlveda et al., 2008). This scale is scored from 0 to 96. A higher score means more negative appraisals on specific aspects of caregiving.

Appendix 3, the Accommodation and Enabling Scale for Eating Disorders (AESED), is used to examine how families organise themselves around the illness. The questionnaire has thirty-three items and five subscales, Avoidance and Modifying Routine, Reassurance Seeking, Meal Ritual, Control of Family and 'Turning a Blind Eye', encapsulating the accommodating behaviours and attitudes expressed by carergivers. The alpha value for the overall scale is 0.92. This scale is scored from 0 to 132. A higher score means more negative appraisals on family accommodation to eating disorder symptoms.

Reference

Sepúlveda, A. R., Whitney, J., Hankins, M. & Treasure, J. (2008). Development and validation of an Eating Disorders Symptom Impact Scale (EDSIS) for carers of people with eating disorders. *Health and Quality of Life Outcomes* 6: 28. Available at www.pubmedcentral.nih.gov/articlerender.fcgi?artid=2365933

Chapter 16

What the patients say

An examination of what patients think about family interventions

Janet Treasure, Pam Macdonald and Liz Goddard

Introduction

The aim of this chapter is to introduce the voice of the patient with an eating disorder. What do they think about this form of intervention? Do they notice any changes in their parents' behaviour? Are these changes welcomed? At the present time we do not have quantitative evidence from the patients themselves to address this question. To date, however, we have obtained some qualitative feedback. We know that the patients themselves may have mixed opinions about this sort of intervention. We have heard of individuals who object to their parents attending workshops and may even act out to interfere with them going. We have heard of individuals having thrown the DVDs away before their carers have had the opportunity to watch them. In the short section that follows, we give the case report of Julie, who reflected on the intervention with her parents. Finally, we also give some examples of qualitative feedback from patients.

Case study: Julie

In this example, the parents had adopted a rhinoceros approach to care. This approach, however, was failing and driving them to become even more punitive. Consequently, a coercive vicious circle was building up and the atmosphere in the home becoming intensely hostile. In this case we report on the development of the formulation and treatment. After Julie had made a significant degree of recovery, she retrospectively reports on the process of treatment.

> Julie had had a relapsing course of anorexia nervosa over ten years. There were exacerbations at the time of exams. However, when she went home in the holidays, she was able to let her weight increase. The family had never gone for help but had managed to give Julie support so that she was well enough to

continue her academic career. Julie's parents were very concerned when she decided to change her career and do a second degree. Julie thought that she was fulfilling a sustained ambition, which was to follow her father into a career in law, but her parents just thought that this would entail further stress with exams and they strongly advised her against this. Nevertheless, Julie succeeded in getting a place on this course, but by the second year exams she was once again having difficulties and had to return home. Her parents were horrified when they returned after a short holiday to find that Julie was at her lowest ever weight. Julie's parents were desperately worried and felt that they could no longer cope. They felt that the time had come for Julie to be admitted into an inpatient unit and they made urgent enquiries to get this organised.

In the individual part of the assessment, the therapist enquired about Julie's functioning in all domains of life, physical, psychological, education, family, social and spiritual. The therapist elicited from Julie some of the concerns she had about her illness and the reasons and need that she had for change. Julie was on the contraceptive pill because she was concerned about her bones. She admitted that one of the reasons that she started to get treatment was because during the time that her parents were away, she woke in the night with chest pain. Her ankles had also started to swell. The therapist elicited the need for change. Julie thought that her anorexia nervosa might impinge on her career. Spirituality was important for her and one of the few times that her cheerful demeanour broke during the interview was when she explained that she did not feel entitled to go to church. She thought that she would be judged as having inflicted this illness upon herself.

The major area in which Julie noted the eating disorder caused difficulties was at home in the family. Julie explained that she thought that her parents considered that she used her eating in order to punish them. She said that her father, who had accompanied her to the appointment, had almost put her suitcase in the car in preparation for her being admitted to hospital immediately. The atmosphere at home had become very tense. There was a great deal of talk about death. Both parents considered that the stress relating to her illness was increasing their blood pressure. After rows they would measure each other's blood pressure. During these 'hot' interactions, Julie's mother accused Julie of killing her father. The atmosphere and comments became more acrimonious and bitter. Her father became so concerned about her that he had made special visits to his family to warn them about how severely ill Julie was.

When the therapist saw Julie's father as part of the assessment, he was very eager to detail his concerns and stressed the severity of Julie's illness. He was extremely sceptical about Julie's ability to make any progress at home. The assessment became derailed into arguments and it was difficult to make any agreed plan of management. Julie's parents wanted her admitted but she was opposed to this. A compromise was agreed which was for a further assessment in a week. This space of time gave everyone a chance to cool down and an opportunity for Julie to demonstrate to her parents that she was actively working to overcome her anorexia nervosa behaviours.

The therapist worked with the family to set up a tight plan to define what would be accepted in terms of feeding and activity at home. The family made a visit to the ward inpatient unit and were able to copy and implement some of the strategies that were used by the nurses. As Julie lived a long way away from the centre, both the family and Julie herself used email to ask questions and get advice when disputes arose. Email was also used when there was uncertainty about where to go forward within the monthly interim period until the next review session was held. Family meetings, however, continued to be extremely difficult. Often heated arguments arose and individuals would leave the room for cooling-down opportunities.

Nevertheless, Julie gained enough weight at home to be able to resume her studies at university. Once back at university, despite engaging in individual therapy, Julie's weight once again gradually fell. Julie's parents went to London for follow-up meetings. During the first four months, Julie did not apply herself fully to her individual therapy. She put off therapeutic homework tasks, such as completing any worksheets. She would fill the sessions with non-stop talk. It was difficult for the therapist to interrupt and get her to stick to the point. The therapist suggested that these interactions could be a form of avoidance, a barrier to working on the real issues. The metaphor that sprung to mind was that Julie was distracting the therapist to join in a merry conversational dance. The level of intimacy and confiding with the therapist contrasted with the barren avoidant relationship she was having with her peers and with the world. The therapist worked hard to keep the focus of the session on the core issues, such as how to implement a strategy for ensuring that her body was well nourished. Julie's parents remained actively involved with some email contact. Eventually the therapist was able to interrupt this avoidance and get her to focus on her eating and to reflect on and alter other unhelpful behaviours. A year later, Julie's weight had markedly improved.

Julie and her parents were later able to reflect on how they worked together. In this passage it is clear that Julie's mother had some kangaroo behaviour that, at times, flipped into being a rhinoceros. When Julie's mother was able to step back and play a less compulsive, caring role, Julie was able to start to make progress.

This passage illustrates how it is important to encourage parents to take time off from their caring duties. It also illustrates how stigma can contribute to the level of difficulty.

Julie's account

I can honestly say there were two people operating in my life. I didn't believe I had anorexia and I got so used to eating so little that what was normal seemed like such an enormous amount of food. I had a completely warped idea of what was normal. Just looking after myself day after day was difficult, I stopped washing my hair, I wore the same clothes all week and I was really going down, total neglect, I probably would have stopped drinking if I had been left to my own devices.

We all need food, that's something I had forgotten because I had spent a lot of time in life on my own with my studies. I started to isolate myself, which was very unlike me . . . not quite believing I could achieve what I am achieving now doing everything. Before I thought I had to spend 99.99 per cent of my day in work in order to achieve my goals, which is not the case. Being isolated was really detrimental I think.

It's like being in this grey black cave. You don't want anyone to come in and disturb you because you are quite happy being unwell, you are desperate not to be but you don't want anyone to come and interrupt your misery. I became incredibly stingy – I wouldn't spend a penny on myself or anyone else.

You really lean on whoever was looking after you the whole time for emotional, physical, every kind of support you can imagine. Certainly when the anorexia takes over I can honestly say I can be a complete monster, especially to my mother at times.

Of course for a mother it must be desperate to see your daughter not looking after herself and not wanting to look after herself and not understanding why and trying to do everything you can possibly do. I remember my mother would drive probably around an hour and a half trip so I can get yoghurt from Sainsbury's, in a little pot, because I knew exactly how many calories that would be.

Carers need not just support from each other but they need to be able to have time away. I think for my mother (who loves golf) she gave everything up for me the whole summer to try and get me well enough to go back to university. Eventually she said to herself 'I have to get time to myself, otherwise I am going to go mad' so she started having time with friends and she would go and play golf a couple of times a week. I used to find it quite hard because I needed her for everything but when she came back her spirits were so much lifted. So I think it's quite important for carers to have some time away to recharge the batteries.

Time away is as important as time with. It makes the person with anorexia suddenly sit up and think, 'Oh', because I sort of let Mum make choices all the time for me, I totally relied on her . . . so I spent the entire day with my mother and so when she went out and did her things, it meant that I had to try and fill my time in the house alone. I found that really hard but when I look it now, it was probably the beginning of me getting better only a tiny step towards it but suddenly having to be on your own and coping with that.

When someone is severely underweight they are not able to look after themselves at all. I had no idea what was going on, I had no idea how much damage I was doing to my bones, body, my brain. I really had no understanding. I lost insight. So I really think it's important, certainly in the beginning stages of recovery, that you got to be there for somebody to make sure they eat, for instance.

As an adult with anorexia you get very clever about knowing how not to put on weight. I think that's probably an area that carers need to be educated about – the kind of nutrition that is needed to actually make a difference. Until you start to gain any tangible weight, you can't even begin to get your head straight and to begin to think about why it happened.

In our family we started off by signing contracts but it just didn't work. I found that I spent hours and hours in my bedroom writing out what I would and wouldn't eat, how much I could eat and then could I have time out to do that this and the other and exercise. If it ended up that I had earned the privilege to go and exercise I ended up exercising far too much. I just had no kind of balance. My walks were then timed and I started to feel as though I was in a prison and then I started to fight against that. Really I was fighting against my mum, which she found so hard because all she wanted to do was to really love and help me.

That's when I think where it helps you to have an intermediary . . . a therapist or a psychiatrist at some meetings. When we met as a family for help, we used to have Mum and Dad there, and me and obviously there would be a big row and Mum would get out and then she would come in and Dad would be exasperated, but by the end of the discussion everyone would be smiling, even though there would have been crying because we would have some kind of plan of action to go forward and something to hang the next few weeks on.

Gradually Mum used to say, 'OK I want you now to be in charge of making your own lunch.' When Mum said to me, 'I want you to do your own lunch', that was really quite a big step forward for me because I had to make my own decisions. She would look at me and what I had made and say, 'You got it wrong'.

I would look at the lettuce and think no one would get through that, not even a rabbit, by next year. But I accepted Mum's decision.

When my mother was able to share the burden with people who weren't looking after people with anorexia I think she found it quite helpful. She eventually realised that she was not going to hide away because of stigma. At first she was sensitive to the stigma of having someone at home, who was training to be a barrister and had suddenly decided not to look after herself. It looks awful – it was really more than my mother could handle. It made her feel like she was a complete failure as a mother.

One of Mum's friends . . . she saw me . . . I saw her face and it was the most awful thing, her face just looked shattered and she just said, 'Your daughter looks like she's got cancer.' As she got to know more about the illness she decided that by isolating herself because of her fear of stigma, she was contributing to the perpetuation of this attitude. She therefore told herself that some people might have prejudices but she was not going to respond to that by hiding but by being open and honest.

Julie's reflection about the role her parents played in her care illustrates several important points. This family had high levels of expressed emotion oscillating between extreme over-protection and bursts of fury. Judging the level of responsibility for eating that can be allowed and balancing this with the parents' need for rest and respite, can be difficult. Similarly, finding the correct balance between developing a career and optimising health is also problematic.

The impact of working with carers

Preliminary findings after delivering the workshops were that more individuals with an eating disorder did re-engage with therapy. It remains to be seen what impact these interventions have upon the overall outcome from the eating disorder. However, some of the qualitative feedback from the patients did indicate that there appeared to be both short-term benefits in respect of better reactions to the illness with the possibility of long-term benefits in closer, more secure attachments and improved patterns of communication.

Parenting skills

In the following section we illustrate some quotes from patients whose parents joined the workshops for carers, while they were being treated on an inpatient unit. The patients themselves were phoned a few weeks after the intervention and asked whether they had noticed any differences in their parents' attitudes or behaviours following the intervention.

Recognising the illness

The intervention for parents enabled them to recognise the behaviours as symptoms and they were able to develop a united front to manage it.

> They supplied a book to my parents and I think ... which helped a lot with understanding what went, the processes that went through my head when I saw the food and I had to eat and the feelings afterwards and all of that. I think they understood that more and instead, as before, I went straight downhill and no one even knew what I had, it's almost like now sometimes I might have a hiccup ... and it would be like 'Oh, oh the illness coming back' and they'd make sure they hit it there rather than letting it go back to where it was.

> I would say that even though that was frustrating, it was a positive aspect of the group that they did identify the things that were, you know, most parents or carers wouldn't be able to see that that was part of the eating disorder and they would fall for the tricks that anorexics play, and I think that was good that they did teach them about that.

Gaining competencies in understanding and managing the illness

Parents understood more about the illness and gained mastery over basic management skills.

> I think mainly the confidence thing, I think they think they know what they're doing more and they feel they understand more. I think that's essential because before they felt panicked, they didn't know what to do. They felt disillusioned with the whole thing, they just thought ... self-doubt as well because it's made them think they were crap parents and all this sort of stuff so I think the confidence issue was the biggest one.

> I mean she's now stricter than she ever was but she's more knowledgeable, knowing what to do. When a situation appears when the eating disorder is getting the better of me, she comes in and says I won't be able to get away with it because she knows more information, whereas before she wouldn't have a clue so she'd probably go with it.

Awareness of psychological aspects of illness

Some patients reported that their parents were more able to understand and recognise the emotional and psychological aspects of the illness which enabled empathy and emotional support from carers.

- Well, it is almost like they are in my head kind of thing, whereas before it was just eat and that is the answer, I think they understand the difficulty in me doing that, whereas before they didn't.

- The way that there can be other things behind the eating disorder than just eating.
- [It] helped a lot with understanding the processes that went through my head when I saw the food and I had to eat and the feelings afterwards and all of that. I think they understood that more.
- I'd say just more understanding of how my mind works and the illness itself, it's how it takes control of things and understanding it more and knowing more about it which is the first step of helping me get rid of it.

Reducing stigma

Some patients recognised that by going to the groups and recognising eating disorders as serious illnesses, stigma and blame was reduced.

- It's not a secret, you don't have to keep it a secret any more.
- So I think in general she's come to understand that it's not something that I want. I think that was her problem: that she thought I really liked doing this, and she saw that it was hurting my dad and my brother and she hated me for that.
- She always used to avoid phrases like eating disorder, or anorexia or bulimia, which irritated me then because you know, I thought, 'Well stop denying it', you know? It's obvious . . . And then I was really ill and that was when she got involved. And I think that was when I, when she was actually going off to groups to actually learn about my problem: that's when I think I realised she did care.

Managing carers' emotional reaction to the symptoms

Parents learned from the intervention the importance of moderating their emotional response to the illness.

- They've learned that if they show too much emotion, it throws up more emotion in me basically.
- It really, really helped, because when she gets angry with me, I then get even angrier, which makes me worse and it's just like a horrible atmosphere, whereas when she stayed calm, I sort of stayed calm myself and just like got over it, if you see what I mean.

Setting boundaries

Parents who had a more permissive style of parenting learned to set boundaries.

I think it's given them more confidence. I think before they were a bit too scared to be tough with me but when someone else says it's OK to be tough with them I think they learn that they can be tough with me. I think that's the biggest thing they've learned . . . that it's OK to be horrible to me and occasionally they need to be.

Benefits for patients

Although some patients who were not ready to change resented their parents becoming more skilled, others noticed general positive effects.

General comments

The long-term benefits of the project were noticed by some of the patients.

- So yeah I would say definitely, if she hadn't had the sort of teaching and support and stuff like that then I might not have got better as well, or as quickly as I have, and I guess we'd still be in a, well . . . further down that road than we are.
- I can't tell you how annoying it was but I think in the long term, if I'm honest, and I think it was probably better because then you know you've got that support there and you know that they actually do care rather than ignoring it.

Communication skills

Some patients noticed an improvement in communication skills, in particular the ability to demonstrate listening.

- I think everyone's more aware of listening to each individual. Instead of someone saying something and over talking them and not listening. I think they just become more aware of listening to their children's opinions and taking it on board.
- I feel like they are more able to or willing to listen to me . . . to try and explain myself because before it was just 'I don't want to hear it, I don't want to hear it'.
- And then afterwards she was – it was just a lot easier to speak with her. She would just kind of listen . . . because I think she stopped trying to understand it and more just listened to what was happening and to what I was saying.

Many patients also mentioned that as communication improved, family members were able to express themselves more freely.

- If he or my mum says something that hurts, I can say that you are hurting my feelings and in some degree they can do the same. Instead of getting upset and walking out, I can, perhaps, five times out of ten I can say that . . . which is really strange, because we did not use to.
- I don't hide anything from her now, like if I'm having a bad time I tell her, whereas before it's silence, cover it up kind of thing.

Attachment

Other patients noticed an improvement in attachments.

- It makes me feel safe to think that I'm not only surrounded by staff but also parents that have some idea of what they are doing rather than going straight home to parents who have no idea what they are on about ... they're more negotiable and more approachable because they seem to grasp how difficult it is and how much internal dialogue there is and they say ... how can I help you, what's going on, what would make this easier.
- It's just because we didn't talk before and it was a bit more strained when I was younger kind of thing, so it's nice now we actually do have a relationship whereas before there wasn't anything there.

Negative or ambivalent aspects of the intervention

Parents as part of the therapeutic team

In some cases, when the individual is not ready to change, they resent the fact that their parents show more competencies and a change from over-protective, kangaroo care to a more guiding approach.

- I'd give excuses and things and they'd know they were excuses and they'd just let me get away with it because they didn't want to fight with me and they thought if they fought with me it would stress me out more.
- When you go home it's supposed to be nice and relaxed and you want to be able to enjoy yourself at home and here's where you are supposed to feel the pressure of things and you are like everyone's ganging up against you, your parents and the staff and you'd rather they were on your side.

Increasing resistance

On some occasions there were some negative aspects of the intervention caused by parents moving into action which fostered resistance.

> Um, I think that was at the point I was still in the heavy grips of the illness so when they would come back and they would have ways to solve it, it would almost um make my illness retaliate. I wouldn't like it at all.

Some individuals found their parents' use of new techniques and skills condescending:

> Yeah, I find again, they come up with phrases, you know, are sort of ... what they've got from somewhere else or like, for example, I know if I say, 'I'm going

to find this hard,' my mum will say, 'It's all right to find it hard' and I think 'I know where you've got that from'. Do you know what I mean? It's ver . . . it just makes me feel a little bit like set up and . . . I'm not just a, you know, I'm not a piece of paper, I'm a person and it makes you feel like . . . yeah, they're practising on me. It makes me feel – it's just patronising.

Misattributions of behaviours

While many patients recognised the positive effects of their carers' increased understanding of the illness, some also mentioned the frustrating experience of their carers using the information they had learnt to explain negative behaviours that were not necessarily symptoms of the eating disorder.

Sometimes it's a bit annoying because he'll attribute too much, you know, and when you are annoyed about something that you've got every right to be annoyed about, he might then put that down to the eating disorder but, you know, for him it's very early days but at least he's willing to try.

Conclusion

Although some patients, especially those who are not ready to change their behaviour, have some reservations about the intervention, many who are in a more advanced stage of change are able to notice benefits. The intervention enables an increased understanding of the illness which, in turn, produces a more authoritative style of parenting, helping those who are overly permissive to set boundaries and those who are too authoritarian to negotiate more. This can have a wider benefit in terms of improving communication and strengthening attachments.

Chapter 17

The professional perspective

Gill Todd, Wendy Whitaker and Pam Macdonald

In conclusion then, we end this book on collaborative caring with contributions from three individuals who have worked in various skills-based training projects. Gill Todd, a psychiatric nurse, has developed programmes for families and carers on an inpatient unit and currently delivers carers' skills workshop training to professionals and carers and also delivers motivational interviewing training for chronic disease management. Wendy Whitaker is a senior practitioner social worker who currently runs the intensive day patient intervention for those families preparing for the transition from inpatient to outpatient care. Pam Macdonald is a carer who is now working on a PhD on the development of a skills training DVD plus telephone coaching for carers of people with eating disorders. She is also involved in delivering telephone coaching to carers, using the principles of motivational interviewing.

Gill Todd

Carers are extremely grateful for any opportunity to express their concerns and be self-reflective about their own behaviour. They appreciate the chance to ask for information from a clinician in a neutral setting, i.e. away from their loved one, and with other carers who understand and sometimes share their experiences. Carers can begin to take a step away from the highly emotional atmosphere at home and express their loss, grief, fear, hopes and expectations for their loved one without feeling as though they are walking on eggshells.

Carers show a great capacity for learning to be flexible and step by step change their own behaviour. They are very generous with other carers in the group by sharing their emotions and seem to quickly learn the power of being able to articulate their feelings in a non-judgemental atmosphere. The amount of learning and change carers engage in is astonishing and the workshops can be a very moving experience for all.

Our carers learn to be parents again, rather than jailers or nurses, and although they say the language we teach is quite artificial, they realise that a change is necessary. Over time, repeated practice in the form of small experiments helps them to be more spontaneous and genuine in their responses.

Finally, carers also learn that showing that they love the person, and not the eating disorder, helps the individual to feel valued and not criticised and also allows the carers to reinforce their individual boundaries without engaging in a character assassination of the sufferer and feeling worse themselves, thus reinforcing a negative cycle. Carers want hope for their loved ones and we can as professionals work with them to the benefit of all.

Wendy Whitaker

Skills-based training workshops have increased my knowledge about working with carers of people with eating disorders, as the collaborative process generates new thinking and ideas. Carers appreciate the way the skills-based model values both their role as carers and the ways they have struggled and survived. As a professional I have found this collaboration creative and more constructive than working individually with carers. Skills-based training workshops have been a collaboration between carers and professionals, synthesising our experiences, ideas, struggles and achievements.

Working in this way, which values carers' experience and knowledge, enables professionals to really get alongside those whose efforts and love for the sufferer far surpasses that of professionals. As a result, not only is it possible to transfer skills, but also it creates a safe place for carers to acknowledge how difficult their job is and also the particular ways in which they personally struggle. Difficult issues, often about family life, are offered by the group members and are collaboratively resolved. Thus, the entire group gain from an individual's difficulties.

Working with carers, whose lives are affected by an eating disorder, can be sad and difficult. However, using the skills-based workshops, the resilience of families is often demonstrated by the frequent laughter – usually at themselves.

The skills-based workshops and manual provide a step-by-step process for not only families but also professionals to learn about the most effective ways of working with people suffering with an eating disorder. It also provides a structure to organise skills workshops for families and carers.

Pam Macdonald

Crossing that bridge from 'carer' to 'professional' has indeed been an enlightening voyage . . . rather like entering the world of the eating disorder itself. What started out as an ominous, lonely, frustrating and horrendously terrifying experience has gradually become an enlightening and self-reflective journey, one that has been a tremendous learning curve for myself, as well as close others around me.

As a carer, I've been the rhinoceros, the jellyfish, the ostrich, the kangaroo; I've also tried extremely hard to overcome such responses – at times, with great success and at other times not quite as well! The adage 'every mistake is a treasure' has certainly helped along the way. Through applying the same determination, effort and focus, displayed by so many of the carers I now work with, I now find myself in the enviable position of struggling to keep up alongside our daughter in the sea of recovery.

Throughout the journey, I have come to recognise and reflect upon those traits that may have helped maintain or accommodate the eating disorder. Now, as a professional wading through the plethora of academic literature, I also find myself mulling over common family characteristics and natural temperaments that may be only too ready to strike again wreaking havoc, perhaps, on a future generation?

Consequently, it is my personal belief that providing families with support, education and collaborative caring facilities is absolutely crucial for families who may find themselves facing the stark prospect of an ED in their midst. I have worked with some remarkable carers over the last years and witnessed first-hand their truly wonderful traits and characteristics. I am sure the same can be said of their daughters and sons. If, through skills-based training and psychoeducation, we can help carers work with their offspring to channel those same strengths through life's more adaptive channels, it will be a job well done.

At this writing there is tremendous rhetoric on the concept of 'change'. As our American cousins ride high on a wave of hope and optimism, it is perhaps worth tapping into these aspirations when we ask ourselves the question, 'Can carers and professionals work collaboratively in the fight against eating disorders?' I personally believe there is no alternative, other than to respond with a resounding 'Yes We Can!'

Appendix I

Toolkit for Carers

The caring role in eating disorders

Introduction

Eating disorder symptoms can have profound social and emotional ramifications for carers. Symptoms are variable in their form and impact and are frightening, intrusive, antisocial, anxiety provoking and frustrating. (In these worksheets, please note that we use 'Edi' to represent the eating disorder – this is to represent the stereotyped clinical presentation which gets confusingly entangled with your child's personality.)

All semblance of normality disappears, social life evaporates, future plans are put on hold and interactions around food increasingly dominate all family relationships. Consequently, it is understandable that responses can be the source of hostile confrontations with family members. Unfortunately, however, the manner in which the carer attempts to *reduce* the symptoms may inadvertently play a role in maintaining or enabling the problems (Treasure et al., 2008). The result can be that the individual feels even more alienated and retreats even further into eating disorder behaviours. Carers often report they lack the skills and resources required to care for their loved ones and acknowledge their need for help and skills to manage these behaviours (Haigh & Treasure, 2003).

Does the eating disorder (Edi) bully you about what, when and how you eat (Figure A.1)? Are you bullied about when and how you can use the kitchen and/or bathroom? Perhaps you are controlled by Edi about what, when and how you shop? . . . Or about when and how mealtimes are arranged?

There again . . . perhaps you are covering up negative consequences of Edi behaviour . . . clearing up mess, dealing with bathroom problems, buying more food (Figure A.2). Perhaps you are turning a blind eye to antisocial behaviour, such as stealing or addictions? Perhaps you have been giving constant reassurance and being sucked in to obsessional rituals or compulsive concerns?

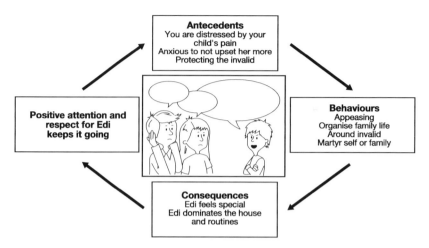

Figure A.1 The ABC of accommodating: bullied by Edi.

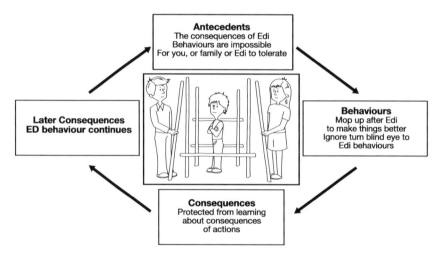

Figure A.2 The ABC of enabling Edi behaviours.

The caring role

Parents are the solution, not the problem. Eating disorders can – and do – put tremendous demands on the coping abilities of family members. Carers and other family members are usually the main support for the sufferer but frequently get caught up in unhelpful patterns of behaviour that, in turn, perpetuate eating disorder behaviours.

Nobody knows the cause of an eating disorder. There is no evidence that family factors are the cause; there may be a small genetic risk but this is not something over which the parent has any control. Consequently guilt and self-blame are futile and inappropriate. There is, however, evidence from naturalistic studies that the outcome of eating disorders is influenced by the emotional reactions of close others which can act as maintaining factors.

It is often necessary for members of the family themselves to change some aspects of their patterns of interacting in response to the eating disorder behaviours. The aim of our carer interventions is to highlight alternative techniques and strategies which allow both carers and sufferers to consider the impact of their responses to eating disordered behaviours and to use this information to reflect on their own unique emotional responses in guiding goal setting and action planning.

The following animal analogies describe some of the common reactions of people who provide care and support for people with eating disorders. Often these reactions can get in the way of providing effective help. Each animal analogy may be your default way of coping with stress and this response could be part of your natural temperament, e.g. over-protective, logical, overtly emotional or avoidant. In order to change these responses, you may have to experiment with trying responses which do not feel natural or spontaneous.

You may not feel motivated to change your responses and behaviour because you are coping with the eating disorder (Edi) and getting results. If this is the case, you can capitalise on what is working for you and enhance your success by sharing your strategies and skills. If you are able to role model flexible coping strategies to the sufferer you may be able to help build their confidence to try and change their behaviour.

You will find more information about these styles and reactions from our book, *Skills-Based Learning for Caring for a Loved One with an Eating Disorder: The New Maudsley Method* (Treasure et al., 2007) and from our website www.eatingresearch.com

The kangaroo: too much emotion and too much control

Kangaroos do everything to protect, taking over all aspects of the sufferer's life. They treat the sufferer with kid gloves, burying them in their pouch in an effort to avoid any upset or stress, accommodating to all possible demands. The downside of this type of caring is that the sufferer fails to learn how to approach and master life's challenges, become trapped in the role of the eternal infant.

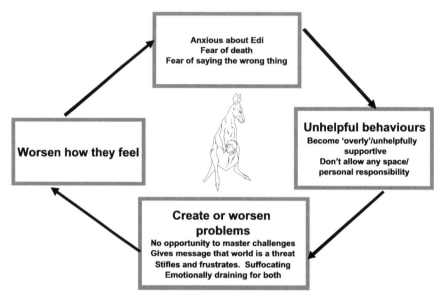

The vicious circle of kangaroo caring.

- Reflect on your kangaroo responses.
- How are they working for you?
- If not, what difficulties are you encountering? Give an example of what's not working for you.
- What aspects of your behaviour can you experiment with?
- How important is it to address some of your kangaroo responses?
- Think back to one of your kangaroo behaviours in recent weeks. How can you change that behaviour a little? What would be the first step?

IMPORTANT! Change is tough . . . remember to congratulate yourself after having attempted the change!

The rhinoceros: too much logic and too little warm emotion

Fuelled by stress, exhaustion and frustration, or simply one's own temperament, the rhinoceros attempts to persuade and convince by argument and confrontation. The downside is that even if the sufferer does obey, confidence to do so without assistance will not be developed. More likely, arguing back with Edi logic will merely produce a deeper hole for the sufferer to hide in.

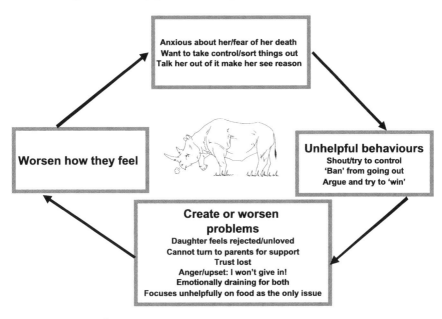

The vicious circle of rhinoceros caring.

- Reflect on your rhinoceros responses. Are they working for you?
- What difficulties are you encountering?
- How can you avoid these obstacles?
- What might be the repercussions of change, both negative and positive?
- We know that any behaviour change may encourage your loved one to up the ante. In the event of this happening, how can you safeguard or protect yourself?
- What can you think of that you can do for yourself to lower your anxiety, stress or anger levels?
- Set a goal or target for yourself?
- How do you think this will make you feel?

IMPORTANT! If possible, try to work in coming up with ideas on how *you* can achieve some 'me' time. Remember the importance of your own well-being in both your physical and mental health. Role modelling self-care will help the sufferer to learn to change.

The ostrich: too little emotion and too little control

Rather than confronting the difficult behaviour, the ostrich finds it difficult to cope with the distress of challenging and confronting the Edi behaviour and so avoids talking and thinking about the problems at all. The downside is that the sufferer may misinterpret this approach as uncaring and feel unloved, thus strengthening low self-esteem.

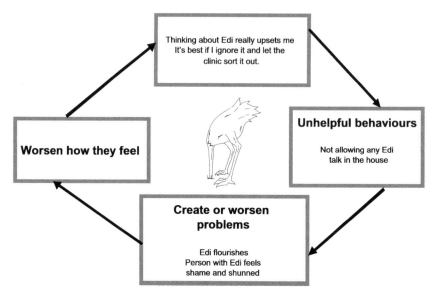

The vicious circle of ostrich caring.

- Reflect on your ostrich tendencies. How do you feel about the vicious circle above?
- It takes courage to change our behaviour. What small step can you take to become less of an ostrich?
- Who can support you in experimenting with new responses?
- What would you want this person to do or say? A list of suggestions is often useful.
- What do you think about involving others?
- How do you feel about making these changes?

IMPORTANT! Change can be difficult and uncomfortable. It may be worthwhile engaging the help of a supportive family member or friend to support you in your quest. Think about your own self-esteem and how role modelling confidence might help the sufferer to take a risk towards change. The fact you're reading this sheet and considering these questions is already a huge step. Well done!

The jellyfish: too much emotion and too little control

Some carers may become engulfed in intense emotional responses. They may hold some false interpretations about the illness, high levels of self-blame, or perfectionist tendencies with regards to parenting skills. The downside is that the 'sad and mad' approach causes tears, anger and sleepless nights and worsens how everybody feels by raising anxiety levels.

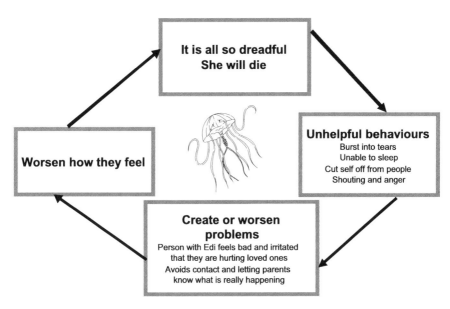

The vicious circle of jellyfish caring.

- Reflect on your jellyfish tendencies. How do they make you feel?
- What are the effects of those responses on yourself? On others?
- How important is it that you work on your 'jellyfish' responses?
- If you were advising a friend with the same problem, what would your advice be?
- What beliefs do you need to work on in order for this change to happen?
- What are the green shoots that make you feel a little bit confident?
- What would you need either yourself or from other people that would help you move forward in terms of your confidence?
- The fact that you are reading these worksheets shows that you are open to new ideas. Well done! What specifically could you do to get started to experimenting with different patterns of responding?

IMPORTANT! All of the aforementioned 'important' points apply. Role modelling calmness and compassion will help the sufferer think about their own self-care as a first step towards change. Well done for considering the first step.

OUR AIMS

The dolphin: just enough caring and control

An optimal way of helping someone with an eating disorder is to gently nudge. Imagine your daughter or son is at sea. The Edi is her or his life vest. She or he is unwilling to give up the safety of this life vest while living in her stressful and dangerous world. You are the dolphin, nudging her or him to safety, at times swimming ahead and leading the way, and at other times, swimming alongside with encouragement, or even quietly swimming behind.

The St Bernard: just enough compassion and consistency

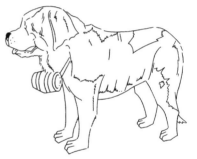

An optimal caring response is one of calmness, warmth and compassion. This involves accepting and processing the pain that is involved with what is lost and developing reserves of kindness, gentleness and love to provide the backdrop of change. A St Bernard responds consistently – unfailing, reliable and dependable in all circumstances. He is calm and collected, even in the most dangerous of situations. He is dedicated to the welfare and safety of those who are lost – calm, warm and nurturing.

Nobody gets it right all of the time – in challenging times it is important to remember the adage, 'every mistake is a treasure'. Tomorrow is a new day. For further information and support on caring for a loved one with an eating disorder, please see the following resources:

- *Skills-Based Learning for Caring for a Loved One with an Eating Disorder: The New Maudsley Method* (Treasure et al., 2007)
- Our website www.eatingresearch.com
- beat (www.b-eat.co.uk) is the leading UK-wide charity providing information, help and support for people affected by eating disorders.

References

Haigh, R. & Treasure, J. (2003). Investigating the needs of carers in the area of eating disorders: Development of the Carers' Needs Assessment Measure (CaNAM). *European Eating Disorders Review* 11: 125–141.

Treasure, J., Smith, G. D. & Crane, A. M. (2007). *Skills-based Learning for Caring for a Loved One with an Eating Disorder: The New Maudsley Method.* London: Routledge.

Treasure, J., Sepúlveda, A., MacDonald, P., Whitaker, P., Lopez, C., Zabala, M. et al. (2008). Interpersonal maintaining factors in eating disorder: Skill sharing interventions for carers. *International Journal of Child and Adolescent Health* 1(4): 331–338.

Appendix 2

Eating Disorders Symptom Impact Scale (EDSIS)

Name:...Date:..

The following pages contain a number of statements that commonly apply to persons who care for relatives or friends with an eating disorder. We would like you to read each one and decide how often it has applied to you over the *past one month*. It is important to note that there are no right or wrong answers. Also, it is best not to spend too long on any one statement. Your first reaction will usually provide the best answer.

Items	Never	Rarely	Sometimes	Often	Nearly always
During the past month how often have you thought about:					
1 How your friends/relatives have stopped visiting	0	1	2	3	4
2 Losing your friends	0	1	2	3	4
3 Feeling unable to go out for evenings, weekends or on holiday	0	1	2	3	4
4 Cancelling or refusing plans to see friends or relatives	0	1	2	3	4
5 Feeling that I should have noticed it before it became so bad	0	1	2	3	4
6 Feeling that I have let her/him down	0	1	2	3	4
7 Feeling that there could have been something that I should have done	0	1	2	3	4
8 Thinking that perhaps I wasn't strict enough	0	1	2	3	4
9 Thinking about where I went wrong	0	1	2	3	4
10 Physically and/or verbally aggressive	0	1	2	3	4
11 Controlling/manipulative	0	1	2	3	4

12	Lying/stealing	0	1	2	3	4
13	Out of control temper	0	1	2	3	4

When the sufferer was living with you at home during the past month, how often:
(if the sufferer was not living at home with you during the past month, please refer to the last time she/he was living at home)

14	Did you experience difficulties preparing meals (i.e. making separate meals for family members, not having correct ingredients)?	0	1	2	3	4
15	Were there arguments with other family members about how to handle mealtimes?	0	1	2	3	4
16	Were there arguments or tension during mealtimes?	0	1	2	3	4
17	Did food disappear from the cupboards?	0	1	2	3	4
18	Did you spend long periods of time shopping for food?	0	1	2	3	4
19	Did you have difficulties with blocked drains, plumbing?	0	1	2	3	4
20	Were there bad smells and hygiene in the bathroom?	0	1	2	3	4
21	Did you have to turn up the heat due to her/him feeling cold?	0	1	2	3	4
22	Did you check on her/him to ensure that she/he was OK?	0	1	2	3	4
23	Did you notice or think about how the illness was affecting her/him physically (e.g. see her/him fall, faint, struggle up the stairs)?	0	1	2	3	4
24	Did you notice or think about how the illness was affecting her/him mentally?	0	1	2	3	4

Source: Sepúlveda et al. (2008), courtesy of BioMed Central.

Appendix 3

Accommodation and Enabling Scale for Eating Disorders (AESED)

Name:...Date:..

The following items contain a number of statements that commonly apply to the family members who live with a relative or a friend with an eating disorder. We would like you to read each one and decide how often it has applied to your family members over the *past one month*. It is important to note that there are no right or wrong answers. Your first reaction will usually provide the best answer.

Items During the past *month* how often have you thought about:					
0 = never 1 = rarely 2 = sometimes 3 = often 4 = every day					
1 The choices of food that you buy?	0	1	2	3	4
2 What other family members do and for how long in the kitchen?	0	1	2	3	4
3 Cooking practice and ingredients you use?	0	1	2	3	4
4 What other family members eat?	0	1	2	3	4
Does your relative engage any family member in repeated conversations:					
5 Asking for reassurance about whether she/he will get fat?	0	1	2	3	4
6 About whether it is safe or acceptable to eat a certain food?	0	1	2	3	4
7 Asking for reassurance about whether she/he look fat in certain clothes?	0	1	2	3	4
8 Their ingredients and amounts, possible substitutes for ingredients?	0	1	2	3	4
9 About negative thoughts and feelings?	0	1	2	3	4
10 About self-harm?	0	1	2	3	4
Do any family members have to accommodate to the following:					
11 What crockery is used?	0	1	2	3	4
12 How crockery is cleaned?	0	1	2	3	4
13 What time food is eaten?	0	1	2	3	4

14	What place food is eaten?	0	1	2	3	4
15	How the kitchen is cleaned?	0	1	2	3	4
16	How food is stored?	0	1	2	3	4
17	The exercise routine of the relative with an ED?	0	1	2	3	4
18	Your relative's checking their body shape or weight?	0	1	2	3	4
19	How the house is cleaned and tidied?	0	1	2	3	4

Do you choose to ignore aspects of your relative's eating disorder that impinge on your family's life in an effort to reconcile or make it tolerable for the rest of the family such as if:

20	Food disappears?	0	1	2	3	4
21	Money is taken?	0	1	2	3	4
22	The kitchen is left a mess?	0	1	2	3	4
23	The bathroom is left a mess?	0	1	2	3	4
24	In general, to what extent would you say that the relative with an eating disorder controls family life and activities?					

None at all			*About half*					*Completely*		
0	1	2	3	4	5	6	7	8	9	10

To continue answering the questionnaire, please bear in mind the following:

If it has never happened, you would circle the number 0. If it has happened 1–3 times per month, you would circle the number 1. If it has happened 1–2 times per week, you would circle the number 2. If it has happened 3–6 times per week you would circle the number 3. If it happens daily, you would circle the number 4. Over the **past one month**:

0 = never 1 = 1–3 times/month 2 = 1–2 times/week 3 = 3–6 times/week 4 = daily	

25	How often did you participate in behaviours related to your relative's compulsions?	0	1	2	3	4
26	How often did you assist your relative in avoiding things that might make her/him more anxious?	0	1	2	3	4

To continue answering:

If the answer is NO, you would circle the number 0. If the answer is MILD; you would circle the number 1. If the answer is MODERATE, you would circle the number 2. If the answer is SEVERE, you would circle the number 3. If the answer is EXTREME, you would circle the number 4. Over the **past one month**:

0 = no 1 = mild 2 = moderate 3 = severe 4 = extreme	

27	Have you avoided doing things, going places, or being with people because of your relative's disorder?	0	1	2	3	4
28	Have you modified your family routine because of your relative's symptoms?	0	1	2	3	4

29	Have you modified your work schedule because of your relative's needs?	0	I	2	3	4
30	Have you modified your leisure activities because of your relative's needs?	0	I	2	3	4
31	Has helping your relative in the before-mentioned ways caused you distress?	0	I	2	3	4
32	Has your relative become distressed/ anxious when you have not provided assistance?	0	I	2	3	4
33	Has your relative become angry/ abusive when you have not provided assistance?	0	I	2	3	4

Source: Sepúlveda et al. (2009), courtesy of BioMed Central.

References

Sepúlveda, A. R., Whitney, J., Hankins, M. & Treasure, J. (2008). Development and validation of an Eating Disorders Symptom Impact Scale (EDSIS) for carers of people with eating disorders. *Health and Quality Life Outcomes* 6: 28.

Sepúlveda, A. R., Kyriacou, O. & Treasure, J. (2009). Development and validation of the Accommodation and Enabling Scale for Eating Disorders. *BMC Health Services Research* 9.

Index

Accommodation and Enabling Scale for Eating Disorders (AESED) 134, 252, 278–80
adult services 5, 36, 37, 39–40, 167
Al-Anon 49
alcohol 48, 49, 81, 132
alexithymia 151
Alzheimer's disease 46
anorexia nervosa 4, 6, 11, 14–15, 22, 37–40, 45, 46–51, 53, 56, 61–82, 84, 88–9, 97, 101, 115, 127, 135–6, 144, 150, 157, 161, 167, 184, 193, 203, 222, 232, 235, 241, 243, 253, 257; adolescent 11, 14–15, 16n2, 37–8, 52, 115; adult 7–8, 10, 12–16, 37, 40, 48, 125, 127, 145, 257; behaviours associated with 45–7, 88–9, 105, 108, 116–19, 127, 130, 231, 233, 255; binge purge type of 7, 138; and bulimia nervosa 7–8, 16; categories/subtypes of 7, 8; causality of 60, 107–8, 130, 136, 156–7; as communication 64–5; and 'conscious intent' 156; consequences of 10; as coping mechanism 61; and decision-making 15, 38–9; and developmental delay 37; and ethical issues 31; and family maintaining factors 63, 80, 107; and fertility 61, 221, 236; and isolation 30, 110, 180, 188; maintenance model for 62–3; and maternity 221; models of 104, 106; and mortality 21, 28n3, 40; onset of 7–8, 10, 155, 112; outcome of 8, 12, 13, 51, 63, 172, 193, 243; persistence of 8, 15; and powerlessness 37, 101; psychological aspects of 40, 259–60; and readiness to change 43, 48, 54–5, 84, 86–90, 96, 170–2, 183, 190, 205;

and reinforcers 143; retracing type of 7; risk factors for 9, 61; and starvation 11, 48, 60, 80; treatment of 125–6, 150, 205; *see also* eating disorders
'anorexia nervosa minx' 75
'anorexic voice' 75, 208
antecedents-behaviour-consequence (ABC) model 116–18, 200–2, 268
antecedents-meaning-consequences (AMC) framework 130–4
Anxiety Control Training (ACT) 205, 215
attachment 37, 133, 262
autonomy 35–40; in children 226, 228–9; culture of 30, 34–5
avoidant traits 90, 158, 162, 185, 205, 255, 269
Avon Longitudinal Study of Parents and Children (ALSPAC) 221

beat (formerly Eating Disorders Association) 16, 20, 24–5, 48, 70, 79
behaviour change 43, 49, 55, 84–8, 92, 110, 130, 145, 172, 197
binge eating 8, 11, 48, 66, 106, 131, 165n1, 201, 205, 222, 227, 242
bioethics 35
bipolar disorder 63
brain 34, 39, 112–13; development of 10, 37, 224; social 60
bulimia nervosa 4, 12, 14–15, 22, 28n2, 45, 46, 49, 81, 106, 132, 167, 222, 225, 242, 243; adolescent 12–13; adult 127; and anorexia nervosa 7–8, 16; and 'conscious intent' 165n1; consequences of 10; and ethical issues 31; and perfectionism 225; onset of 7; risk factors for 9; *see also* eating disorders

Printed in Great Britain
by Amazon

46835033R00174